Riding High with Jesus

Colleen Hurd

Riding High with Jesus

Onwards and Upwards Publishers
Berkeley House
11 Nightingale Crescent
Leatherhead
Surrey
KT24 6PD
United Kingdom
www.onwardsandupwards.org

Copyright © Colleen Hurd 2016

The right of Colleen Hurd to be identified as the author of this work has been asserted by the author in accordance with the Copyright, Designs and Patents Act 1988.

All rights reserved.

No part of this publication may be reproduced or transmitted in any form or by any means, electronic or mechanical, including photocopy, recording or any information storage and retrieval system, without permission in writing from the author or publisher.

Printed in the UK by 4edge Limited, Essex.

ISBN: 978-1-911086-31-4
Cover design: LM Graphic Design

Unless otherwise indicated, Scripture quotations are taken from THE HOLY BIBLE, NEW INTERNATIONAL VERSION®, NIV® Copyright © 1973, 1978, 1984, 2010 by Biblica, Inc.™ Used by permission. All rights reserved worldwide.

Scripture quotations marked (KJV) are from The Authorized (King James) Version. Rights in the Authorized Version in the United Kingdom are vested in the Crown. Reproduced by permission of the Crown's patentee, Cambridge University Press.

Dedicated with grateful thanks to

God my Father,

Jesus my Saviour,

*and my family,
who have all had a part
in this story.*

Riding High with Jesus

Contents

Preface 7

PART ONE 9

1. The Story Begins 11
2. My Childhood Home 43
3. Marriage and Parenthood 125

PART TWO 265

4. A New Beginning 267
5. New Horizons Beckon 327
6. A New Life in England 343

Appendix 406

Riding High with Jesus

Preface

"Colleen, you should write a book about your life's adventures," I've had several people say to me over the years. From a young age I've enjoyed reading and writing, using my imagination in school compositions and keeping diaries, so after my husband Peter died in 1992 I felt inspired to start writing my memoirs for our family. Now in my 70s, friends have encouraged me to publish my story, so I invite you to come on a journey with me through what has been a wonderful adventure of living life to the full with Jesus as my companion and Lord.

I know people who have very sketchy memories about their childhood, so I feel blessed to recall much of my life in wonderful detail. Mum told me that she and Dad named me Colleen because my colouring resembled that of a little Irish colleen[1] with my curly dark hair, clear complexion and deep violet eyes. How apt that named has proved to be because I am still a girl on the inside, brimming over with zest for life and adventure. I ask myself, "Where have all the years gone?" Looking back over my life, I am filled with gratitude to God for the unmistakable thread of his Fatherly love and care flowing through the colourful tapestry of experiences, the memories of which now rise like bubbles from a pond, each one sparking off another.

For most of us it's only as we grow older that we think about preserving memories of the past for future generations and have the time to do so. Before that, we're caught up in the fast pace of life carving out careers or raising families. So it was that nearing my 60th birthday I bought my first computer and launched into the challenging and exciting world of technology to begin writing my story! Those readers who have learned to master a computer at my age will agree that the adventure is both daunting and exhilarating!

---

[1] 'girl' in Gaelic

I owe a debt of thanks to friends and colleagues who over the years have patiently come to my aid in moments of panic – "HELP! I pressed something and I've lost everything!" – or answered countless requests starting with, "Please can you show me how to..." With their help, my grasp of the workings of my computer and the Internet has expanded steadily, spurred on by high praise from my children and young friends. Now, after twenty years of adding to the manuscript, I've been urged to bring this tale of adventure to print as an encouragement to others along the journey of life. I do so with tremendous joy and the hope that readers may experience for themselves the wonder of entering into relationship with the Living God and walking with Him daily.

Part One

Riding High with Jesus

Approximate Map of Natal

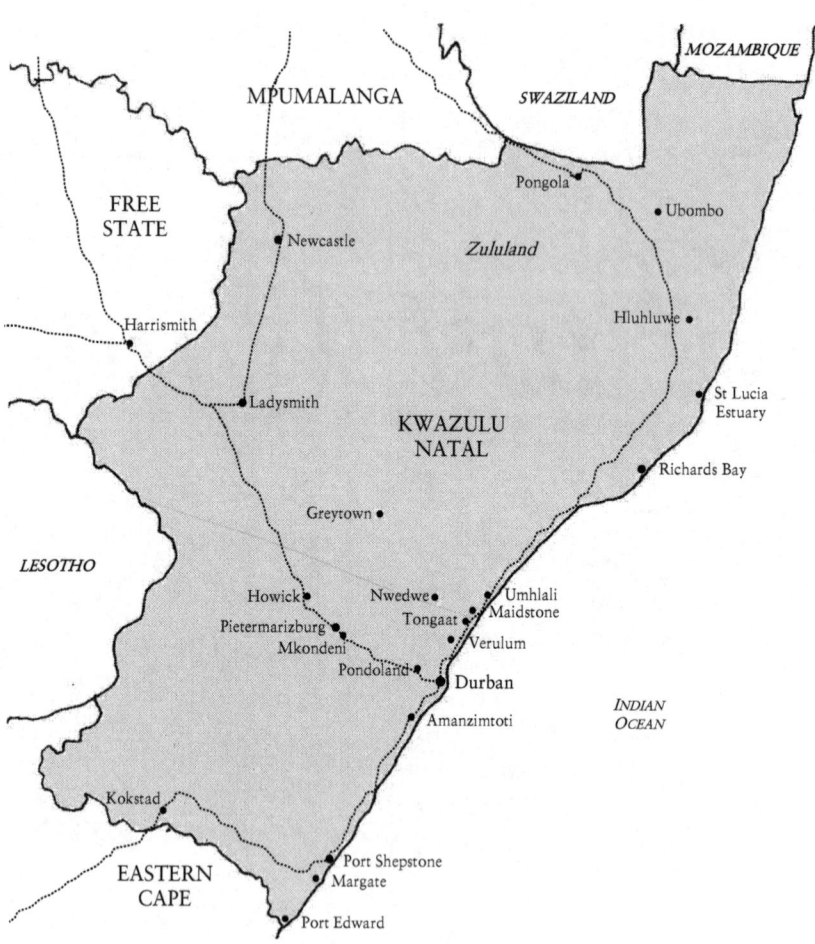

1

The Story Begins

Born at the tail end of the Second World War to wonderful parents, Colin and Marjorie Eckersley, I had four older siblings – Lorna, John Stanley, Enid Rose and Coral Norma – and two younger sisters – Madeline Claire and Marjorie Elizabeth. We enjoyed the freedom of farm life in sunny South Africa on the east coast of Natal, surrounded by sugar cane fields. Our small farm was only a few miles from the village of Tongaat where Dad had grown up with his six sisters – Hilda, Maude, Fanny, Florence, Natalie and Madeline.

Both Dad's and Mum's paternal roots are British, Mum the second and Dad the third generation to be born in South Africa. Their families still referred to England as 'home' and growing up we loved to listen to the older folks chatting about their simple pattern of life, far removed from ours in many ways. For years we took for granted that they would be there to fill us in on interesting facts about our ancestors and the past. Now they've gone and we deeply miss their presence, their wisdom, their laughter and their stories. We miss, too, their link with the past in which Christian faith and moral values laid the firm foundation for stability in our nation, which has been eroded by compromising modern standards.

Suddenly, it seemed, the truth dawned on me that we are now the oldest living members of our Eckersley clan, and my siblings and I feel a responsibility to leave a record of our lives for the generations to come. So a few years ago we set out with mounting enthusiasm to compile our own stories and records, delving into the archives at home and abroad for birth, marriage and death certificates, and appealing to relatives and friends for any contributions they could add to the collection. I was not aware until after Mum's death that she had been recording the stories of her and Dad in great detail over several years, and we have no idea how many hours she spent typing with two fingers on a little old portable typewriter.

We're grateful to our niece Heather Farr for retyping Mum's original manuscript into a wonderfully clear copy, but the original with all its errors has a special place in my heart, because I can picture her sitting in her cottage through the lonely years after Daddy's death, tapping away with two fingers to capture for us the priceless record of family history. We owe a huge debt to our sister Enid for buying a photocopier and devoting herself to the amazing task of photocopying all of Mum's memoirs and photographs stretching back over many years. Enid created albums for each of her six siblings and her five children, and I can remember visiting her when she was in full flow, with twelve growing piles of pages spread around her large dining room table – an incredible labour of love! These memories form a wonderful foundation to build on with our new discoveries, and we enjoy getting together with our brother Stan to exchange individual memories, reminisce about shared experiences and check facts with one another to keep the records straight.

From all that I have gleaned, I began to create my family tree by drawing the earliest available strands of our ancestry together into a unique blend of characters that contributed to making us who we are today. For the full ancestral tree turn to the Appendix but here is an abbreviated summary for the story.

Our Eckersley Ancestors

The records of Dad's paternal Eckersley line begin with his great-grandfather George Eckersley, who was born in 1793 in

The Story Begins

Lancashire, England. He died in Salford, Manchester in 1848. George married Susannah Blacklock from Newbury, Berkshire in Middlesex in July 1824. On their Marriage Certificate George is listed as a hostler/servant in Hulme, Manchester.

Their eldest son, John Eckersley, born in 1825, had nine siblings – Ann, William, Elizabeth, Henry, Thomas, Mary, Martha, George and Fanny. John married Ann Thomas, daughter of Rowland and Margaret Thomas in Holywell, Flintshire, Wales, in March 1848 in Manchester Cathedral. I am fascinated by the fact that at the time of their marriage, Welsh-speaking Ann could hardly speak a word of English.

Towards the latter half of the 1800s many families left Manchester, England to escape the harsh conditions of life in the industrial cotton mills era for the sunny British Colonies of Australia or South Africa. In eager anticipation of a new life, my great-grandfather John Eckersley was among those who braved the three-month-long journey to South Africa in 1849 on the sailing ship 'King William' with his wife Ann and their infant daughter Martha. Travel aboard sailing ships in those days must have taken great courage in conditions that were primitive, with rampant sickness claiming the lives of many children and the journeys made hazardous by unpredictable elements and rough seas.

Together with William and Edith Jane Dore from Newport, Isle of Wight, their passages were paid by TW Galloway in exchange for the land which had been promised to them as 'Byrne & Company Emigrants'. Arriving in the province of Natal in South Africa, life for the first settlers was basic and very hard as they battled to find work and eke out an existence.

By early 1851 the Eckersleys were at Mount Moreland where John was employed as a labourer. By 1854 he was farming for a living and by September 1855 they had moved to Tongaat. Great-grandfather John is recorded as having helped to build the first primitive hand-operated sugar mill in 1854 and the first simple bridge across the Tongaati River.

He also appears from the 'Natal Almanac' of 1879 to have moved inland from Umhlali to the farm 'Riet Valley' where he

13

became a sugar farmer, registered in the South African archives as one of the earliest farmers to start growing sugar cane for the Tongaat Sugar Mill. John was later financially in a position to build a large house in Tongaat village which he named 'Victoria House' where he lived with his wife Ann and some of their children until his death in August 1900. Two generations later, our Dad still referred to it as the 'Old Home' when we were children.

John and Ann Eckersley had nine children: Martha, William Henry, George Thomas, John Stanley, Frederick Owen, Agnes Ann, Fanny Amelia, Emma Elvinia and Alfred Ernest Renault.

Dad's father, William Henry, was born in July 1853 at Mount Moreland, Natal. As a boy William herded pigs for a farmer at La Mercy, Natal, and had to pass regularly through virgin bush which was inhabited by wild animals. He told the story of how on one occasion he had the frightening experience of encountering a leopard but passed by unharmed. He married Alice Eliza Catterall in March 1880 and is listed as transport rider, carrier and later sugar planter. William Henry was one of the colonist farmers recorded in the 1870s Annals of Natal. He died in Tongaat in December 1934.

John Stanley (nicknamed Jack) was born in Tongaat in July 1855 and became a trader in Zululand. Being a fluent Zulu linguist he was highly respected among the natives as close adviser to the Zulu Chief Zhibhebhu. He was given a Zulu wife by whom he bore several coloured children, settled to tribal life and died in 1933 in Nongoma district, Zululand, leaving an extended family bearing the Eckersley name. Frederick Owen, born in Tongaat in 1859, became a transport rider with his brother Jack and lived in Nongoma district. He married a black wife, Ntambose Matabela, and in the 1880s owned a store in Swaziland. He died in Babanango, Zululand in 1936.

Dad's maternal grandmother, Alice Eliza, was a descendant of the Quested family from Kent, England. Thomas Quested married Harriet Susannah Coulter, born in 1799 in England, and had five children. After Thomas died his widow Harriet left Maidstone in Kent to sail to South Africa in 1853 with her children – William, George, Harriet Susannah, Caroline and Eliza Ann. She established an inn on a property in West Street, Durban, helped by her youngest daughter, Eliza Ann, as together they made ginger beer for sale in their inn which later became well-known as 'The Kentish Tavern'.

Eliza Ann Quested married James Catterall in South Africa in 1857. James was born in England in 1824, most likely in the County of Lancashire where Catteralls had been established for some generations. He sailed from Liverpool in the ship 'Henrietta' which reached Port Natal in 1850. Described in the ship's passenger list as a 'Byrne settler' he had his passage paid for him and was allocated twenty acres of land at the Dunbar-on-Illovo Estate in the Byrne Valley, Natal which he sold on arrival. After their wedding James and Eliza Ann lived at Tongaat where James was an overseer on the Tongaati Estate. Harriet Quested died in Durban in 1876.

Family Links to the New Sugar Industry

Our Eckersley forebears have a strong connection to the start of the sugar industry in Natal, and I have referenced much of the following information about that era from the book by RGT Watson entitled 'Tongaati – An African Experiment',[2] which contains a wealth of fascinating details too numerous to include here.

While our great-grandfather John Eckersley was farming in Mount Moreland, a young man called James Renault Saunders arrived in South Africa from England. He was the grandson of Robert Saunders whose family had originated in the north of Scotland. Robert qualified as a Surgeon in Scotland, moved to India as Assistant Surgeon in the city of Monghyr, married and after the birth of his third child, James Ferguson, Robert Saunders returned to England. Several years later his grandson James,

---

[2] Published 1960 by Hutchinson & Co. (Publishers) Ltd.

nicknamed 'Monghyr', moved to the Island of Mauritius as an Officer of the British Crown where he established himself in the sugar industry. There he married and had four children, his eldest son, James Renault, being born in 1818.

In 1823 Monghyr Saunders was appointed as one of a group of agents representing the Mauritian Sugar Industry to the British Parliament and moved to England with his family. At the age of nineteen, after spending fourteen years of his childhood and youth in England, his young son James Renault decided to return to Mauritius in 1837. Having neither the capital nor the experience to start as an independent sugar farmer, he gained some knowledge of the sugar industry by working as an employee on several sugar plantations. On the island he met Captain Laffan, who was interested in investing in land in South Africa. He introduced James to a Mr Norsworthy, who had visited the Cape of Southern Africa and believed there was money to be made by acquiring land in the new colony of Natal to the north-east. James had visions of developing his own sugar company and, through his association with Mr Norsworthy, was admitted to a syndicate of shareholders. In time he was appointed Manager of the company to handle the affairs of the new property venture, and became the founder of the Tongaat Sugar Company.

James Renault Saunders at thirty-five years of age, with his wife Katherine and baby daughter Laura, boarded the steamship 'Hotspur' at Portsmouth harbour to set sail for South Africa in 1854. At the end of the long journey the little family disembarked in Table Bay and continued round the coast from the Cape by packet vessel to the very rural settlement of D'Urban[3].

At this time D'Urban was no more than a cluster of primitive buildings facing on to the dusty, potholed streets marking out the rectangular blocks of the developing town, which became rivers of mud when it rained. There were several simple dwellings, a market square, a brick church under construction and one two-storey building identified by the sign 'McDonald's Hotel'. Next to it a

---

[3] the original name of the town of Durban

The Story Begins

low thatched building had several doors leading on to the wide verandah[4] which looked out on to wild fig trees shading the courtyard. Seated around rustic tables and chairs made of knobthorn and flatcrown wood, the guests, mostly men, sprawled in the shade dressed in corduroy or moleskin trousers, coloured cotton or woollen shirts, velskoen[5] and low crowned hats with wide brims. The genial owner, Hugh McDonald, moved among his guests making sure they were all being promptly served with Geneva gin or English bottled beer by male native servants.

Here at McDonald's Hotel, James and Katherine Saunders were met by a Dutch farmer Jan Meyer. As a boy Jan had ridden into Natal on the Voortrekker wagons of the early 1820 Dutch settlers as they set off on their historic pioneering journey inland from the Cape known as the 'Great Trek'. He had come prepared with two oxen-drawn wagons, the second of which was to transport items of furniture, provisions and stocks of implements. His intention had been to take the newcomers straight to their farm, which was known as 'The Tongaati Estate' and also 'The House by the Drift'. However, they chose to pay social calls in the capital Pietermarizburg first, so Jan Meyer had no option but to make the long journey home to his 'Klipfontein' farm and return three weeks later.

The Tongaati Estate ran down to the river of the same name, derived from the ancient Bantu name 'U-tho-ngathi' given to the river by local natives who were incensed when passing travellers asked the way to the river to bathe. On seeing it they made the derogatory remark, "Do you really call that a river? It's nothing more than an insignificant trickle!" to which the indignant locals replied, "U-tho-ngathi." ("It is a thing of importance for us.")

---

[4] porch
[5] handmade leather shoes

The Tongaat Sugar Company is Born

In the very early days of the sugar industry the labourers were all low caste Indians known as 'coolies', meaning unskilled, low paid labourers, brought out on five-year contracts because the local Zulus were not interested in doing this work. The sugarcane was planted and cut by workers with sharp pangas[6]. At the mill the cane was fed by hand between rollers and crushed in much the same way as wheat was ground in England.

When James Renault Saunders arrived in the area in 1853, the village of Tongaat in the County of Victoria had grown very little beyond its simple beginnings. Because it had never attracted a growing white population in forty-four years, numbers had dwindled and many plot owners had sold to Indians. When the contracts of indentured Indians expired, many stayed and became tenant farmers and the population was further increased by the arrival of Hindu and Muslim traders from India.

Under James Renault's strong leadership, in 1898 the move was made from the primitive hand-fed mill to a steam-driven machine. At a certain point the system of importing Indian workers on contract was stopped because natives willing to work in the cane fields were brought in from Pondoland in the Eastern Cape. Years later the railway was extended to reach the village and the oxen-drawn wagons transporting the sugarcane to the mill were replaced by rail. The rail also linked the mill to ports for exporting refined sugar, and many years later when James' son Douglas floated the estate as the Tongaat Sugar Company Limited, a much larger mill was constructed in the village of Maidstone, which was still in operation when I was child.

Dad's Ancestry

Dad's parents, William Henry and Alice Eliza Eckersley, had seven children: Hilda, Florence, Maude, Fanny, Colin, Natalie and

---

[6] cane knives with a hooked tip

The Story Begins

Madeline. Their home in the village of Tongaat was the central hub of entertainment and hospitality, and the Eckersley family was well respected and loved by the whole community. Two other old Tongaat families of the time were the Boltons (as a very little girl I remember Ina Bolton being the postmistress in the village post office) and the Waughs (stern-faced old Mr Willy Waugh scared us little girls by hooking us around the neck with the crook of his walking stick).

In his early days Grandpa William Henry Eckersley was a 'transport rider'. On one occasion while riding through dense bush he was attacked by a lion which he shot and removed the ivory claws to give to each of his daughters. Maud was very proud of hers and had it mounted in gold as a brooch, which became an interesting conversation piece, especially in the company of visitors from abroad. Grandpa later became Manager to Mr Starling, brother-in-law of Edward Saunders of the Tongaat Sugar Company, and worked for him until he retired after a heart attack. Grandma Alice died when her little girls, Natalie and Madeline, were only eleven and nine years of age.

Grandpa's eldest sister, Martha, who came to South Africa as a baby, married John Alexander Dore, son of William Dore, and settled next door to Victoria House with their three sons. Alfred became Postmaster, Frederick worked on the railway and Lindsay worked in judicial circles. Alfred was still living in this small family home when we were children. Fred Dore married Ada Nash and lived in Durban with their two sons, Lance and Patrick. Once a year these outgoing, friendly cousins Fred and Ada visited the Old Home and made a lasting impression on me as a little girl. Both were incredibly tall, standing head and shoulders above everyone else, and their sons Lance and Patrick followed the Dore tradition in height. I remember Fred most notably for his very bushy eyebrows and Ada for her freckled face and sparkly eyes when she smiled. They were great walkers and had a youthful spirit with a keen sense of humour and zest for life.

After our dad and five of his sisters had married and left home, Florence devoted her life to caring for their father, William, until his death in 1933. By this time Hilda and her husband Samuel McAravey ('Mac') had returned to live in the Old Home with their three children, after losing their farm and livelihood at Mooi River.

In the course of time, after Uncle Mac passed away, Hilda and Flo were sadly forced by the new South African Group Areas Act to sell the Eckersley property to Indians, who demolished the house and built a block of flats in its place. The two sisters were invited by their niece Edna Holmes to live with her in her old family home 'The Rambles' at Mkondeni near Pietermaritzburg, and later in a small modern house she built next door. After Hilda's death our mother invited Flo to live with her until she passed away. Cousin Alfred's old house was left standing but the home of the Rogers family further up the hill was replaced by a large modern Indian High School.

In 1930 the Tongaat Sugar Company took a decision to create a Tongaat Health Committee to eliminate the shocking living conditions of the Pondo workers who were squatting in Indian-owned hovels. Serious epidemics of malignant malaria were taking their toll, and in 1944 the plan to create separate areas for Indians and natives was put forward. Work began on the development of an Indian housing settlement on Ghandi's Hill in Tongaat, and a property was purchased outside the village for the creation of a Housing Scheme for local black residents.

In 1938 this became the 'Hambanati Model Native Village' named after the 'Hambanati Mission' meaning 'let us go together' which was started by Allen Gardiner, an ex-Naval Officer. The neat brick houses leased to Zulu tenants had small gardens for growing vegetables – pumpkins, cabbages, spinach, sweet potatoes, madumbes[7] and maize[8] – all staple foods of the Zulu people. With nothing going to waste, the cobs and maize leaves provided fuel for open fires under their large three-legged cast iron cooking pots.

---

[7] a root crop
[8] corn

Dad's Work Environment

Dad was appointed Superintendent of this well-established Model Native Village during my primary school years. Being a fluent Zulu-linguist he was the perfect choice for the position under the supervision of Mr R. G. T. Watson, the Tongaat town board chairman.

Adjacent to the village was a large walled community centre called the 'Machen'. Along the inside wall Zulu women rented space to set up stalls and sell their home-grown vegetables, fruit, traditional herbs, potions, handmade articles and beadwork. On busy market days there was always a loud buzz of conversation between customers and the clamour of vendors' voices at top volume trying to attract the attention of customers to their wares.

At the far end of the enclosure was a brewery where tshwala[9] was fermented in huge vats. Next to it was the meeting hall where beer was sold by tin measures to the Zulu men, who sat at long wooden tables around the hall, chatting while they enjoyed their refreshing drink. Every so often Daddy made an inspection tour of the brewery to test the level of fermentation in the vats and sometimes allowed us to go in with him. The strong acrid aroma of the fermenting grain caught in my throat and I could never understand how Daddy enjoyed sampling the beer to test its readiness!

Dad's spartanly furnished office was tucked into the corner near the entrance, and it was his responsibility to collect rental in cash from the cottage tenants and stall holders. I loved to stand beside his big desk and watch him cashing up and when I was old enough to learn the identity of the denominations would ask, "Please, Daddy, can I put the money away?" Under his watchful eye he taught me to put the coins in the right compartments of the cashbox, which made me feel very important.

---

[9] sorgham beer

The Tongaat I Knew as a Child

By the time I was born the only remaining relatives living in Victoria House on the hill overlooking Tongaat village were Auntie Hilda, Uncle Mac, Auntie Flo and Cousin Alfred. They were part of a very small minority of white residents including Lewis Dykes, his wife Marie and their three children, Helen, Edward and John. They owned a black Doberman Pincer dog named Squire who frightened the daylights out of me with his ferocious approach and loud barking every time we came to play.

Just below their property the South African Railways owned a modest cottage occupied by a young Afrikaans-speaking railway worker Mr van Rensburg, with his pretty wife and three children – daughter Everlee, little brother 'Boetie' and a tiny baby. The homes in between Alfred's cottage and the Dykes' home had long since made way for the building of a large, red brick high school for hundreds of eager Indian pupils. In the village itself the only other white residents were the owner of the Central Tongaat Hotel, the Afrikaans Police Sergeant's family and the Greek Tsampiras family who owned the Tongaat Bakery.

Surrounding this small remnant of whites, the Indian population of Tongaat Village increased enormously over the years. Shopkeepers from India had brought a natural flair for trading which resulted in many small shops springing up throughout the village to line the main road and the narrow side streets such as 'Stink Street' which had been so named in its earliest days to describe the squalor.

They catered mainly for their own Indian population selling clothing, beautiful traditional saris, dress fabrics, jewellery, cotton thread, pins and needles, scissors, knitting wool and needles, traditional Indian foods, curry and spices, paraffin, torch batteries, lamps and every household item imaginable. These shops were crammed to the hilt with all their wares, many items hanging from the ceiling, which gave the feeling of entering an Aladdin's cave of fascinating treasures to be explored.

The Story Begins

Many of the older generation couldn't speak a word of English and depended on younger family members to communicate. As children, when we stepped with Mummy into the blend of strange aromas from burning incense and spices, we entered the territory of another culture, and browsing the shelves discovered all sorts of unexpected surprises. In addition to incense, a strong musty smell rose from open sacks of dried beans, peanuts and grain, with big tin scoops for weighing goods on old-fashioned scales. Of course, as was the Indian custom, there was often a 'bargain' to be had after some haggling over the price!

The largest Indian General Dealer, called 'Ghandis', on the main road running through Tongaat, was owned by the refined Desai brothers of superior caste. This modern store catered for the white community and stocked almost everything we needed – clothing, jewellery, torches and batteries, bolts of dress materials, knitting wool and needles, liquid paraffin, candles, food, soft drinks and sweets to name a few. As a child I was fascinated by their system of sending cash payment to a central Cashier's Office situated on a level above the ground floor, like that used in Durban's large departmental stores. The cash was placed with invoice in a tiny metal capsule and sent electronically on overhead wires to the cashier, who returned the change and receipt the same way. An added advantage of shopping at Ghandis was having the petrol station right in front of the store. Heading north out of the village toward the Tongaat River, Maidstone Station nestled in the valley with its cluster of Afrikaans-speaking railway workers' cottages on the hillside above.

On occasion we came across a Hindu festival procession making its way through the village to the river, which both intrigued and frightened me when I was small. Hundreds of Hindu worshippers wearing marigold garlands around their necks surrounded a colourful pagoda carrying statues of their gods on a cart as it made its way to the sound of loud Hindu music. What frightened me was the sight of weird-looking men with matted hair, painted faces and chests, pulling the cart by huge fish hooks inserted in the flesh on their backs! Daddy would not allow us to get caught up in the procession but I remember watching from a distance how the pagoda was lowered into the river to be swept away with marigold blossoms as an offering to the Hindu gods.

Skeletons in the Cupboard

In Dad's generation intermarriage between whites and blacks across racial lines was totally taboo in South Africa. Consequently, the fact about Dad's uncles Jack and Frederick having "gone wild", as the aunties described it, brought deep shame upon the family. Both brothers were living in Zululand with Zulu wives and bearing children of mixed race[10] and the stigma ran so deep that on occasions when Jack called at the family home in Tongaat, he was never invited in but given a mug of tea at the kitchen steps. As innocent children we overheard conversations in hushed tones between Dad and his sisters, but any attempts we made to ask questions about these two uncles were silenced, which lent an air of intrigue and mystery to their disappearance from the local scene.

In today's changed world I regret the breakdown in family relationships between these brothers and their family. My earliest awareness of the stigma of mixed marriage took root subconsciously at the home of our aunties in Tongaat when I was a little girl. Every afternoon a light-skinned lady called Mrs Choonoo walked past on the road, and knowing that she had an Indian name I sensed a sort of unspoken scandal in the hushed references to her. When I discovered much later that it was due to her marrying an Indian man, I felt compassion for her living with the unveiled scorn and discriminating attitude of other whites.

I Discover Our Mixed Race Cousins

More than a hundred years after John and Frederick Eckersley had settled in Zululand, I was to encounter descendants

---

[10] known as 'coloureds'

The Story Begins

of our mixed-race cousins in a totally unexpected and, for me as a very shy young teenager, quite startling way. I had been on a building project in the rural area of Northern Zululand with a group of young Methodists and was returning to civilization alone ahead of the others.

Being the only white person on a local bus full of black passengers, I was allocated the front seat beside the driver. As we bumped along the dusty country road far from civilization, I became aware of a loaf of bread bouncing on the shelf between us. At first glance I noticed faint pencil lettering on the tissue paper wrapper and out of pure curiosity bent down to read it more closely. Imagine my shock when I saw my name "ECKERSLEY" on the wrapper! My mind 'did a bender' with shock: in this very remote area, where on earth had it come from, and to whom was it going with my surname on it? Eager to find answers but feeling very nervous, I plucked up courage to ask the black driver in Zulu who owned the bread. He replied that he was taking it to the storekeepers at the Ubombo Trading Store where the bus would be stopping. Now I was intrigued as we journeyed on.

Suddenly realization dawned! I was travelling through the country of the Zulus in which Uncle Jack and his brother had settled. So the Ubombo storekeepers must be some of the Eckersley cousins we had never met! For many people today, ugly attitudes of past discrimination have vanished but such was the shame instilled in us by the older generation that my heart began to race with the anticipation of coming face to face with coloured cousins! Being so shy, I felt caught between wanting to see what they looked like and a totally irrational fear that my Eckersley identity would somehow be exposed if I was seen and I wouldn't know what to do or say. So when the bus pulled up outside the trading store, I approached the steps cautiously and stood nervously at the door, peering through the bustling crowd of local Zulu customers and bus passengers buying food for the journey. Edging just inside the door I could see three tall, fine-looking young men busy serving behind counters and studied them from a distance until the bus driver emerged and I followed him back on to the bus with pounding heart.

As we covered the miles back to civilization I relaxed and began to feel quite foolish about my fears. If they had seen me in the crowd, there was no way on earth they could have known my identity! I continued the long journey mulling over this strange experience, eager to share it with my family and ask Dad for the full truth. Many times since then I've wished that I'd had the courage and confidence to conquer my fears and introduce myself to those Ubombo members of our extended clan. However, while I matured into adulthood, attitudes in our generation toward racial issues in South Africa changed so much that my siblings and I felt free to bring the skeleton out of the cupboard and put the family taboo to rest.

My next interesting contact with Zululand relatives came nearly ten years later after I was married. Out of the blue I received a letter from my sister-in-law Gill Hand living in Mkuze, Zululand with surprising news that she'd met a man by the name of Patrick Eckersley – a real gentleman, she said, who was managing Mr Rutherford's bottle store. When she told Patrick that her brother Peter Hurd had married an Eckersley, both were intrigued to find out the connection between us. With the silence broken over our family's dark secret, I wrote back to tell Gill the story about the "wild" uncles, and Peter and I arranged to visit Patrick on a trip to Swaziland.

With heart-warming appreciation of our coming, Patrick greeted us and took us into his humble home to meet Martha, his second wife. Over tea he brought out his well-worn photograph album full of faded pictures. I sat paging through photos of the old Eckersley home and family in Tongaat with the same strange sense of unreality I'd felt over my loaf of bread experience. There was our Grandpa William sitting on the verandah of Victoria House with my baby brother Stanley on his knee! With Cousin Alfred and the aunts and uncles we knew well, here was positive proof of our mutual ancestry!

After a long chat in which Patrick and I exchanged family news, we took photos and hugged each other warmly before Peter and I left feeling the richer for having met this fine cousin, truly a man of integrity. Our brother Stan met a young Eckersley youth from one of the Zululand families working in Durban, and more recently through the Internet I have established contact with Laurens who took on his mother Alice's name of Eckersley. Not much is known by us about Frederick's offspring but the Eckersleys we've met carry the name with pride.

On a visit to Tongaat village in 2010 I took my daughter-in-law Annie for a drive up the hill to see if there were any reminders of our Eckersley past but as I expected the landmarks had all disappeared. However, we are recording for our young ones the precious memories of bygone days before they are lost, and value the many photos in our possession.

Dad's Boyhood and Batchelor Adventures

Our dad, William Colin Eckersley, was born at Otto's Bluff, Natal on 13th June 1886, while his Mother Alice Eliza was on holiday there. He was brought up with six sisters – Hilda, Fanny, Maude, Florence, Natalie and Madeline – in Tongaat and started his education in the local school just down the hill from their large family home Victoria House. Later he transferred to the government school in Verulam under the headmaster Mr. Buss, travelling daily by train which sometimes broke down when he would have to finish the journey on foot.

As a boy he learned to speak fluent Zulu from his little black playmates, and gleaned a great deal of knowledge about the customs and superstitions of the Zulu people. This was a great asset when he left school and started work as a clerk of the court in the Native Affairs Department at Ndwedwe. He later became Prosecutor and Interpreter there, and from the court moved into storekeeping at Ndwedwe for a time, running a postal service and telephone exchange for the Government with the daily mail being conveyed on foot by a native 'runner' to and from Verulam some distance away.

Tiring of that lifestyle, with a friend Charles Rathbone he decided to seek his fortune in the British colony of Northern Rhodesia[11] where he got his first job as clerk of the court in Livingstone, just beyond the Victoria Falls. He was a handsome, virile young man of adventurous spirit and initiative, and once there, the call of the wild became stronger so he applied for a post as Labour Recruiter for the Gold Mines in the Transvaal. In his early twenties he recruited labour from tribes in remote areas of Northern Rhodesia, travelling right up to the Congo border from village to village on foot or riding a bicycle, made to a specific design with raised pedals and chain to cope in the long grass and rough terrain full of sizeable anthills. With a contingent of strong black men – thirty porters, five policemen and one mail runner – Dad covered vast areas of this unexplored country.

Being out in the bush for months meant carrying every commodity they needed: camping equipment; basic medical supplies, especially quinine for Malaria; bedding, food; cooking utensils; ammunition for his shotgun; and personal effects. The currency of payment for the porters and policemen was rashers of salted bacon and lengths of limbo[12], both welcome items in the extreme heat of Africa. These were in addition to a regular issue of rations and fresh meat from buck which Dad shot.

In some tribal villages where no white man had been seen before, Dad encountered fear and strong superstition from the local natives. The women and children fled from him in fright and only crept out of hiding when the translator explained their mission of recruiting men to work in the mines of South Africa. Dad smoked a pipe and after striking a match it amused him to watch the children running to pick up the dead match, thinking that it held some magical power!

---

[11] now Zambia
[12] a thin type of gauzy fabric used for loincloths

The Story Begins

As little girls we loved nothing more than to gather of an evening around Daddy's feet in the pool of lamplight, to listen to the tales of his brave adventures. With the skill of a good storyteller, he kept us spellbound and wide-eyed with exciting details of his experiences. He told us how he slept in his tent at night, gun close at hand, aware that only the canvass sides separated him from wild animals such as cheetahs and leopards, which he could hear prowling round his tent in the darkness. No matter how many times we heard the stories they never lost their power to set our little hearts racing.

We hung on every word as Daddy re-lived his near-death experience from a burst appendix and the dreaded Malaria fever common even today in some mosquito-ridden parts of Africa. In spite of taking strong doses of quinine, he succumbed to the fever and became so ill that he had to be carried for miles in a hammock slung between the shoulders of his bearers. On arrival at the nearest hospital, he was in a state of delirium close to death. Thanks to his faithful native bearers and the medical care and attention he received, he survived and returned home to Natal.

With his recruiting days over, it was while running his trading store at Ndwedwe that Colin met his shy young bride-to-be, Marjorie Long. For many years afterwards Dad suffered recurring bouts of malaria, so severe in the early days of their marriage that Mum feared for his life as he thrashed about in delirium from the high fever.

Mum's Ancestry

Mum's father, Frederick Ernest Long, was born on 16th October 1867 in the British County of Essex, into a very different family lifestyle from Dad's ancestors in Manchester. Fred's parents, John William and Rachel Long (née Cant), lived in Manningtree, the smallest town in Essex, at the mouth of the Stour River. His father was a lay preacher in the Methodist Church and a butcher master by trade, so as a young boy Fred had the job of delivering meat to local customers.

Riding High with Jesus

In 1890, at the age of twenty-three years, Fred obeyed the call of God to the mission fields of South Africa, and left his parents and siblings – Elizabeth, William, Rosa, Frank and May – to train as a Wesleyan/Methodist preacher in the Eastern Cape. While in Cape Town he met and married our grandmother, the beautiful and talented young artist and teacher, Frances Echardt.

Born in Cape Town on Christmas Day 1869, Frances was one of six survivors from a family of thirteen children, with four sisters – Clara, Bertha, Maggie and Alice – and a half-brother, George, from her mother's first marriage. Her father John was a prominent shipbuilder of Huguenot descent and trader with the East. Her mother, Elizabeth, died when Frances was only seven and her father died three years later, but we have no record of what happened to their estate. Following the girls' education at an Anglican Church school, two of her sisters married very young and Frances became a teacher, rising to the position of Headmistress of a girls' school in Grahamstown in the Eastern Cape, at the young age of twenty-one.

Frances had been trampled by an epileptic as the age of six and suffered severe internal injuries, which left her lungs in a weakened state. For health reasons, at one point she was advised to take up a post as Governess to the Leppan family living in the dry climate of the Karroo area of the Eastern Cape. Two of her pupils turned out to be young men about her own age, who played a boyish prank on her which had painful consequences. Their father was entertaining an eminent Dutch guest and the lads told Frances they would teach her some phrases in Afrikaans to honour the guest at table. In the language derived from Dutch which the early settlers brought to South Africa, they taught her a vulgar expression used only for gluttons and animals. In all innocence she turned to their guest to enquire if he'd had sufficient to eat using the words she had learned: "Het jy genoeg ge_vreet_?" instead of "ge_eet_?" Thinking she had mastered a polite phrase, she was mortified when there was shocked reaction from the family around the table. The amused faces of his sons gave the game away to their angry father, who made them apologise to the visiting guest

The Story Begins

and their embarrassed young governess, before giving them a good thrashing.

During her time of employment with the Leppan family, Frances met and fell in love with the young Methodist preacher Frederick Long who was stationed at Maclear. They were married in 1898 and took up their first post in Idutywa, Transkei, where Mum was born on 21st May 1899.

In 1900 Granddad took his first furlough and followed his wife Frances and little Marjorie, nearly two, to introduce them to his widowed mother and family in England. Granny Frances, heavily pregnant with her second child, had gone ahead by sailing ship and became so severely ill with seasickness that they feared for her life. However, she rallied and Granddad arrived in time for the birth of their baby Doreen on 24th September 1901 in the ivy-covered two-storey family home. To their deep disappointment Fred's eighty-three-year-old mother had passed away two weeks before Granny's arrival but his Aunt Lizzie, who had never married, made them welcome for the duration of their stay. Frederick returned to his ministry work in South Africa but Frances stayed on with her little girls until she was strong enough to face the return journey almost two years later, when Marjorie was nearly four. During their stay, Granny Frances enjoyed many opportunities to give expression to her talent by painting the English landscape in watercolours.

The family joined Granddad at his post at Dordrecht before moving to Ncera in the East London district. Later he was posted to Hilton in the Cape, with Cathcart, Whittlesea, Waku and Queenstown all falling within the extended circuit he covered on horseback. Mum described her father as having the heart of lion, despite being only five foot three inches tall. In the course of his ministry, preaching and visiting parishioners he was away for two to three weeks at a time, leaving Granny alone with two little girls in their remote surroundings. Frances played the piano and violin and filled many lonely hours singing to her own accompaniment. She nursed the girls through a serious bout of measles and other childhood illnesses, and coped with the challenges of poisonous snakes and a serious veld[13] fire which got out of control on the farm next door. When the flames swept up the hill, threatening the wooden parsonage and church buildings, with her maidservant she beat out the flames with heavy sacks soaked in a tin bath of water. In spite of her limiting poor health she was a brave and remarkable young woman, exceptionally intelligent, sensitive and artistically gifted. Living on a minister's meagre stipend[14] there was no money to buy toys for her children, so with vivid imagination she created handmade dolls out of fabric, to the delight of the little girls.

Looking back over Granny's life, I am full of admiration for her pluck and spirit of resilience through years of failing health and other challenges. In the year 1909-1910 her deteriorating health warranted a serious operation which had only been attempted three times before in the country. The operation was successful and she was the first patient in South African history to survive what is now known as a hysterectomy. While their mother underwent surgery and regained her strength over a nine-month recuperation, the little girls were taken on the long journey to Jaggersfontein in the Orange Free State to stay with Granny's eldest sister, Aunt Clara. Mum recalled that their stay was not a happy one with this family of strangers – strict Aunt Clara, her mine manager husband at Jaggersfontein Diamond Mines, and their family.

Granddad and Granny moved from the Cape to Greytown in Natal in 1911. Within three years, at age forty-one, Frances developed a serious form of angina and had to be nursed back to health. Here the girls Marjorie and Doreen attended the government school and learned to ride horses with friends, which was a great joy. In 1914, when they moved to Verulam, Frances spent two years on her back nursed by a friend, Miss Braithwaite. Slowly she began to improve but sadly her friend was called away to care for her own father, so her daughter Marjorie was called in

---

[13] grass
[14] salary

The Story Begins

to become her carer for two years until she was strong enough to take up active life again.

In 1920, the year of our mum's twenty-first birthday, Granddad was sent back into the European Circuit at Malvern near Durban. In better health, with great tenacity Granny started an Anti-waste Organization with volunteers in the basement of the Durban City Hall. The group worked closely with the Welfare Society and were highly respected and appreciated for their efforts. It was during this period that she discovered she had breast cancer and underwent successful surgery at Berea Nursing Home to have one breast removed. She carried on courageously with her work for ten years before it was discovered that the cancer had spread – but this time she declined surgery. Nursed by Marjorie, she died peacefully in her sleep at age sixty-one on the 24th September 1930 after bearing two years of suffering bravely.

Sadly, Granny Frances was only able to enjoy two grandchildren, Lorna and Stan, as she died when Enid was two months old. Though we younger ones didn't have the pleasure of knowing her, Mum described her as a strong personality, compassionate and warm, with wonderfully creative gifting expressed in painting, fine stitchery and other exciting ways. She was a prolific painter in watercolours and oils, honoured to have her striking oil painting of three horses drinking at a water trough selected by the South African Artists' Society for exhibition in London. In this painting she captured with amazing skill the alert expression in the horses' eyes, their veins standing out boldly against the magnificent glossy sheen of their coats. To everyone's great disappointment, the sailing ship was delayed by bad weather en route from Cape Town to England so the painting arrived too late for the exhibition, but it continues to be greatly admired by everyone who sees it. The original is with one member of our family and we've had professional copies made of this family treasure for each of us to enjoy.

One of Granny's favourite pastimes was collecting pieces of driftwood on the seashore after high tide, which she transformed into amusing animal shapes and creatures of fantasy with her vivid imagination and palette of oil paints. It is thrilling to see that the legacy of her wonderful artistic gifting is being passed down through the generations in all branches of our family. My sisters and I regret that we did not get to know our gifted Granny Frances, but in many ways her strong character was epitomised in our mother. Mum's strong faith and godly values of courage, compassion and tenacity were imparted to all her children as the secret of victorious living, combined with a keen sense of humour, vivid imagination and girlish ability to enjoy simple pleasures. Her creative gifting of improvisation and needlework enabled Mum to dress her six daughters at minimal cost, and our farmhouse family meals were always wholesome and delicious.

Mum's Early Days

Our mother, Marjorie Elizabeth, elder daughter of Frederick and Frances Long, was born in the tiny town of Idutywa in the Queenstown district of the Eastern Cape, called the Transkei. Her memories of childhood spent in the remoteness of rural mission life were happy, as their imaginative mother taught her girls to enjoy simple pleasures and appreciate nature, including the creepy-crawly insects they encountered which she called "cosy neighbours". Mum remembered being taught by their old coloured maid to knit with two sharpened matchsticks and a short length of wool, and after battling to master the skill graduated to needles and her own ball of red wool.

In her early years Marjorie adapted to several moves with her parents around the Eastern Cape. Their means of transport was a horse-drawn Cape cart which had no overhead covering, so in heavy rain the little girls lay down under a canvass sheet which leaked and sent cold trickles of water down their necks, while their parents seated above took the full force of the storm and arrived home soaked to the skin. Mum recalled how good it was to get home to a hot bath and bowls of warming soup.

She described how on days when Granddad was expected home from his time away, Granny walked her girls along the road

The Story Begins

to meet him and taught them to put their ears to the ground to listen for the vibration and then the clip-clopping of the horse's hooves before they came into view. On one journey to East London, the choppy crossing by ferry over the Buffalo River was an anxious time for Granddad, as the horses became extremely nervous and it was only his firm hand and calming voice that stopped them from leaping overboard.

In 1911 the family moved up to Natal. While living in Greytown, the girls enjoyed several holidays with friends in Rietfontein, where young Marjorie learnt to ride a horse, enabling her in later life to go riding with Dad when they were courting. Her great joy at this time was being able to take piano and violin lessons which gave her the only breaks she had from nursing her mother. Because she was needed to run the home for years, Mum had little public schooling but was home-schooled by Granny who taught her girls to read and discover things for themselves. Living some distance from the village, they spent their time learning the skills of housewifery, cooking, needlework and simple dressmaking. Mum was a quiet, reserved girl, sacrificing her own secret desires to nurse her mother suffering from breast cancer, while her outgoing sister Doreen was free to accompany their dad to social gatherings and tennis afternoons.

Granddad was moved from Greytown to the native Mission Station in Verulam in 1917. On arrival he was shocked to discover that the previous minister, the Rev. Abraham, in his mid-eighties had not vacated the parsonage. He had become a naturalist and refused to move until he could find accommodation for all his pets, creatures, insects and spiders! So the Long family was obliged to return to Durban and stay in the Marine hotel for three weeks until the matter was resolved by the circuit leaders.

When they eventually moved into the very old thatched Mission House they were dismayed to find it in a serious state of disrepair, with numerous leaks in the roof, thick spider webs festooned in every corner, the bathroom window blacked out and the bath so stained with photographic chemicals it took months to clean! The house stood on the same property as the African

35

school, where Mum was called upon in place of her ailing mother to teach the girls domestic skills and the boys gardening. The local Zulu headmaster, Mr Mhlongo, helped her to master the Zulu language, which was a great asset to her in later years. A caring local Zulu woman, Mrs Matiwane, helped to bathe Granny Frances and sat with her on Wednesday afternoons so that Mum could enjoy an occasional game of tennis on the village courts. In this village Marjorie and Doreen were able to take piano lessons with Miss Marjorie Williams, and Mum was given violin lessons by a gifted German professor, until he was sadly interned with other Germans when the First World War broke out.

Romance in the Air

In 1917 after a severe bout of bronchitis, Marjorie, aged eighteen, was invited by one of her mother's art students, Bill Windsor, to the home of May Kirkman in 'The Residency' at Ndwedwe. It was here that she met a handsome bachelor, Colin Eckersley, in a group of friends from the village enjoying tea after a game of tennis. Over the years our girlish hearts delighted to hear the romantic story of how Mum and Dad met in the home of these friends.

Mum was warmly welcomed by her hostess and joined the jovial company including Colin's youngest sisters seated round the lounge. Suddenly their host's tiny pet monkey, which had freedom of the house, leapt on to Mum's lap spilling her cup of scalding tea on to her. Colin leapt gallantly to the rescue of the shy young guest and pulled out his silk handkerchief to mop her skirt. He made sure she was not seriously burnt before putting her at her ease, and from that moment a spark was lit in both their hearts. Their love was put to the test over a number of years, because Granddad insisted on their waiting until Mum came of age before giving his consent to their engagement.

Living in Verulam it was possible for Mum to take singing lessons in Durban with the renowned singing teacher Grogan Caney. To celebrate her nineteenth birthday, she invited a number of young friends to come to her party and spend the night. Having arranged to meet the seven o'clock train from Zululand, she rose early that morning and began to set out everything for the party. In haste to get a draught into the stove to heat her bath water quickly, she opened the stove door and the backdraught forced the flames out, burning her forehead, nose and chin and singeing eyebrows, hair and eyelashes! The happy day she had planned was ruined and, sadly, she had to spend the next twenty-four hours swathed in oiled bandages to relieve the pain and start the healing process. Needless to say, someone else went to meet her guests from the train and her party continued without the birthday girl!

The romantic heart of the lovely Marjorie's 'Prince Charming' is borne out in love letters to his "Girlie" which were the link throughout their seven-year wait of patient courtship. Once Dad had made his intentions known to his beloved, on one of their happy outdoor picnics he secretly sized her dainty ring finger by weaving a tiny circlet of grass. From this carefully preserved sample he ordered a beautiful engagement ring to be made with a cluster of seven small diamonds, which happily was the number of children they would later have!

In 1920, Granddad was sent back into the European Circuit at Malvern, and this was to be his last circuit. After Granny died he lived at the YMCA in Durban and continued to preach on occasion as a supernumerary preacher, until in his last years he moved to live with Mum and Dad.

Dad had originally planned to settle with his bride in Southern Rhodesia, as four of his sisters had done. He purchased 'Stormvale', a farm near the town of Gwelo (now Gweru) adjoining 'Springvale', the home of his sister Fanny. She and her husband Donald Wilkinson had five children: Joyce, Barbara, Ivor, Eric and Alice. Joyce married Scotsman Tommy Hall and moved to Scotland after the Second World War. They had three children: Tommy, Aileen and Denise. Barbara (Bobbie) married Alexander Eccles who ran the post office in Nyanga, where they lived and raised their two daughters Dawn and Audrey, who later married and settled in the UK. Their son Gordon served time in the

Riding High with Jesus

Rhodesian Army before moving to England and later Kenya. Alex and Bobbie Eccles lived in Nyanga until despot President Mugabe's regime made it unsafe to remain, and they emigrated to Exeter in Dorset, England. Natalie and her husband Jack Scott settled in Gatooma and had one son, Colin. Madeline and her husband Noel Woodrow lived in Que Que with one daughter, Norma, who married Fenwick Corbett.

Grandfather William Henry fell seriously ill so Dad shelved his plan to move to Rhodesia, in favour of remaining close by. Springvale was sold and Dad settled with his new bride on a smaller parcel of land given to him by his father in the Inanda District of Natal, which may well have belonged initially to his early settler father, our great-grandfather John Eckersley. Mum and Dad rode up to the top of the hill on horseback to view the spot overlooking the Tongaat River and together planned their home and dreamed of the family they would raise there. Their marriage ceremony took place in Durban on 23rd June 1923, conducted by Mum's father, the Reverend Fred Long, and an assistant clergyman.

Following a short honeymoon at the Inchanga Hotel between Durban and Pietermaritzburg, the newly-weds moved into the simple, homely dwelling which Dad had built on the farm named 'Nqabeni'[15], because of the remnant of virgin bush in one corner. During the days of unrest between Zulu tribes, Dad came close to being attacked when he was challenged by spear-wielding natives while travelling through this dark bush. Fortunately, being a Zulu linguist he was able to call out and identify himself so they allowed him to pass without incident.

---

[15] Zulu for 'indigenous bush'

The Story Begins

Eckersley Ancestors

Ann Thomas

William Henry Eckersley (centre)

William Eckersley, Colin and five sisters

1914 Colin and police interpreters

Riding High with Jesus

Colin Recruiting Labour in Zambia, 1914

William Colin Eckersley

Colin's home on Safari

Bachelor safari days in Rhodesia

If Dad was unwell, he would be carried to the nearest First Aid station

Dedicated companions

Children doing their chores

The Story Begins

Long Ancestors and Parents

Colin and Marjorie's wedding

Fred and Frances Long with Marjorie and Doreen

Frances Echardt, 21 years old

Rev. Fred Long

41

Riding High with Jesus

2

My Childhood Home

Our childhood home may have been simple in structure but Mum and Dad's love for each other and their children created warmth and comfort that made it a happy family home that I remember vividly.

The inner walls of the home that Daddy built were lined with wooden tongue-and-groove panels, and the pitched roof was covered with waterproof malthoid. Two large front bedrooms opened into the spacious lounge-cum-dining room, and their outer doors led on to a wide front verandah with low wall and green wooden latch-gate. From the front lawn through a gap between the gum trees, there was a clear view of the Maidstone Sugar Mill in the valley below, and the Indian Ocean in the far distance.

Leading off the lounge was a narrow single bedroom, and on the opposite side a small pantry where Mum's paraffin fridge gave off its homely aroma. I loved to help Mummy with simple tasks like filling the long metal tank under the fridge. When I grew strong enough to hold it steady, I would pull it out on its runners to reach the cap and watch as Mum poured the paraffin up to the mark through a long funnel. After she had lit the wick with a match, I replaced the pretty cobalt blue glass chimney and slowly pushed the full tank back into place.

The fridge was always full of assorted items of food, but my abiding memory is of a daily supply of rich Jersey cream from our cows. Before setting off for school every morning, Madeline and I helped ourselves to a generous helping for breakfast, coating spoons of thick cream with dry Cornflakes. Little wonder that we developed well-rounded, healthy little bodies, strong bones and teeth to see us through to old age. On a low cupboard at the pantry window, Mum kept a basket of eggs gathered daily from our farmyard hens. The smallest were the first laying of the young pullets, and every egg counted in the large family-size omelettes or bowls of scrambled egg which Mum produced. The view from this pantry window extended over the violet patch under the window, past the splash of bright orange from the triangle of Barberton daisies, down the long drive and beyond to the district road in the far distance.

At the back door of the house Daddy had sunk a heavy metal scraper to clean the red mud from boots and shoes before entering the short back passage, which had a row of strong coat hooks on the wall for outdoor jackets and hats. The kitchen to the right had Mum's anthracite-burning Aga stove at its heart, giving off constant warmth. Dad was an early riser and every morning put a large enamel pot of creamy milk on the stove with his favourite 'Bev' coffee essence to simmer until the family woke. Without electricity on the farm, in the rainy season the rack suspended over the stove on a pulley was a godsend for drying clothes. On rainy days when we arrived home on foot drenched to the skin, Mum would rub down our little bodies before the comforting warmth of the Aga before we changed into dry clothes and tucked into welcome cups of hot Milo. The smooth rings of the Aga hotplate provided the perfect heat for Mum to turn out mountains of the most perfect crumpets or drop scones for tea, all the more delicious with farm butter, fresh cream and honey.

Opposite the kitchen was a sunny family breakfast room, where we spent happy hours when not enjoying the outdoors. Leading off was a small cosy bedroom which held happy childhood memories for me, except for the occasion I stole big sister Lorna's Vicks cough drops! She was home for a weekend and being a working lady who had started to smoke, always carried a packet of these medicinal drops. I found the flavour of these drops irresistible, so when everyone was gathered in the front of the house I crept under the bed with her handbag. Enjoyment was short-lived however, because Lorna returned and caught me in my hiding place with a mouth full of aromatic evidence! Her gentle but firm chastisement underlined the lesson in honesty.

To alleviate the financial struggle in the early years of establishing the farm, Mum had started a dairy with a herd of Jersey cows and supplied fresh milk to customers in Maidstone village. The milk was delivered on foot by two Zulu farm labourers, Mabasa and Xijimpi, who carried the milk cans on their shoulders through the neighbouring cane fields and across the Tongaat River. As Dad was doing shift work at the mill to release young men to the war effort, it was Mum who rose at 4am every morning to supervise the milking, even in the months after she had delivered her first three babies at home with the help of a midwife. In later years she reduced the herd and stopped supplying milk to the village, but maintained an adequate supply of milk and cream for her growing family and staff.

With the urgent need to find a water source, Daddy had called in water diviners who located a good water table near the house. A borehole was sunk and a windmill erected to pump the supply into a pressure tank on a tall stand. We grew up with the familiar clonking sound of the corrugated iron tail of the blades catching the wind, and the quiet thumping of the long pipes as they rose and fell in their casing below the ground. The concrete steps of the tall tank stand served as a good launching pad when Madeline and I were learning to ride the large men's bicycle belonging to John, our cook from Mozambique. With hindsight I truly regret taking advantage of John's long-suffering kindness, because my early attempts at learning to balance usually ended in headlong crashes into the orange trees lining the vegetable garden! After several such accidents John wisely locked his bike away, and resisted our pleas for just one more ride!

At the entrance to the farm Dad planted an orchard of five hundred young litchi trees for additional income. By the time I was born, these were mature trees giving a fine yield which brought significant financial help in the good years. Indian vendors bought and harvested the annual crop, except for a few trees close to Mum's vegetable garden, which Dad kept for our personal use. These trees benefitted from run-off water from the garden and bore the most delicious, plump fruit. There were, however, hard years of devastating loss when a scorching north wind burnt off all the blossoms and the crop failed. On those occasions we saw a deep despondency settle on our beloved Dad's face as he contemplated the consequences of the devastating loss.

Until I was about ten the wooden privy was literally down the garden path. Having to go out in all weathers was a challenge, and on hot summer days I dreaded being hit by the enormous bluebottle flies that rose up from the pit. There was also the scary possibility of finding a snake which had crept in and settled itself on the warm concrete floor. When I grew to an age regarded by my sisters as old enough to go alone, they ignored my desperate pleas to accompany me after dark, so urgent evening calls presented the severe discipline of heading out on my own into the blackness of night. Swinging the beam of torchlight down the path ahead, I would stamp my feet and sing loudly to scare away any creatures in the vicinity, hoping that there were no spiders or snakes waiting to keep me company! It was a great relief when Dad built a bathroom and indoor toilet on to the back of the house, just a few stepping stones away from the two thatched rondawels[16] used at weekends by our older sisters and brother Stan.

The blue morning glory creeper that Mum planted along the chicken-wire fence from the rondawel down to the privy spread like a wide green curtain covering the wire. In full bloom the massed display of beautiful sky blue trumpets delighted my heart, and I loved to watch the tightly curled buds opening up like magic in the warmth of the sun. In different flowerbeds there were deep purple violets, dainty lobelias, creamy lily-of-the-valley, roses and coral red Barberton daisies. Wonderful splashes of colour came

---

[16] round huts

from the flame red and gold blossoms of two magnificent flamboyant trees and the pink, white and purple bougainvillea hedges. The drive was bordered by rows of succulent Kalanchoe plants with pretty pink bell-like blossoms on long stems, and silvery-green leaves so thick that we used them as slates to carve letters when we played schools.

At the far end of the fenced vegetable garden stood an enormous mulberry tree whose canopy of leaves reached to the ground. As little girls Madeline, Beth and I could stand shielded from view under this umbrella of leaves to eat our fill of the juicy fruit, emerging with telltale stains on fingers, mouths and bare feet. Close to the gate into the garden Mummy gave us each a small patch of earth and some flower seeds to plant. To this day I remember how proud I felt when my little patch was filled with tall pink and white larkspurs, dainty pink linarias and miniature carnations with their sweet, strong perfume.

Precious Memories of Mum and Dad

Life must have been tough for Mum and Dad raising a large family with limited finance, yet as children we never felt in want, thanks to home-grown produce and Mum's ingenuity. We grew up in the wonderfully secure knowledge that we were loved and affirmed by parents whose deep commitment to one other and their children was never in question. Mum used her imagination and creative gifting to devise entertainment for her children. Such was her skill that we were never fully aware of the financial stress and challenge of bringing up a large family with scant means. I thank God for her wonderful example of living in the presence of God which impacted my life powerfully up to the day she died at the age of eighty-eight years, enabling me when I had five children of my own to trust God implicitly in times of severe testing.

Having married in his thirties, Daddy was already fifty years old when I was born, a man of great integrity and commitment to his family. Lorna, Stan and Enid knew him as a young man, and our brother has vivid memories of the stern discipline meted out to him by Dad on occasion when his escapades got him into trouble. But we younger ones only knew him as a silver-haired, gentle, ageing Dad who loved us all with quiet pride and deep affection.

The simple lessons we learned from Daddy have remained with me for life, positive habits which I'm proud to attribute to a father who cared about training his children in the old traditions of good behaviour and sound values. One of Dad's qualities I determined to master was his beautiful cursive writing, the perfect copybook style of his schooldays. In this age, when writing by hand is replaced by computers and other technical devices such as mobile phones, iPads and tablets, I often receive compliments for my neat hand and think of Dad with gratitude every time.

He taught us never to cut knots in string or fishing line, but to tease them until they loosened so that the string or line could be unravelled for future use. On holidays at the seaside Dad would sit patiently for hours, untangling our fishing line from messy overwinds. In an effort to teach us thrifty habits, he reminded us frequently to take a small dab of toothpaste instead of a wasteful large blob which fell off the brush and down the drain! Our Dad was fastidious and neat in his person and in everything he did, whether it was shaving, trimming his moustache, mixing his tobacco, buttering a slice of toast or preparing a dose of rat poison for troublesome rodents!

When Daddy prepared rat poison, we girls sat beside him at the end of the long dining room table, and watched enthralled as faint wisps of smoke rose from the tube of sulphurous 'Ratnip' cream. First he cut a slice of bread into minute squares, then very precisely lifted a little dab of cream with the tip of a knife to spread evenly on each square. In general I hated the killing of any living creatures with the exception of flies and mosquitoes, but somehow the fascination of watching this process distracted from the sad demise of the troublesome rats who would tuck into this carefully prepared meal!

Daddy taught us to conquer fear by facing up to scary situations with courage, and gave us ample opportunity to prove to ourselves that we could be brave. Madeline and I were given the task on alternate nights of going out into the dark farmyard with a lamp, to let our large bull mastiff dogs loose from their daytime chains! I admit to childhood fear of the dark, but equally daunting was the task of undoing the chain while the dogs leapt and growled with wild excitement at the prospect of being free. Once loose, these huge animals jumped all over me with exuberant joy, while I fended them off with the swinging lantern. As they raced off into the dark barking loudly, I ran back as fast as my legs could carry me and burst puffing and panting into the comfort of the family circle. With teasing smiles of reassurance Daddy would say, "You see, my girl, I knew you could do it!" But his reassurance was small comfort knowing that within two days I would have to repeat the exercise!

One of our happiest memories of Dad's fine attention to detail was his tradition of bunching litchis[17] at Christmas time for family and friends. Litchis have a thick layer of delicious, juicy white flesh over a shiny brown pip, and a rough skin which turns deep red when ripe. Dad taught us to look for the heart-shaped fruit which have the smallest pips and thickest flesh! At bunching time, it was a joy to sit companionably on a little stool beside him, under the shade of the huge flamboyant tree's canopy. Around the clusters of ripe fruit from our private trees, Daddy arranged fans of leaves and tied them with pre-cut pieces of brown string which I held ready to pass to him. Prepared bunches were arranged in a box, like beautiful bouquets, to be delivered to friends. The flamboyant tree was one of our favourite climbing trees, with boughs strong and wide enough for making a treehouse with rugs to put our dolls to sleep in. Over the years, borers ate away a deep bowl at its centre, but the tree lived on through our years on the farm.

Dad was a confirmed pipe smoker and we little girls were fascinated by his simple evening ritual of mixing tobacco. When we saw him lay newspaper on the carpet, we knew he was about to blend two of his favourite varieties that I remember in my day as being Greyhound and A1 Magaliesberg. We would scramble to

---

[17] lychees

sit beside him and pick out the dry stalks while Dad sifted and re-sifted the pile, saying, "Be careful, girls, don't let it spill on to the carpet." When he was satisfied that it was well mixed, he filled his pipe, then stored the rest away in an ebony tobacco jar with a tight lid that stood on the bookshelf. He pressed the wad of fresh tobacco firmly into the bowl of his pipe, carefully struck a match and held the flame to it. With a couple of strong draws the little bowl began to glow and Dad settled down to enjoy a relaxing smoke while he read the paper in the light from the lamp. After every smoke he emptied his pipe, scraping the old ash into a bin with the tiny blade of his penknife, or knocking the bowl against the heel of his shoe if he was out of doors. These simple everyday rituals are etched into the bank of sweet memories we have of our beloved Dad.

Our little Mother was industrious and selfless in her role as wife and mother to seven children. Coming from her early life as a missionary's daughter, marriage to Dad with the demands of carving out a life on the farm must have held many challenges, which she faced with courage and a true sense of adventure. As a child I remember her being constantly busy during the day. In between attending to the demands of the youngest members of the family in succession, she cooked meals, supervised our Portuguese servant John in the kitchen and dairy, baked scones or made piles of crumpets on the ring of the Aga stove, bottled marmalade, mended clothes and sewed new garments on her Singer sewing machine – and still had time to give us loving attention.

Some of my favourite moments were spent sitting beside Mummy on a tiny footstool, helping to sort rice grains on a tray. When her shoulder muscles ached, I would try to ease the pain by rubbing her shoulders with my small hands. Of an evening she would sit quietly in the arc of lamplight with her knitting or crochet work, from time to time chatting to Dad about daily happenings or items of news he read in the newspaper.

Mum and Dad must have had differences of opinion, but I can't recall hearing heated quarrels or anxious conversations about finance in front of us. Only years later when I became a mum myself, could I appreciate the heavy toll on both of our parents in raising a large family. The dad I knew was a gentle man who lived his life with quiet dedication, not given to talking about his faith but living by godly principles. Our little mother left a wonderful legacy for her children and grandchildren to follow of selfless devotion, childlike enjoyment of new discoveries and total fulfilment in everyday tasks. They have both been sorely missed by our whole family and all who knew them.

My Siblings

Lorna was born on the farm, delivered by a capable midwife, Sister Foy, on 17th May 1925. At six years she started her schooling at the government school in Tongaat, under the headship of Mr Plant followed by Mr Armitage, a short, rotund gentleman. She and little brother Stan were driven to school daily by horse and cart and taught by their Aunt Madeline, Dad's youngest sister. Rhona Kean and Eileen Coleman were both single young teachers then, who later married and remained on the staff after the school was transferred to Maidstone village. Lorna inherited her love of babies from Mum and helped with each successive arrival in the family, until she left home to work. Her childhood was very different from mine, being the eldest and without a sister for five years until Enid was born. Looking back to that time, she remembers feeling quite lonely, especially when little Stan was born and Mum was laid up with milk fever.

Lorna left school at the age of sixteen, when I was five years old, spent a year at Natal Business College and began work at Hind Brothers Factory in Durban, manufacturers of 'Nutrine' which for generations was the most popular baby feed. She started as understudy to Mrs Dorothy Wood who ran the Nutrine Clinic, advising mothers on feeding their babies, and was later promoted to Mrs Wood's position as Clinic Advisor long before she had babies of her own. Launching out from farm and village life into the business world of the city must have been daunting for Lorna at such a young age, but she was blessed to find boarding with friends of the family in Durban and found her feet in the big wide world.

Being eleven years younger than my big sister, I was very impressed by her stylish town image – the 1940s' quiff hairstyle, bright red lipstick, high-heeled shoes and handbag to match. When she prepared to catch the train back to Durban, I watched with fascination while Lorna powdered her face with a soft powder puff and applied her lipstick. In contrast to Mummy's soft pink 'Tangee' lipstick, red lips were an exciting novelty and as I watched her trace the outline of her lips very carefully with bright colour and blot them with a tissue, I found my own lips moving to mirror hers. These feminine tips laid the foundation for the day that I looked forward to, when I would be old enough to wear make-up!

Lorna married her handsome sailor, Brian Fennel Christian, in Durban on 29th May 1948 and settled in Durban North. They had three children: Meryl (1st April 1952) who married Pieter Horn, Colin (23rd September 1954) who married Karen and divorced, and Heather (4th May 1959) who married Barry Farr. Many years later they moved to Pietermaritzburg and helped to landscape and establish the gardens on the African Enterprise estate in Town Bush Valley. Eventually they moved into 'Twilanga', a Retirement Home in Umhlanga, until Brian's death, after which Lorna moved to live with their daughter Heather and son-in-law Barry in Edenvale, Johannesburg.

John Stanley was born on the farm on 15th March 1928 but, sadly, due to careless nursing procedures by the attending sister, Mummy developed a breast abscess and had to be hospitalized at the Durban Sanitorium for an operation soon after he was born. During this difficult time, Dad's sisters Hilda and Flo cared for her new baby, and on Mum's return he flourished and even won first prize at a baby show. He started his schooling in Tongaat, but once the village of Maidstone was established by the Tongaat Sugar Company for their employees, he and his five younger sisters became pupils in the primary school under Nic Strydom's headship. The old Tongaat school was taken over by the growing

My Childhood Home

population of zealous Indian pupils in the village, many of whom are direct descendants of indentured labourers (coolies) brought over many years before to work in the sugar cane fields, and others from families who came at their own expense to start a new life in South Africa as traders.

Stan was a typical farm boy spending his weekends swimming or fishing with the little Zulu boys[18] in the nearby river. They made tiny clay models of cattle, and fashioned toy lorries out of wire that had long pieces of steering wire connected to the wheels. In his teens he made balsa wood models of aeroplanes which he hung from the rafters in his rondawel. I loved to watch him painstakingly sticking the tiny pieces together guided by the printed plan until the model was complete and ready to be painted. Stan followed Lorna to Durban a couple of years later for his schooling at Mansfield High. Unfortunately, he had contracted bilharzia from the polluted water of the Tongaat River and had to undergo a lengthy course of severe treatment. He also lost many days of schooling through bouts of appendicitis. As a result of missing so much of his high school education at Mansfield High in Durban, Stan took a gap year to build up his strength by helping Dad on the farm. The Mansfield headmaster advised Dad and Mum to put him to a trade, so he started an Artisan's Apprenticeship with the Hind Bros Building Dept and attended the technical college. He later became foreman to the brothers Arthur and Townley Jones in the city.

Stan married Eileen Cuffley in Durban on 17th November 1952 and had one little daughter, Susan, born in 1957. Sadly, their marriage came to an end in 1963. Three years later Stan married a widow, Joy Harris, and they moved from the Stanger area down to Pennington on the South Coast, where Stan built and repaired homes for several years before taking a job with the Durban Corporation and moving to Yellowwood Park, Durban. Stan and Joy retired to a flat at Poinsettia Park Retirement Village, Amanzimtoti, where Stan remained after Joy's death. Our brother

---

[18] umfaans

Riding High with Jesus

is the epitome of an immaculately dressed gentleman, in his neat shorts, matching shirts and silver moustache trimmed to perfection!

Enid Rose was born on 25th July 1930, an auburn-haired little girl who endured hurtful teasing as a girl because of her freckles and red hair. At age five she suffered a traumatic separation from her family, being hospitalized for six weeks in the Infectious Diseases Hospital in Durban with a serious case of diphtheria. At age six, she started school at Maidstone under headmaster Mr Armfield and later Nic Strydom, and was made Head Girl in her last year. Excelling at athletics in her primary years made me very proud of my big sister on annual sports days when she won her races and scaled impressive heights in the high-jump. Enid moved to Durban for secondary education at Mitchell High School and became a weekly boarder with Granddad's widowed friend Bill Windsor. His Swiss housekeeper, Lily Bernard, ran the home for his young daughter Heather and later married Bill's son Michael.

Enid was the first in our family to express artistic gifting when she took a Commercial Art Course in ceramics, dress design and modelling at Durban Technical College. Her first job was with Tromp von Diggelin's nephew in his fine art studio, painting and firing ceramics pieces of pottery. In 1948 she decided to switch to a career in nursing, qualified as a Sister at Greys Hospital in Prince Alfred Street, Pietermaritzburg and went into private nursing before marrying Douglas James Crankshaw, the only son in the Crankshaw family of Newcastle. As a newly ordained Methodist minister, Douglas and his bride started their ministry in the East London district, and small towns of Hylton and Nanaga in the Eastern Cape, where our missionary Granddad had served many years before.

After fourteen years their ministry ended in Stanger on the north coast of Natal, and Douglas moved into the Insurance field of business which took them to the Transvaal. Enid and Doug reared five fine sons in a lovely large family home in Northcliff: Owen, who married Sue; Anthony, who married Jackie (divorced)

My Childhood Home

and later married Donné; Paul, who married Marjorie; Grant, who married Danielle; and Timothy, who married Bev (divorced) and later married Debbie. After many years Enid and Doug retired to a charming apartment with river frontage in Rivonia, Johannesburg. Our beautiful Enid Rose continues to bloom into her senior years with graceful poise and flair.

Coral Norma was the first in the family to be born at Mothers' Hospital, Durban, on 18th November 1933. With her blue eyes and curly dark brown hair, I recall that as a teenager she attracted the attention of admirers whenever family friends gathered for annual holidays. After schooling at Maidstone Primary School, Coral attended Mitchell High School and became Head Girl in her final year. With her commercial qualifications of shorthand, typing and bookkeeping, she held down several secretarial positions in Durban with great efficiency. Coral shared a rented flat in Durban with her friend Pat Pollard and later our youngest sister Beth while she attended Business College.

During the years she worked for The Master Builders, Coral met Andrew Porter, a widower with two grown children, Elaine and Anthony, from Bloemfontein, Orange Free State. They were married on 6th April 1968 and honeymooned on the Greek Islands.

In 1971 Andrew decided to move to Natal and bought a property called 'The Shack'[19] from our brother Stan at Tongaat Beach, which was his portion of our inheritance. He and Coral had two children: Bradley, who married Melissa in the UK (divorced) and later married Chantal; and a precious little daughter, Diane, born with Downs Syndrome. 'Didi' delighted everyone with her sunshine nature for nine years before she went to be with the Lord Jesus, whom she loved, on 18th March 1982.

Coral was widowed on 8th October 1984 and living so close to Mum was of great assistance to her in her later years. She ended her working years at Whiteheads Textile Company near

---

[19] See page 82 for more about the building of The Shack and the acquisition of the land.

Maidstone, sold the large home that Andrew had built at Tongaat Beach and moved into her own retirement cottage in Pioneer Park, Umhlanga on the North Coast. Well into her senior years, Coral has maintained her high level of concern for others and her energetic get-up-and-go spirit is enabling her to enjoy her first little grandson Oliver Porter to the full.

I, Colleen Margaret, was born on 18th June 1936 at Mothers' Hospital, Durban, two-and-a-half years after Coral. Enid has described her joy at helping Mum with each new baby sister and remembers me clearly as a happy, contented baby enjoying bath time and the 'rub-a-dub-dub' on Mummy's knee. In spite of having a sunny disposition, I entered my teens feeling shy and the 'odd one out' among my blue-eyed, fresh-complexioned sisters, with my sallow olive skin colouring inherited from Granny Frances. Shyness and lack of confidence weren't detected by siblings, who teased me unaware of the negative effect which caused me to withdraw into my own little world. In fact, years later as adults we discovered that we'd all battled with hidden complexes until we established our identity in Christ Jesus, and we've been able to laugh about them together.

Having trained as a primary school teacher I taught for five years before meeting my 'Prince Charming', Peter Graham Hurd, in 1959. We were married on 7th January 1961 and raised five children: Andrew Graham, who married Lynne Robertson; Stephen Bradley, partner to Annie Webber; Murray, who married Michelle Lewis; Shelley Anne, who married Nicholas van Rensburg; and Justin Peter, who married Michelle (Mish) Brits. Well into my senior years I have retained a youthful zest for living through my faith in Jesus and a very deep appreciation of the beauty of God's creation. Being blessed with good health has enabled me to move abroad at God's calling, to serve Him in ministry that is both joyful and fulfilling.

Our little 'tough guy' sister Madeline Claire was born on 5th December 1938 when I was two-and-a-half years old. She was named after Dad's favourite sister and loved to be Daddy's helper. Though younger than me, Madeline didn't suffer with my shyness and had much more confidence. When the older girls went off to school in Durban, she and I spent a number of years in close companionship which has lasted throughout our adult lives. We married in the same year and had our first three children within weeks of each other.

When Madeline married Harry Cockerill in 1961, they rented a flat until Harry built a beautiful home in Cowies Hill, Durban where they raised their family of four: Karen, who married Len McAllister (divorced) and later married Jono Rundle; Kenrick, who married Karen Walls; Shaun, who married Laurian (divorced) with one son Tristan (born 2001); and Jacqui, who married and divorced Ewan Cochran. Our two families shared many memorable holidays together building wonderful memories. In later years Jacqui and her husband rented the family home and Madeline retired into a lovely flat attached to the home of her daughter Karen and Jono in Pinetown, Durban.

Throughout her life Madeline Claire was the epitome of strength, wisdom, compassion and good humour towards all her extended family, her children and many friends. In her later years she fought lymph cancer and the severe effects of radium radiotherapy and chemotherapy on her lungs and heart with utmost courage, tenacity and fortitude. After seven years of bravely adapting her lifestyle to diminishing energy levels, her system began to register increasingly debilitating effects, and our beloved Madeline Claire passed quietly into her eternal rest on 23rd June 2013, the day on which her husband Harry had died seventeen years before. We miss her presence more deeply than words can say, but rejoice in the fact that she has been lifted out of physical pain and stress into her eternal rest with her Heavenly Father and Saviour Jesus. Her death at seventy-five broke the sibling circle spanning seventy-one years, reminding us all how blessed we have been to have each other for so long.

Our youngest sister, Marjorie Elizabeth – known as Beth or, to some, Liz – was born three-and-a-half years after Madeline on 13th May 1942. Once Madeline started school, Beth had to spend a lot of time on her own. As a result, she was a shy, sensitive little girl who found leaving Mummy's company for school a daunting experience. On one occasion, pushed to the limit by her teacher's harsh remarks, she rose up with uncharacteristic boldness to declare, "I don't like you and neither do my sisters!" which resulted in Madeline and I being called to the office.

When Madeline and I moved on to high school, Beth was alone at school for three difficult years and suffered with a lack of confidence that blighted her enjoyment of school days. She went on to Business College in Durban and worked as a secretary until she married Kenneth Reardon and raised their family of eight children in Durban North: Lara, who married James Grobler; Nicholas, who married Dene Timpany; Lucas, who married Kim (divorced) and later married Rae Edmunds; Christopher, who married Cathy; Daniela, who married Marc Ferguson; Jarrett, who married Debbie Unger; Matthew; and Louise.

Beth has always had a deep love for children. Having raised her family of eight, she now fills her days in the company of grandchildren and little people at a preschool where she works. As I write, she has recently fulfilled her lifelong dream to build a home in the foothills of the Drakensberg Mountains with the vision of possibly running a small preschool for local children.

The Old Eckersley Home, Victoria House

Dad's three sisters Maud, Hilda and Florence, who had not gone to Rhodesia, remained in Natal. Hilda and her Irish husband, Samuel McAravey, lived for some years on a small farm in Hidcote, Natal, with their children Sheila, Dennis and Aubrey. Sadly, during the hard time of recession they were forced to leave and were living in the old family home, Victoria House, when I was growing up. The Auntie Hilda we knew had a gentle nature, an infectious laugh and a distinctive little habit of whistling through her teeth. She had picked up some Irish expressions from Uncle Mac and called us by the affectionate term of 'Ducky'. In spite of constant pain from chronic ulcers on her leg, she was always cheerful and never complained, but could often be seen

My Childhood Home

standing at the stove with her bandaged leg raised at the knee to ease the pain. The aunts spent all their leisure time with crochet hooks and cottons following intricate patterns to make dainty doilies, table centres and beautifully covered coat-hangers as gifts for all of us. We were surprised to discover they had never been taught to knit in their young days and envied us being able to knit garments, while we on the other hand thought their fine crochet work was amazing.

Uncle Mac raised chickens and ducks in a wire run next to the water tank behind the house, and ran a little business selling eggs and dressed birds in the village. A lasting memory I have from all our visits to the Old Home is of the strong, sour aroma emanating from a large pot of vegetable peelings and maize meal cooking on the Aga stove in the kitchen, to feed Uncle's caged birds. Uncle Mac seemed to be a man of few words in all the conversations we overheard as children, and my fond memory of him is sitting in his chair on the verandah catching a nap, his head tilted back with his well-worn old felt hat covering his face.

Aunty Flo always seemed to be very stern and lacking in humour, so we were careful not to incur her wrath. However, Madeline and I share the vivid memory of the day we disobeyed her instruction: "Do not touch the red chillies on the bush growing by the back steps of the house!" The beautifully shiny little red chillies looked so inviting that we couldn't resist just a little taste! Instant punishment followed the first tentative lick, as these little devil chillies set our mouths on fire. We rushed to Mary the maid for a drink of water which only accentuated the burning and our cries were heard by Auntie Flo who came to investigate. Preceded by stern words of "I told you so!" she came to our rescue with dry bread and glasses of milk which gradually tempered the heat and the pain receded. When old enough to understand that Auntie Flo had lost her young suitor during the war years, we felt sad that she had never had a family of her own.

Many years later when Hilda and Flo had sold Victoria House and gone to live with Cousin Edna in The Rambles at Mkondeni, I was married and living in Pietermarizburg. I drove

Riding High with Jesus

out to visit them with our little sons, Andy and Steve, and after Auntie Hilda broke her hip and passed away, Auntie Flo spent days with us to ease her loneliness while Edna was at work. She had mellowed so much over the years, and watching her with our little boys I realized that she loved babies. I've always been grateful that I had time to change my childhood attitude and show her love as an adult. In her last years, Mummy graciously offered Auntie Flo a home in her beach cottage and cared for her until she fell ill.

Just before Peter and I left to travel down to the beach on holiday, I heard from Mum that Auntie Flo was in Addington Hospital in Durban so I bought her a bouquet of flowers. We headed to the seafront where Pete took the children on to the beach while I went into the hospital. Entering the General Ward, I stopped a young nurse to ask directions to Auntie Flo's bed. She looked hesitant before telling me with regret that Auntie had died that morning. Hit severely by the shock, I turned and walked out of the hospital with an aching heart, to give way to tears before going to find Peter and the children on the seashore.

I've always felt relaxed in the slower pace of our parents' lifestyle and feel I would have been happy living in the simplicity of their generation. On our many visits to the Old Home we girls enjoyed exploring the property while Dad chatted to his sisters and Uncle Mac.

Being used to native labourers on our farm, it was a fascinating discovery for me as a little girl to find an old Indian dhobi[20] doing the aunties' washing on a concrete block in the backyard. From a comfortable distance I studied his barefoot figure stooped over the block, white tunic tucked up around his knees. His white beard matched the turban covering his head, and following the Indian custom he chewed beetle-nut which stained his teeth red and coloured the saliva that he spat out at regular intervals. The dhobi was later replaced at the washing block by the young Indian maid Mary.

---

[20] laundryman

My Childhood Home

On very rare occasions when Mum and Dad went away for a night or two, we girls stayed with our aunties at the Old Home. Before darkness fell, Mary would heat water on the stove and pour it into the galvanized bath in the kitchen for us to have a sponge down. Then one of the aunties, carrying a candle, would accompany us to the front bedroom. Lying side by side in the big four-poster bed with a large ceramic chamber pot underneath, we amused ourselves by studying the watermarks on the ceiling by the dim light of our candle. It was fun making out imaginary creatures in the shapes of the dark stains, but as the candle melted and the giant shadows thrown across the walls grew longer, I was always very glad to have my sisters close beside me.

In the days before water-borne toilets were installed in most homes, the Old Home privy stood across the yard under the spreading branches of a massive tree which had big surface roots and large seed pods the size of huge conkers. Unlike our home 'loo' constructed over a long-drop pit, here in the village a black worker of the Tongaat Town Board brought a donkey cart up the hill at dusk every night with the task of emptying all the neighbourhood pails into a drum on the cart. Years before I was born, the Eckersley aunts had jokingly named the sewerage cart 'The Kimberley Mail' after the diamond mining town of Kimberley in early South African history where the first diamonds were found. And the name had stuck!

Every night as we lay in bed in the front room, through the silence we could hear the echoing *clip-clop* of the donkey's hooves coming up the hill as the cart approached, then the *crunch* of the black man's gumboots as he crossed the yard to fetch the pail. These sounds in the dark set my tiny mind racing with an air of suspense, and if the window was slightly ajar the potent smell of Jeyes fluid[21] would waft into the bedroom.

---

[21] Jeyes fluid is an inky black liquid which turns magically to creamy white in water. Whenever I catch an unexpected whiff of Jeyes fluid, memories of the Kimberley Mail spring to mind and I'm transported back to my childhood with a smile.

Riding High with Jesus

As a young girl I had an experience with the Kimberley Mail that we've laughed about for years. One summer evening at dusk I was down the garden path balancing carefully on the wooden seat and lost in thought as I looked out through the open door, when suddenly I registered the *crunch* of heavy footsteps and the back trapdoor of the privy opened under me! I leapt off the seat in fright, pressed my back against the wall and watched with hammering heart as a black hand reached in a few inches away to take out the bucket and replace it with an empty one! The trapdoor closed and only when I heard the *crunch* of boots receding into the distance could I relax and race back to tell my sisters what had happened, which had Auntie Hilda and the girls in stitches of laughter!

Without electricity the dark bedrooms at the Old Home always had an eerie sense of mystery about them even in the daytime, with their musty smell and dark wooden furniture. Accustomed to our sunny farmhouse, childish curiosity drove us to peer from the passage into Auntie Flo's spooky bedroom but we dared not go in. All we could see in the dim light was the silhouette of the furniture, the dull gleam of the white china chamber pot under her bed and the vague outline of a large ceramic jug standing in a basin on the dressing table.

The lounge at the front of the house was only used for family gatherings, so on our frequent visits we girls usually spent the time playing out of doors or on the wide verandah. The aunts had their main meal at midday so Auntie Flo served light suppers at five o'clock sharp. On Fridays when we waited for our sisters to come home from Durban, we looked forward to Auntie Flo's delicious home-baked white bread with simple egg custard, sago or rice pudding baked in enamel bowls in the Aga stove. On rare occasions while the adults sat around the dining room table listening to the six o'clock news on radio, we girls crept into the lounge to explore family treasures. I stood and stared at the large photographs of stern-faced Victorian ancestors looking down from the walls in dark wooden frames, with smaller sepia photos of cousins Aubrey, Dennis and Sheila in army uniform on the old honkytonk piano. Beside these stood two large antique ceramic vases and pewter candlesticks with grapevine embellishment.

Items of great interest to us were mementos brought back from Egypt by Dennis and Aubrey, who had served there in the Second World War. One was a model of a coiled cobra in striking pose which looked solidly made, until Madeline and I made the awful mistake of sitting on it and discovered to our dismay that it was only made of paper-maché when the top coil broke off! Too afraid to own up, we tried to balance the piece in place on the damaged snake and hurried out of the lounge! Of course the aunties must have known we were to blame but I can't remember being scolded about it. If we were, the memory has been lost in the mists of time and hopefully Uncle Mac was able to glue it together again!

The front yard at Victoria House was daily swept clean of leaves by the Indian gardener, with a homemade broom of twigs that made a *scritch-scratch* sound on the bare earth. We sometimes asked Daddy's permission to visit our elderly bachelor cousin Alfred in his old home on the other side of the hedge. Alfred had suffered with TB as a young man and never married. I remember him as always neatly turned out in cream linen trousers and shirt, and when I was about six, Coral and I were taken on a never-to-be-forgotten ride to visit the Dykes family in Verulam in the dicky-seat of his Willys car with 'liquorice' tyres. Every year the Dykes sisters, Sybil and Elaine, planted a sizeable patch of green mealies[22] which were ready for sale in the summer holidays, and at every opportunity Dad bought sacks full of their large succulent cobs to steam for a favourite corn-on-the-cob meal.

In Alfred's home Madeline and I never ventured beyond the front porch, but looking into the dark dining room which had a musty smell we could see that the house was spartanly furnished. Because Alfred usually had his main meal with Mac and the aunties, all the food we ever saw in his mesh 'safe' on a wooden frame in the dining room were blocks of dried cheese and butter.

---

[22] maize

Riding High with Jesus

In his garden there was a rare custard-apple tree and it was a real treat to share the delicious creamy soft flesh around the shiny black pips of the ripe fruit.

It was in Alfred's home that our innocent little minds were first exposed to the scandals of British high society in newsprint publications of 'The Mirror'. Alfred subscribed to the thick overseas magazine with soft yellow cover which we sometimes found lying on an old chaise lounge in the front porch. They had no illustrations or lewd content but contained stories of marriage, divorces and society gossip. Dad sometimes borrowed these magazines from Alfred, much to Mummy's strong disapproval as she didn't want her girls exposed to the sordid content of society divorces and misdemeanours, so we didn't ever confess to having already read them!

Dad's sister Maude married Donald's brother Fred Wilkinson and lived in The Rambles at Mkondeni, Pietermaritzburg, which was then known as the 'Star and Garter Pub'. They had two sons, Ken and Leslie; and a daughter, Edna, who had an only child called Roma. We might have visited these relatives more than once in their rambling old house with its dark, spooky interior but the only visit I recall as a child was at Easter time. Growing over the verandah trellis was a flourishing Catawba grapevine, a variety I'd never seen or tasted before. The sour skin put my teeth on edge but the sweetness of the marble of purple flesh inside tempted me to keep eating the fruit off the laden vine. Another memory of that visit was a treasure hunt for Easter eggs which Mum had hidden under the sprawling vine and shrubs in the front garden. I ought to have enjoyed the novelty hunt, but having a deep fear of disturbing snakes in the undergrowth, I was greatly relieved to spy a chocolate egg without delay.

Simple Delights of Farm Life

On long summer evenings while Mummy and Daddy sat on the front verandah chatting quietly, we attempted handstands or played catches on the front lawn. As the light began to fade we

My Childhood Home

chased fireflies, whooping with delight when we caught one, and studied its magical little glowing tail in our hands before releasing it again. At weekends there was a timeless feel to the evenings, but on schooldays all too quickly these precious moments passed and we had to go inside to bath, put out our school clothes ready for the morning and get to bed.

Every summer we delighted in the first sweet chirpings of our dear little swallows which announced their return after the incredible migration flight from abroad. Peeping carefully from inside through the lounge window so as not to disturb them, we watched as the adults flew back and forth with lumps of mud to build a fresh tunnel at the entrance to the half calabash[23] which Daddy had nailed on to a board in the corner of the front verandah. Little eggs appeared in the nest and very soon the insistent chirping of the baby hatchlings kept their parents busy all day, darting back and forth with beaks full of insects to feed their young. We kept a careful watch, to chase off the cheeky swifts that swooped in to try and take over the nest. Daddy taught us to recognize the swifts by their longer forked tails, and the swallows by their blue-black hoods and backs, russet throats and white chest spots.

For me the lazy mood of hot summer days on the farm was captured in the memory of a family outing with our Samuelson friends. The soft droning of bees around blossoms and the sound of far-off voices floated on the hushed air as we walked to the Tongaat River along the lower road past the farm. Adelaide Samuelson had been friends with Mum since they'd met ten years before at Mothers' Hospital in Durban, when our Coral and her Joy were born within days of each other. On this occasion she was visiting from Pietermaritzburg with her children Vernon, Clare, Joy and Liz. While our mothers sat chatting quietly we played on the huge flat rocks at the water's edge, a safe distance from the cattle wading in the cool water. Nearby, the little Zulu herd boys enjoyed a playful splash in the river, bodies gleaming like liquid

---

[23] gourd

chocolate in the bright sunlight. Our friends had brought a bottle of caramel butterballs and no sweet has ever surpassed the delicious creamy flavour of that big, round butterball as it dissolved slowly in my cheek!

How different our life on the farm was from that of city children, without all the modern conveniences which are taken for granted. Throughout my childhood we had no telephone nor electricity, but used candles and simple paraffin lamps which gave off a warm, kindly light. Later Dad replaced these with more efficient benzine-burning Coleman lamps, and every evening at dusk I watched his lamp-lighting ritual with fascination. First he pumped the small plunger to build up pressure in the bowl, then filled a little cup inside the glass with methylated spirits from a small metal container with an S-shaped funnel. A lighted match was put to the 'meths' and there was a soft *plop* as the fragile mantle burst into life, ignited by the flame. The darkening room was flooded with light and I felt a quiet sense of security and comfort as the warm glow lit up the dark corners of the lounge.

One summer day when we'd acquired a few pennies, Coral, Madeline and I had the bright idea of walking through sugarcane fields to the nearest Indian store in the village to buy a bottle of fizzy red lemonade. It was a two mile walk there and back so what had seemed a fun idea at the start lost its appeal by the time we arrived home, hot and bone-weary, with our lukewarm drink. Not even a few blocks of ice could create the illusion of an exotic drink but we gulped down the bright red liquid and agreed that the effort was definitely not worth repeating!

We seldom went on journeys beyond our own village with Dad, so the few we did take left strong impressions on my young mind. One such was a trip to a farm at Mooi River in the Midlands of Natal, to buy a bullmastiff dog from a farmer called Mr Pickering. We stopped en route for a meal, my first exciting experience in a hotel at six years old. I remember the novelty of sitting in the dining room with a waiter standing by to take our orders while Mum studied the menu. As she was about to speak to the waiter, little sister Madeline, all of three years, piped up with

My Childhood Home

an insistent, "I want to see the cardboard!" which caused a ripple of laughter from Mum, Dad and the other guests. On arrival at Mr Pickering's farm, I stayed close to Daddy as the farmer's boisterous dogs followed us through an orchard of laden plum trees to the puppies' enclosure.

From the time I learnt my ABC, reading was my favourite pastime and from the age of ten I enjoyed spreading a rug under the gum trees below the cattle track to read, Nancy Drew or Hardy Boys mysteries being among the favourites. I loved to listen to the strong breeze rustling the gum leaves overhead as I lay and watch clouds drifting across the sky above. Moving into my teens, girlish fancies were stirred with romantic ideas of maidens being rescued by knights in shining armour and I began to dream of the day I would meet *my* Prince Charming! Living on the farm beyond the reach of worldly influences, my dreams of the future were innocent and unsullied if somewhat detached from real life! I smile now as I remember climbing a gum tree with friend Heather Windsor at the age of twelve, to sit among the branches and compose our own love stories in the true spirit of romance – of happy endings with maidens and their rescuing knights living happily ever after!

We were very blessed to grow up with plenty of climbing trees. One of our favourites was a gum tree that had a low, deeply curved bough, the perfect shape for holding a pillow saddle and bouncy enough to be a bucking bronco. When the huge guava tree was in season we climbed high into the branches and filled our tummies with the choicest golden fruit, making sure to avoid the overripe ones with tiny worms.

One day Madeline and I collected all the loose bricks we could find and beneath the guava tree built a little brick structure big enough to creep into. We set a square fireplace out of bricks, lit a small fire and proudly sat watching our potatoes boil in one of Mum's tiny aluminium pots. When big brother Stan passed by, he was alarmed at a precarious angle of the walls of our structure, and in spite of our wailing protests insisted that we dismantle it before it collapsed on us! We were bitterly disappointed but he explained the danger and showed us how to lay bricks safely, which stood us in good stead many years later when we made mission trips into northern Zululand to build for the locals.

Next to the guava tree stood the 'longan' tree from South East Asia, whose strange marble-sized fruit had a rough, olive-brown skin and a thin layer of flesh around a large shiny pip. We don't know where Dad bought it and I've never seen another like it but found its origin on the website. From six small China guava trees growing alongside the Barberton daisy patch we ate our fill in season. These and several orange and grapefruit trees along the vegetable garden fence provided us with a good fresh source of vitamin C and many jars of Mum's delicious homemade jellies and marmalade.

The farm driveway, bordered by tall gum trees, curved past the simple dwellings of our cook John, his wife Alice and two farm labourers. It continued straight up the hill to the house and farmyard. Running parallel to the drive opposite the litchi orchard on the left, a second row of gum trees formed an avenue to serve as a cattle track. At the top corner of the drive Dad had sunk a pipe across the yard to carry water to a deep trough, where the dairy cows could slake their thirst in the heat of the day and on their walk round the track to the shed before afternoon milking.

Opposite the trough was a flamboyant tree which we climbed to get a clear view of the district road in the distance that we called 'the flat'. From this vantage point we watched for a sighting of Daddy's car or expected guests, then raced home to tell Mum, "They're coming!" She would pop a batch of cheese scones into her Aga stove and ten minutes later greeted her guests with a welcoming tray of tea and hot scones straight from the oven. From a safe distance up the tree, we could also watch our fierce black bull, Dorni, grazing in the paddock, recognizable by his distinctive cream back and thick bronze nose-ring.

The driveway divided as it crested the hill, curving left to the kitchen door and in a wide sweep to the right past the front of the house to an open garage. Mum had filled the broad V-shaped

My Childhood Home

garden with a mass of coral Barberton daisies, which made a brilliant splash of colour in bloom.

Every little girl loves the thrill of secrets, and Madeline and I devised our own game of secrets using the pompom balls of fluff left when the blossoms died. We dug hiding places in the damp violet patch under the kitchen window and buried black canna seeds in the holes lined with leaves and Barberton fluff. Fortunately, the canna seeds didn't ever germinate among Mum's violets! Our major failed experiment was an attempt to make cigarettes by crushing dried leaves to fill dried Barberton daisy stalks! Needless to say we were saved from becoming smokers as the stalks turned immediately to ash when lit!

The wide front drive provided a perfect space for me to practise tennis strokes with Madeline, except after rain when the soft earth turned to mud and car tyres left deep ruts that dried into hard ridges and hurt our bare feet. However, once these had been flattened by the car, we could resume our games and our tennis balls and soles were stained bright orange from the rich red soil. In the rainy season we made sure to put on our oldest clothes to play outside and rinsed off well at the garden tap before coming inside. I salute Mummy's level of tolerance in allowing us the freedom to enjoy these fun times in spite of the muddy consequences and stained clothing!

Opposite the Barberton daisy patch on the driveway, Dad hung a swing from the peppercorn tree, another favourite for climbing except at a certain time of the year when its grey, uneven bark provided perfect cover for hordes of tiny hairy caterpillars. These grew into large, brilliantly coloured adults covered with stinging hairs and having once been stung, we were careful to give the tree a wide berth, so I don't remember ever seeing the transition from pupae to moths which must have flown away leaving it safe for us to climb again.

In their early years Mummy had trained a pink Natalia bougainvillea hedge into a shady summerhouse in the corner of the garden. On rare occasions when she took time out from household chores to relax, it was a treat to sit and share a tray of tea with her in this little nook. Here on the lawn we played with successive litters of glossy brown puppies from our gentle bull-mastiff bitch, Bhubezi[24]. I enjoyed watching my older sisters giving her an occasional bath on the grass, and squealed when she shook her wet coat over us. I absolutely adored the newly hatched little Bantam chicks, tiny balls of fluff that scrambled after their mothers who meandered through the flowerbeds scratching for worms. I couldn't bring myself to watch our cook, John, wringing the fowls' necks for the table, but I was able to watch with interest how he plucked and cleaned the dead birds for the pot after plunging them into a paraffin tin of very hot water to loosen the feathers.

I recall a hot summer day when my older sisters Enid and Coral had a visit from their friend Gwen Johnston from Maidstone village. They climbed up a long ladder on to the flat corrugated iron roof of the old shed to eat sweet lemons and chat in the cool breeze. On this occasion they allowed me to join them because I'd grown tall enough to span the gap from the ladder to the roof of the shed. I remember the heady sensation of feeling on top of the world as I looked right over the litchi orchard to the blue hills in the distance. From this dizzy height I looked down on our servant John boiling sheets in a paraffin tin over a fire in the paddock below, and managed to climb safely down the ladder to the ground in a carefully executed manoeuvre.

Not so lucky on another occasion was my descent from the roof of the old school bus that Dad had bought for us, which he had towed to the farm and parked beside the 'veggie' garden. I spent many happy hours holding school inside, using the panel behind the driver's seat as a blackboard, until it rusted away. One memorable day my older siblings had climbed from the window ledges on to the roof of the bus, but at nine or ten years my legs were still too short to reach. When I begged to join them, long arms reached down to pull me up from the window ledge. It felt grand to be one of the gang up there looking down on the world

---

[24] meaning 'lion'

until it was time to get down. Someone told me to place my feet on the window ledge as I was lowered, but unfortunately they let me go before I had found my footing and I hit the ground so hard that I was completely winded. The pain of the air rushing back into my lungs was excruciating, so needless to say I didn't repeat that lark until I had grown somewhat taller!

One of my favourite chores was helping John to fold sheets in the ironing room before he pressed them with the heavy charcoal iron. He was very patient with me when my small hands lost their grip at the corners in the cross-pulling to square up for folding. On the wooden table in the milking parlour next door stood the separator, a fascinating piece of equipment with two funnels that magically separated milk from the thick Jersey cream by centrifugal force. While John turned the handle I waited for the low humming sound of the machine to rise in pitch as the handle turned faster, watching intently up the spout for the flow to begin. As often as I watched the process it never lost its fascination, and if he was not in a hurry John would let me turn the handle. My treat was being allowed to lick the cream in the stainless steel bowl afterwards! The next process I never tired of watching was cream being churned into butter, which Mummy cut into blocks and pressed firmly between ridged wooden paddles to squeeze out the water.

Next to the cattle stalls Dad had built a block of cement sties to keep a few pigs. When the sows gave birth we walked gingerly along the top of the low walls of the enclosure to watch the tiny, pink newborn piglets suckling in a line along their mother's large body, always careful to keep a safe distance because Daddy had warned us that mother sows can be very aggressive in protecting their young.

In the storeroom between the milking parlour and the garage, Mum kept her wooden metal-banded pirate's chest full of fancy dress clothes. There was always great excitement when big sister Enid was given permission to unlock the chest. The old lid gave an agonized groan as it was prized open on its rusting hinges, and we could choose from the musty-smelling assortment of garments for

Riding High with Jesus

our imaginary games. For me the price to be paid for this pleasure was plucking up courage to sidle under the huge, fearsome-looking black and yellow spiders that lived in their incredibly strong webs along the beams of the old shed. The next fear I had to overcome was of the scuttling rats in the storeroom, which in their panic scrambled desperately in every direction to escape from the light that streamed into their dark world when the door was opened! After we'd had our fun Enid locked the chest and returned the key safely to Mum.

On rare occasions at weekends Lorna, Stan, Enid and Coral borrowed Dad's car to drive to Saturday night movies at the Maidstone Clubhouse. I sobbed at being told I was too young to go, but my sisters cheered me up with the promise of a sweetie surprise under my pillow! True to their promise, the next morning I would wake to find a little brown paper bag of nutty toffees or other penny assortments! In that same little bedroom off the lounge, I have clear memories of being confined to bed with chickenpox and reading a little book called 'Marigold Visits Grandmother' with an unusual illustration which captured my imagination, of a little girl stepping into a small round bath sunk into the bedroom floor!

It wasn't often that I was allowed to tag along with Stan and my older sisters on their teenage escapades. But one memorable occasion was a dusk raid on the mango trees of neighbouring Indian farmers! The fun of being included in the gang was short-lived however, as I plunged blindly through the razor-sharp leaves of the sugar cane desperately trying to keep up with them. The adventure turned to a nightmare for me when the Indian neighbour's dogs were alerted before we got anywhere near the mangoes. The others turned and ran for their lives, and I felt my lungs would burst as I raced back through the cutting leaves to escape. Back home in the bathtub, with the cuts on my body stinging painfully in the hot water, I decided some adventures were not worth the effort.

Madeline and I felt very important when we were invited to help our brother Stan and his friend Ian Hobbs catch mullet from

My Childhood Home

a boat on the Tongaat River lagoon. In the inky darkness of a moonless night, our job was to hold the lantern steady while they caught the fish that leaped toward the bright beam into the boat. Madeline was the brave one who enjoyed the experience, while on my shift I sat in trepidation of being slapped by the slippery, wet fish as they flung themselves out of the water in the direction of the light I was holding! Ian lived with his parents a couple of doors from our beach cottage[25]. His mother ran a guest house, and my lasting memory of Mrs Hobbs is of a stern-looking lady dressed at all hours in a kind of flowing kimono, with a perpetual cigarette between her nicotine-stained fingers!

When I was about nine years old, Coral, Madeline and I were sent by train to stay with family friends, Archie and Audrey Mitchell in Port Shepstone. I am not sure why, but it is possible that Mum had gone into hospital for the birth of our little sister Beth. Madeline and I remember feeling lost and homesick, but one enjoyable outing was a trip to a huge collective farm called 'Red Rhino' where acres of carrots and peas were growing. I was amazed at the sweetness of the crunchy green peas in pods and the size of the sweetest carrots I'd ever seen, which we rinsed off at the water well in the centre of the vast garden.

What should have been a happy day at the local village fair was ruined for me by bitter disappointment. We had never been to a village fair before so my excitement mounted as the day approached, eager to see what I could buy with my pocket money. We left early as Aunty Audrey was in charge of the handicraft stall and while she set up her stand, I stood looking at the dolls' clothes for sale. I fell instantly in love with the most beautiful, dainty soft pink knitted set that was the perfect size for my doll at home. As soon as the fair was declared open, I asked Aunty Audrey the price and was crushed with disappointment when she told me I didn't have enough. Clutching my money, I walked away in misery as that was the only thing I wanted. When the fair closed and left-over items were being packed away, Auntie Audrey offered me the

---

[25] The Shack. See page 82.

consolation of buying a dark pink set in thick wool, and not to appear ungrateful I accepted the compromise, but with a heavy heart. My doll Priscilla wore the consolation set for many years, a constant reminder of my first hard lesson in having to let go of disappointment before it turns to resentment.

Dancing Classes

Five Eckersley girls – Enid, Coral, Colleen, Madeline and Beth – had the opportunity of taking ballet lessons on Monday afternoons at the Maidstone Clubhouse. Enid led the way and became firm friends with Joan Brickhill, our first ballet teacher, who became a famous theatrical personality later in life. Village resident Mrs McKeon played the piano for us week by week, and Joan later handed over the classes to her pupil Patti Berry. We girls didn't all have star quality, but the dancing helped us to develop a measure of graceful deportment and we thoroughly enjoyed our classes.

We very seldom had pocket money to spend at the Clubhouse, but on very rare occasions Daddy would have a 'tickey'[26] for us to share. Every penny bought us four Nutties, chewy toffies with chips of nut; four black licorice Niggerballs, which changed to all the colours of the rainbow; or two gobstopper Apricots. I savoured my sweets slowly and was often teased by Coral and Madeline for making mine last long after theirs were finished, accused of deliberately trying to make them envious, which wasn't so.

It was at one of our ballet classes that I fell from grace over a tickey. Madeline's friend Myra Geraghty always had money for sweets at dancing classes, and on the fateful day Madeline was given a tickey too. I begged her to share her sweets with me, but contrary to her nature, this day she refused, saying, "If you want a tickey, go and ask Mrs Geraghty for your own." For me to overcome my shyness and do such a bold thing as to ask Mrs

---

[26] three pence

Geraghty for money would have required a lot of courage; I can only conclude that I must have been desperate! Of course, she graciously gave me a tickey too, but enjoyment was short-lived when my disgrace was relayed to Daddy on the drive home, while I stood in misery behind the front seat. Without any harsh words Daddy just turned his head to me, looked into my eyes and said firmly, "Don't *ever* do that again, my girl. We do not ask people for money." Daddy's quiet disapproval was all I needed to keep me from ever repeating the mistake.

V-J Day

Towards the end of the Second World War in 1945, when I was nine years old, my sisters and I were at our Monday afternoon dancing class at the Club House when we heard the Maidstone Sugar Mill hooter sending out unusually loud blasts. The sound continued for some minutes, and suddenly the exciting news spread rapidly from mouth to mouth: the hooter was declaring the good news of "V-J Day[27] victory" in resounding blasts that reached the whole village.

Living in South Africa, far removed from the realities of war, we only heard of the horrors taking place across the world on BBC News Broadcasts, so we children weren't aware of the full implication of the armistice. But from the talk among the mill workers who travelled home on the bus with us that day, we sensed that this was a momentous occasion. Listening to the BBC news that night on our old battery-operated radio was a joyful time for our parents, giving thanks to God for a step of hope toward peace in the world. The end of the war heralded the safe return to civilian life of our cousins Aubrey and Dennis McAravey who had enlisted in the army and served with the British forces in North Africa. Free to return to their families, too, were the sailor boys from the British Isles who had become deeply bonded with our family during their onshore leave visits. Mum continued to

---

[27] Victory over Japan Day

write to them, and later to their wives, for many years after their last visits.

Scary Happenings

One day our Zulu labourers on the farm reported that they had seen a very large, highly poisonous black mamba among the paraffin tins in the storeroom. Sending us back to the house, Dad and Stan, armed with shotguns, approached very cautiously and managed to catch a glimpse of the fast-moving mamba before it disappeared among the tins where it lived on a plentiful supply of rats. From a safe distance, we watched with bated breath as it was flushed out and shot by Dad who kept the nine-foot skin as a topic of lively conversation with visitors for years.

Lorna and Stan remember a terrifying earthquake which hit the farm when they were young, sending the windmill rocking back and forth on its base. A scary occasion of much lesser proportions in my young life was the arrival of a massive swarm of brown locusts on our farm. The sky was darkened by the oppressive cloud of large flying bodies overhead, accompanied by the unnerving sound of thousands of rustling wings as these ravenous insects descended and gobbled up every green leaf in sight. Like a combine harvester they moved through the green crops in the vegetable garden, the pasture in the paddock and the fruit trees, while the farm labourers tried unsuccessfully to frighten them off by banging paraffin tin lids together. Only when they had eaten everything in sight did the swarm move on as quickly as they had come, leaving the devastation of barren fields where a couple of hours before there had been the promise of good crops.

The most frightening experience I remember was a raging fire in the sugarcane fields of our Indian neighbours on an excessively hot, dry summer's day. Gale force north winds brought the huge flames leaping through the gum tree borders of our farm, totally beyond the control of staff and neighbours trying desperately to contain it. We children were hustled out of possible danger into the safety of our home but we could still feel the scorching heat

My Childhood Home

carried right across the farmyard by the force of the wind. Fortunately, the herd of milking cows was out grazing and the walls of the pigsty protected our sow and piglets from the flames. As the fire blazed through the cane and died down, many cane rats, snakes and even small buck were not so lucky, caught and incinerated in the cane fields by the galloping flames.

War Time Radio

During the war years before transistor radios, we gathered with Daddy and Mummy in the outside rondawel around our cumbersome old wireless powered by a car battery to listen to the BBC World News. When the battery charge ran out at the crucial moment of a programme and the reception grew more and more faint, there would be a frustrated chorus of voices: "Oh no! Not now!" On a light note, with the battery fully charged, we shared many laughs when we tuned in to the entertaining British programmes of the time: 'John and Julie', 'The Goons', 'Take it from Here', 'My Music' and our home-grown South African comedy 'Applesammy and Naidoo'.

Christmas Times

Because we weren't spoilt with material things, Christmas was an exciting time of eager anticipation. One thing we looked forward to each year was a new dress which Mummy found time to sew in the midst of all her chores, probably burning midnight oil while we slept. In a cubbyhole in her writing desk, she kept a small, green-covered notebook in which she recorded her secret lists of gift ideas for the family. As each Christmas approached, the temptation grew very strong to peep into the book. The day Madeline and I succumbed, we discovered that the pages were clean! Crafty Mum had fooled us with an identical book of emptiness while the secret list lay well hidden!

Mum's ingenuity came to the fore as she bought gifts through the year and came up with inexpensive ideas to fill not just a stocking, but a pillowcase! We always had one 'main' gift accompanied by smaller ones – a current Girls Annual, new items of clothing and other practical gifts which were a joy to receive because Mum knew each of her children's interests so well. My bag usually included chalks for my blackboard, wax crayons with a colouring book and a book from the 'Secret Seven', 'Nancy Drew' or 'Hardy Boys' series. Before the advent of ball pens, one of my most thrilling gifts as a high school pupil was a green Easterbrook fountain pen with an ink tube and smooth nib that was a real pleasure to write with. At the bottom of the pillowcase would be tasty treats: a rosy apple, walnuts, almonds and hazel nuts in their shells, a tin of caramelised Condensed milk and sweets in novelty packing.

Just once I made the mistake of crawling to the foot of my bed at dawn on Christmas morning to peep while everyone else slept. In the half light I could just make out the shape of a racquet handle poking from the pillowcase and, although I managed to drop off to sleep again, suffered the miserable anti-climax of hearing Madeline's whoops of surprise when she woke. We had received tennis and badminton racquets, which gave us great pleasure.

Every year up to the age of ten I looked forward to receiving a new doll. In fact, they weren't *new,* but an older sister's doll that Mum had sent to the Dolls' Hospital in Durban for a fresh coat of paint and repair to fingers and toes worn down with loving. Because Mummy dressed them in new outfits, the dolls took on new character, and I was quite content to choose a new name for each inherited baby. I do remember one year getting a brand new 'Wetums' doll which had a little feeding bottle that fitted into a tiny hole in her rosebud mouth and an inner tube that carried water inside the body to the nappy. I guess I must have passed her on to Madeline because the last doll that I kept was 'Priscilla'. Priscilla was passed on to my daughter Shelley Anne and at the time of writing is safe in the hands of her daughter Hayley Beth.

During my last years at primary school, Friday evenings were filled with anticipation when big sisters Enid and Coral were due

My Childhood Home

to come home from high school in Durban. Once Dad had closed his office, we drove to the Old Home and waited with the aunties and Uncle Mac for the train to arrive at 6.30pm. While the grown-ups sat chatting in low tones on the verandah, Madeline and I lay on the broad concrete steps warmed by the sun and listened to the raucous noise of dozens of starlings fighting for a roosting place in the massive wild fig tree in front of the house. On winter evenings we counted the stars as they began to appear with the rising moon in the darkening sky.

As the train left the railway siding at La Mercy and whistled to announce its approach, Dad would say, "Come on, girls!" and bidding the aunties goodbye, we climbed into the car and drove down the hill to Tongaat Station just as the train drew in. We were so delighted to have our big sisters home it took a lot of restraint next morning not to creep into their thatched rondawel and wake them.

Once they had started working, Stan and the girls bought 78" shellac records of top artists of the moment and brought them home at weekends to play on the old wind-up gramophone. Some I remember came from the Musical Shows, others were by popular singers and musicians of the day – Frank Sinatra, Bing Crosby, Louis Armstrong, Glen Miller, Frank Ifield, Johnny Ray, Shirley Bassey and Danny Kay to name just a few. Mummy had a good selection of old records which included piano-playing Charlie Kunz and several of the classics. Later came LPs – long playing vinyl records capturing every genre of music from jazz to the classics, which broke on to the market with huge success.

When I was twelve years old, a Zulu mother approached Dad with a request to employ her deaf and dumb son Moti as a herd boy. Dad was very sceptical about employing a lad who could neither hear nor speak, but she begged Dad to give him a chance, promising that he would be vigilant about keeping the cattle out of the neighbours' cane fields. Dad eventually agreed to take him on trial and he proved to be not only very bright, but the most reliable herdsman we ever had. Years later when our house servant John retired, Mum took Moti into the kitchen and with her own devised sign language, trained him in everything he needed to know. We all learnt to communicate with him and Moti became a much appreciated part of our family. He was with us for many years, saw all of us married, and delighted in the arrival of each new grandchild.

Fun Times and Holidays at Tongaat Beach

I am grateful to have two faded sepia photos taken on Mummy's 'Brownie' box camera of me at two years, standing in a rock pool in knitted swimsuit with striped bib, short dark brown hair and fringe framing my serious little face. But my first actual childhood memories go back to when I was three or four years old. Favourite outings were family picnics at Tongaat Beach, and setting off for the beach was great fun.

Walking barefoot down the narrow bush path to the beach, everyone carried some item of food, drink and huge watermelons in the summer. When a perfect spot was found sheltered from the wind in the lee of the big rocks, Mummy spread the colourful tablecloth on the sand. We watched with eager anticipation as she opened the wicker picnic basket lined with pretty checked fabric, and unbuckled little straps that held sets of plates, cutlery and cups in place. The cloth was soon covered with a mouth-watering array of boiled green mealies, hard-boiled eggs, cold meats and salads, buttered bread and little cheese wedges in silver paper. After playing in the rock pools we didn't need to be called twice to come to lunch.

Kneeling in our 'cozzies' around the edge of the cloth, careful not to kick sand into the food, we tucked into the tasty treats. During the December holidays meals ended with a generous supply of luscious ripe litchis from our own orchard on the farm, or thick slices of chilled juicy watermelons. We stood in the warm sunshine having competitions to see who could spit the shiny black pips the furthest, while the cool juice dripping from our elbows made patterns in the sand.

My Childhood Home

For a number of years Mum and Dad rented the Acutt family's cottage at Tongaat Beach on the north coast of Natal for the duration of long July and December school holidays. There was much activity in advance as Mum checked that we had all we needed in food, farm milk, drinks, clothes, costumes, towels and extras before the car was eventually packed to the hilt and we set off all keyed up with excitement. Our family game was vying to be the first to get a glimpse of the sea when we crested the hill before descending to the seafront, and inevitably after the chorus of little voices rang out in unison, "I see the sea first," there would be a squabble as to who was the winner.

Acutts' property was the most child-friendly, delightful place to spend carefree holidays, with mkhuhla[28] trees that spread their branches so low across the lawn that even the smallest child could climb them with ease. On arrival at the cottage, while Daddy opened the boot of the car to unpack, Mummy turned the key in the rusty old lock and opened the front door to be met by the dank, musty smell of the cottage which had been closed for months.

Following Mum into the house, I felt uneasy in the darkened rooms until Daddy removed the wooden shutters on the windows and daylight flooded in to reveal the familiar shapes of the furniture. There were the old beds with sagging, creaky springs, coir mattresses filled with coarse fibre that pricked through our cotton sheets, and hard pillows in their striped ticking. Because there was no refrigerator, one of Mum's first tasks was to boil the supply of fresh milk we had brought and stand it in the coolest place to chill. I loved the thick crust of cream that formed on the boiled milk when it cooled.

After we'd helped to offload the car, our first instinct was to run down the path through the fringe of indigenous bush on to the shore. On the bush path it was my delight to stop and sift bare toes through the fine grey powdery sand, so soft and different from the course sea sand.

---

[28] Zulu for 'milkwood'

Not far from the cottage was a large rock pool named 'Marots' Pool' because it was in line with the Marot family's cottage. Here we swam safely within the circle of protective rocks until high tide brought huge waves crashing in. A sober memory for me was a game that could have ended in tragedy. We were having fun in the pool linking hands in a wide circle and taking turns to jump over the arms of those opposite. The tide turned and suddenly a massive wave crashed over us, breaking the circle. As the wave receded I felt myself being swept out to sea by the strong current through a narrow gully. Fortunately, my older siblings realized what was happening and dragged me back in the nick of time, shaking with fear but having learned the vital lesson of respecting the power of the sea.

In the days before chemical effluent from factories began to destroy the seaweed and shell life on our shoreline, we spent hours playing at low tide on the wide rocky reef. Our childlike imagination ran riot, creating scenes of wonder in rock pools with the wide variety of beautiful seaweeds of every colour that grew in abundance. We learned not to walk barefoot on the rocks covered with razor-sharp barnacles, because painful cuts from their poisonous casings took a long time to heal even in the salt water.

Sailor Boys' Visits

Some of our most special memories at Acutts' cottage were made during the wartime visits of young sailors from British warships, from the time I was six or seven. They were billeted to our family over Christmas while their ships were docked in Durban harbour. The first sailor boys to come were Johnnie Lowe from Scotland, Bob Chaffey from Devon, Glynn Davies from Scotland, and Ron Fentum from England. Christmas dinners were joyous times around the long table with Mummy's imaginative decorations at the centre. One centrepiece I remember well was a big cardboard model of the lads' own ship, the 'Vanguard', with streamers from each place setting tied to simple gifts on the deck. The sailor boys were generous in bringing us their issue of whole boxes of 'Wrigleys' and 'PK' chewing gum, a rare treat which we enjoyed to the full.

Holiday Friendships

For many years, friends Marcus and Erin Mason from Pietermaritzburg camped out in tents in the indigenous bush at the Tongaat River mouth with their son Ainsley and daughter Leonie, who were Stan and Enid's ages. Enid had the frightening experience in her youth of being dragged out through a narrow gulley at Fynney's Rocks by the strong current at high tide. Being a very powerful swimmer, Ainsley was able to swim out and save her from being swept out to sea.

Every year when I was little, I remember walking with Mummy along the sandy beach road to visit a lady called Grace Plough, who came to her little rondawel cottages near the river mouth for a few weeks at a time. I was fascinated by this theatrical lady who always wore bright red lipstick, dressed in kimono-type flowing garments and wore a turban scarf around her head. She held a lighted cigarette in a holder between her ringed fingers, and as she came to welcome us was surrounded by half a dozen little yapping Pekinese dogs that made me very nervous as they pranced wildly around us.

We made lots of friends who came from far and wide to holiday at Tongaat Beach every year. Dr 'Maf' Helm, who practised in the Reef Mining area of the Transvaal, and his wife Peggy had built a secluded cottage in the bush above the beach road next door to us. They came down to the coast with their four little girls, Priscilla (Micky), Margaret (Doozy) and twin girls Elizabeth (Icky Pick) and Susan (Wobs). Maf's sister Heidel and her husband Dr Nico Viljoen owned the large cottage on the seafront. They came down from the Transvaal with their young daughter Veronica, nicknamed 'Daughty', and sometimes her older half-brother Bunjohn. 'Aunt' Heidel was a flamboyant, outgoing person, with thinning fair hair which she gathered up in a tiny bun on the top of her head, while 'Uncle' Nico wore a neat moustache, spectacles and always had a twinkle in his eyes with a perpetual smile for us. Being a 'laat lammetjie'[29], Daughty was old-fashioned in her ways but enjoyed our girlish company.

Cousins Jasper and Emden Pons, with their quietly-spoken mother, completed the extended family that we saw year after year. We girls always looked forward to visiting the Viljoen cottage because of the relaxed elegance of their lifestyle, even on holiday. For them the cottage was home from home, abounding with all sorts of interesting objects, sculptures, glossy magazines and books on every topic – not to mention good food and cocktails of an evening! The large table on the spacious porch was always strewn with signs of life, and tea trays held multiple cups at any sitting.

Our busy little mother seldom found time to rest during the day, so it was a novelty for us to find their cottage wrapped in silence for a couple of hours after lunch, while Nico, Heidel and other adults took a daily nap. Their black servants living nearby on beach property served afternoon tea on the porch at the appropriate time of four o'clock. Dr Nico told us that there were so many girls in our family that he couldn't remember all our names, so he named us by numbers: Daughter 1 to Daughter 6!

Heidel, who was keenly interested in theatre, encouraged us to put on annual concerts in their cottage. Every year she entertained us with her personal charade of a Chinaman chasing, or being chased, up many flights of stairs to the top of a castle. Then it was our turn to entertain the adults with our plays, wearing makeshift costumes raided from all their wardrobes and cupboards. I was useless at contributing ideas to the plots but, shy or not, was roped into joining the action as best I could, and many were the happy afternoons spent in their spacious lounge. I have never forgotten one little ditty that Heidel taught us with simple actions, which I've used as an item in charades when pressed into participating.

---

[29] born to older parents

My Childhood Home

A little boy and a little girl in an ecstasy of bliss...
Said the little boy to the little girl,
"Pray give me just one kiss."
The girl drew back in great surprise;
"You're a stranger, sir," said she,
"but I will give you just one kiss,
when apples grow on the lilac tree."

The boy felt so downhearted;
she was the only one!
The girl felt quite remorseful
at the terrible thing she had done.
So early in the morning on the very next day,
he was quite surprised to see
his little girlfriend standing in the garden,
tying apples on the lilac tree!

Mrs Tippler, a mother from Rhodesia, came for several holidays with her lovely large brood of children. I can't remember all their names but in my early teens secretly fancied the eldest son, Ted. Our relaxed days passed in happy group activities, swimming in the waves, building sandcastles, playing card games, listening to 78 rpm shellac records on the wind-up gramophone in our Shack cottage and laughing a lot. Adelaide Samuelson from Pietermaritzburg, with her children Vernon, Clare, Joy and Elizabeth, were also welcome additions to our circle of friends. Studious daughter Liz with theatrical leanings was the brain behind the exciting action game of 'Highwaymen' which we girls acted out on the sandy beach road, using green leaves for currency which we robbed from the rich. Names of other friends that spring to mind are Carl Clayton and our next door neighbours David, Anne, Dorothy and John Bass. The big brown rock below the Basses' cottage had taken its name from their grandfather's era and became known as Grooms' Rock.

Daddy and Stan were both keen fishermen who went out at dusk or early morning with rods and reels, often coming home with sizeable catches including enormous salmon. Sadly, fish of that size have long disappeared from our coastal waters and today even the smaller bream, striped karanteen and shad have almost been fished to extinction too. Daddy made his little girls small bamboo rods with simple bent pin hooks that caught pinkies which he used as bait. The fun was in catching a fish but I was too wary of the sharp fins to pick up the fish and retrieve the hook from its mouth, so patient Dad had to put down his rod and free my hook for the next catch. The one fish all fishermen dreaded on the end of the line was the poisonous toby fish, which blew its body into a balloon and cut through the line with razor sharp teeth so hook and sinker were lost.

Every July for many years we experienced the amazing phenomenon of the 'sardine run' when shoals of millions of shimmering little sardines came close enough to shore for people to wade in and scoop them up in whatever container was handy – buckets, basins, plastic bags, picnic baskets and even skirts and jackets! The novelty of their sudden arrival in such huge quantities caused a state of hysteria among holidaymakers and fishermen, who fought to collect as many as possible. For the gulls and other seabirds there was an overabundance of ready meals, while for the fishermen the sardine run often heralded good catches of the larger fish which came to feed on the shoals.

Our Own Bush Cottage

After years of holidaying at Acutts' rented cottage, Dad bought a piece of land covered with virgin bush above the beach road. There he built The Shack, a rustic wood and corrugated iron cottage. Labourers from our farm cleared a large patch in the bush and planted a lawn of tough kikuyu grass before the building was completed. In those early days, to boil water for tea Mum hung a kettle from a tripod of green sticks of wood bent over an open fire in true Girl Guide fashion. She created outdoor tables and stools by weaving strong green vines into mats for seats and tabletops, which she nailed on to four stout posts driven into the earth.

My Childhood Home

Between two trees Mum hung a string hammock which offered a wonderfully relaxing spot under the canopy of leaves on hot summer days.

Once The Shack was completed, the holidays we spent there in the virgin bush had a simple Robinson Crusoe quality. We swung on monkey ropes as thick as our arms, which hung from the tops of tall trees, and examined at close quarters all the woodland flowers, insects and creatures – birds, beetles, spiders, frogs, ants, lizards, crabs and songololos[30] which curled up into a ball when touched. Troops of grey vervet monkeys were frequent visitors, watching us closely from the treetops. We loved to watch the tiny babies clinging on to their mothers' tummies as they leapt from branch to branch.

Not as plentiful but always present were the nocturnal bushbabies which moved about under cover of darkness. Their plaintive cry could be heard clearly on the quiet night air but all we could see were two large glistening eyes by the light of the moon or a torch beam. One inky black night I had an experience with a bushbaby which has provided the family with many laughs at my expense. While everyone else was inside the cottage I was sitting in the semi-dark on the edge of the front porch washing my feet in a basin of water. Suddenly, out of the stillness the loud cry of a bushbaby rang out from a branch hanging right over my head. It gave me such a fright that I leapt up, sent the basin of water and soap flying and hurtled into the room with hammering heart to be met by a roar of laughter from the family. The memory still brings chuckles as the tale of 'Colleen and the bushbaby' is recalled from time to time!

We young ones were usually content to play our own childish games but sometimes asked to join our older siblings in their pursuits. A favourite game played among the sand dunes in the pitch dark on moonless nights was 'Jack, Jack, strike your light'. The person with a torch moved constantly and flashed the light briefly when someone called for him to signal his whereabouts.

---

[30] Zulu for 'millipedes'

Everyone would then dash wildly after the beam to catch him and take over the light. As exciting as it was to be included in the game, I felt very scared when cut off from everyone else in the inky blackness of the silent dunes, my little legs struggling through heavy sand to keep pace with the ever-moving light.

Mummy devised simple indoor games for us to play with our friends after dark and on rainy days. One game she made to test our observation skills was that of sticking portions of product labels on a large cardboard, and points were won for recognizing the full name of each product. Another memory-teaser was a random selection of small articles laid on a tray under a cloth. The cloth was lifted for a few quick seconds then replaced, and to win the prize we had to note how many things we could remember. 'Beetle' was another old favourite, played with a dice on orange-coloured scorecards. The numbers on the dice represented parts of the beetle's body and the first person to complete the full beetle with abdomen, six legs, two feelers and two eyes was the winner. Packs of playing cards often saved the day with games such as 'Happy Families', 'Snap', 'Rummy' and 'Patience', and of course the old wind-up gramophone was constantly in use, playing our selection of favourites of the day. Sometimes during the summer rains, bored with being indoors we put on our swimming costumes and braved the cold, stinging raindrops to run down for a swim. The ocean felt surprisingly warm by contrast and when we eventually got out of the water, it was to race helter-skelter for home to get warm and dry again.

Ocean View Cottage

The cottage overlooking the ocean in front of The Shack had been the property of the Stranack family for many years, but was now owned by Mr and Mrs Bill Broad from Durban. As we had right of way through their property to the beach, Mum extended the hand of friendship to Mr and Mrs Broad and we girls soon made friends with Jennifer, their only child about my age. We discovered she was a lonesome little girl and tried to include her in

My Childhood Home

our games, but she wasn't accustomed to our energetic outdoor activities so we played lots of indoor board games and cards with her. Her parents were fascinated to see how the Eckersley family enjoyed carefree holidays on a shoestring budget in our simple wood and iron cottage. When Mrs Broad heard that we had no refrigeration in our rustic cottage in the heat of summer, she offered Mum fridge space for perishables and butter, little knowing that her friendly outreach would later open the door to a significant blessing for our whole family.

After some months it became clear to Jennifer's parents that she wasn't interested in the beach so they decided to sell the cottage, giving Mum and Dad first option to purchase. For many years the worries of the farm and financial pressures had placed Dad under tremendous strain and eventually Mum persuaded him to sell the farm, buy 'Ocean View' from the Broads and move down to make it their home. Mum told us of the frustration she had felt years before, when the cottage had come on to the market at a much lower price and she had tried to persuade Dad to buy it but he felt they couldn't afford it and it had slipped out of their fingers. This time Mum made sure that didn't happen again!

In due course things came full circle and the little cottage became a haven of tremendous blessing to Mum, Dad and the extended family of children and grandchildren. Our builder brother Stan, with the help of labourers, added another bedroom, bathroom and indoor toilet at the back, with a separate outdoor shower to rinse off the salt water after swimming. He also enclosed the front porch with large glass windows and a front door, which gave extended living space in all kinds of weather.

The magnificent view from the porch stretched along the beach from Groom's rock directly below to Durban Channel, enabling Dad to watch us through his binoculars anywhere on the beach or swimming in the bay. We studied the ocean tides and currents and learned that as long as the tide was coming in, we were safe to swim out to the breakers and enjoy the huge swells that would bring us back to land. Being a non-swimmer, Dad became anxious at times about us being far out and would say to

Mum, "Girlie, shouldn't those girls come closer in?" She reassured him that the tide was coming in so we'd be safe. And we were. The cottage was transformed by Mum into a charming home which we and our children came to love dearly on our visits. Mum's faithful deaf and dumb servant Moti moved with them from the farm and continued to serve the family for many years.

The Royal Family Visit to South Africa

I was eleven years old in 1947 when South Africa, a Commonwealth colony, prepared for an occasion of very special significance to our country, the Royal visit of King George VI, Queen Elizabeth and Princesses Elizabeth and Margaret. Madeline and I felt honoured to be in the group chosen to represent our Maidstone Primary School at the impressive Floral Pageant enacted by thousands of school children at the Greyville Stadium in Durban. We were driven to the big city in our school bus, bubbling over with excitement all the way.

On arrival at the stadium, we were shepherded through thousands of other school children to allocated seats in the stands. Tightly clutching the little wooden suitcase which Mummy had filled with our picnic lunch, we felt proud of the bright patriotic Union Jack flag she'd painted on the lid. For two little country bumpkins who seldom travelled beyond the confines of our village, it was an outing never to be forgotten! The precision of the synchronized movements of thousands of children creating beautiful floral patterns left us enthralled, with much to tell Mummy and Daddy when we got home.

Not long afterwards the Royal train was due to pass through our village on its way up the north coast. At Maidstone Station the whole school gathered on the platform with a crowd of adults to greet the Royals, and our friend Maureen Groom was waiting to present the Queen with a bouquet of flowers. We watched in excited anticipation as the train approached, but it was running late and had no time for the Royal party to engage with the waiting crowd. So it simply slowed down for us to catch a glimpse of the warm smiles and waves of the Royal family through the open windows before it glided out of the station and was gone. The crowd on the platform stood in shocked silence; one disappointed little girl stood clutching the bouquet of flowers the Queen would never see.

A few days later Mum, Dad, Enid, Coral and I had a wonderful close-up view of the Royal Family from the garage roof of Bill Windsor's home overlooking the street in Durban. Having been advised that the Royal cavalcade was scheduled to travel past the house, we settled ourselves well ahead of time. It was a beautiful sunny day and to our delight we were rewarded with a fantastic view of the family in their open-top cars as they drove slowly past. The King, Queen and Princesses looked directly up at us and waved, a thrilling moment after our long wait! It was not long after their visit that the sad news hit the world of King George's untimely death during Princess Elizabeth's honeymoon in Africa. She was catapulted into the role of Queen as suddenly as her father George had been when his older brother Edward had abdicated from the throne to marry Mrs Wallace Simpson.

'Shanks's Pony'

With finances limited for keeping our family car on the road, throughout our childhood we accepted walking as a matter of course. The daily distance to catch the school bus on the main road was two-and-a-half miles of dusty road, come rain or shine. On hot summer afternoons Mum would have cold juice waiting for her tired little brood as we trudged up the last stretch of the road, often in tears of sheer exhaustion. On rainy days it would be steaming mugs of hot Milo waiting to welcome us home, after Mummy had peeled off our soaking clothes and rubbed us down in the cosy warmth of the kitchen.

Still vivid are memories of being the little one at six years in my first school year, struggling at times to keep up with my older sisters Enid and Coral on the long walks home. It didn't help to sit down in the dust and cry for them to wait for me as my little legs just couldn't go any faster. Being tired and eager to get home they weren't keen to stop, so I would have to get up and run even faster to catch up!

In the cutting season we hailed the drivers of sugarcane trucks for lifts as they returned empty from the sugar mill, but some drivers ignored our pleading eyes and roared past leaving us in clouds of choking dust. The exceptions were Mr P. G. Naidoo's drivers, an Indian farmer who had good relations with Dad who had instructed his drivers to stop for us and we clambered gratefully on board. I don't know how the cordial relationship developed between Dad and Mr Naidoo, but every year he gave us an iced Christmas cake with Father Christmas decorations and Dad gave him a generous gift of litchis.

Those years of walking long distances produced strong calf muscles in my legs, and empathy in my heart for others on foot so it was my pleasure many years later to offer lifts in my car to pedestrians of all races.

At the bridge where we waited daily for the school bus, a little stream ran under the main road. Every day I looked longingly over the wall at the pretty blue wild flowers growing down the grassy bank and wished I could pick some for my teacher. One day, in spite of my older sisters' warnings about the danger of falling into the river, I clambered down to the bottom clinging on to the strong grass roots and just managed to scramble up again in time for the approaching bus. What a sense of achievement as I clutched my little posy of bruised offerings and presented them to my teacher!

On hot summer afternoons after school we would call at Dad's office at the beer hall to leave our shoes, socks and satchels in the car and walk home barefoot. A short section of the clay road shaded from the sun by the high bank was pressed as smooth as glass, a delightfully cool balm to our burning soles. Sometimes I knelt down and pressed my cheeks against the smooth earth to feel the welcome coolness on my face! An Indian family by the name of Govender lived beside the road and one of the sons took a shine to Coral. One day as we walked past he was waiting with a bunch of roses which he offered her. Sadly, in the days of racial discrimination in South Africa it was a bold thing to do, and Coral put up with a lot of teasing from the family about her admirer!

After dancing class on Monday afternoons, we walked to the sugar mill to catch the 4.30pm workers' bus to the beer hall. It would be almost closing time for Daddy and I loved to stand beside his large desk and watch him writing out stall holders' receipts in his beautiful copybook handwriting. Once he had balanced the takings with the receipt book, he locked the cash box in the big safe in the corner, which was our cue to gather satchels, shoes and lunchboxes. Dad put on his jacket and hat before locking the office door, and we followed him along the outside path bordered by a spiky Christ-thorn hedge with bright red flowers to where the car was parked at the rear of the beer hall, and settled ourselves for the journey home, hungry for one of Mummy's tasty dinners.

One section of the road which became impassable in rainy weather was the very steep hill running past the property of an Indian farmer, Mr Inkster. In rainy weather he gave Dad permission to take a detour drive through his property to avoid having to put chains on the wheels. Near the summit of the big hill above a small quarry stood the remains of a building like a small Hindu temple, next to a leaning tree which produced beautiful red blossoms on its starkly bare branches. One day Mr Inkster invited us to a family wedding, conducted according to their traditional Hindu custom. As a child I was puzzled and quite concerned that the young bride and groom in traditional finery had to sit engulfed in a veil of smoke from the open ceremonial fire burning in front of them! A fascinating first for us was sitting cross-legged on the ground, in true Indian fashion, eating curry and rice off banana leaves with our fingers.

Another problematic stretch of the road in the rainy season was where our farm drive branched off the public road in front of the property of our Indian neighbour, Mr Timal. There was a dangerously steep drop from the road if the car skidded, so Dad had no option but to use their private driveway to bypass the dangerous section. For reasons I never knew as a child, I picked up from older siblings that feelings between our families were strained and I do remember Daddy becoming irate on occasions when they had put a chain across their road to prevent us from coming through.

Fancy Dress Parties

Every year the Tongaat Sugar Company held a children's fancy dress competition for their employees, to which our Eckersley family was invited. With very little money to spend, Mummy devised wonderfully imaginative costumes which usually won prizes. While still a baby just able to stand alone, I received my earliest prize when Mummy entered me as 'Doll in a Box'. Unfortunately, camera spools were hard to come by during those war years so we have no photos, but Mum described how she dressed me exactly like a baby doll in simple calico nappy and vest and carried me round the parade in the box. The judges asked her to stand the box on the floor and I stood so still they couldn't believe I was real. Calling Mum to the table they turned me round to inspect my outfit more closely, and the authentic detail of a small, gold safety-pin at the neck of the vest was the final attention to detail that clinched Mum's well-deserved Special Prize. How I wish that I had a photo of that special occasion, but I do have other black and white snapshots of fancy dress entries, including one at three years dressed as Red Riding Hood in little gathered hood and cape, short frock and black buttoned shoes.

At age four or five I won a Special Prize with my big sister Lorna when we represented the two grannies on the 'Mazawattee Tea' caddies, wearing long dresses, shawls, lace collars and little gold-rimmed spectacles. Later, at age ten or eleven, I was a Zulu 'tombi'[31] with special theatrical powder to tan my body a rich brown, a black peppercorn wig, handcrafted beadwork and genuine traditional tribal cotton wraps. Winning the Special Prize

---

[31] girl

was great fun, but not so the painful process of removing the stubborn brown stain from my whole body! Screened from view by the bush next to the privy in the late afternoon chill, my shivering body was soaped and vigorously scrubbed from top to toe by Mum and an older sister.

Considering that we weren't employees of the Sugar Company, I felt very honoured at the age of twelve to be chosen by the committee to be Father Christmas's fairy at their Christmas Tree Party. At Mrs McKeon's home near the clubhouse, Mum helped me dress in the pretty white frock she had made, with a halo of tinsel in my hair, sparkly slippers and silver wand topped by a shimmering star. I was very excited when Father Christmas and I set off for the clubhouse on the back of a truck, but on arrival was overwhelmed by the thunderous applause from hundreds of cheering children waiting at the front steps. I was lifted down and made my way on to the stage to take my place among the gifts. Happily, once the children began to receive their gifts from me, I forgot my fears and was able to enjoy the occasion.

Primary School Days

My school life started at Maidstone government school in the year I turned six while Stan, Enid and Coral were still pupils there, and my rather vague memory of the Class 1 teacher, Miss Jacobs, is that she was a kind lady. I remember the novelty of lunchbreaks in my first year when there were five of us at school, because Mum sent a picnic hamper full of interesting lunches with one of the farm labourers on foot. In the shade of peppercorn trees lining the pathway, we gathered round the basket with anticipation. The sweet aroma of cold steamed mealies and other treats flowed out the moment the lid was lifted, and we sat down on large, flat sandstones to tuck into our refreshing meal, to the envy of many onlookers. Later when Madeline and I were the only ones at school, we filled our lunchboxes with more modest fare,

Riding High with Jesus

sometimes ground up maize in 'maas'[32] or leftover mince on sandwiches.

When a school was built in Maidstone next to the Anglican Church, Mr Armfield the rotund old Headmaster at the Tongaat School retired and was succeeded by the Afrikaans-speaking headmaster Nic Strydom. Nic was tall and slim, always wore cream linen suits and at times displayed a fiery temper, so as a little girl I lived very much in awe of him. On Friday afternoons a few of us in the first grades had to wait for older siblings, and Mr Strydom brought us into the senior classroom, while he continued to teach his class. He kept us occupied by copying lists of Afrikaans words from the blackboard and I felt very important sitting in one of the enormous desks at the back of the room, diligently copying the list into my blue notebook. Looking back, I know it was during these early lessons that my love for the Afrikaans language was born.

I remember my Standard 2 teacher, Mrs Eichstedt, for a subtle German influence she tried to introduce to her class, teaching us that the proper way to walk was toe before heel. When I showed Daddy that night what we had been taught, he emphatically insisted that this was *not* the correct way to walk but made no further comment. I accepted without question what Daddy said, and only years later did it dawn on me that she had actually been teaching us the Nazi goose step!

Our Standards 3 and 4 combined teacher, Mrs Rhona Kean, was such a gentle, kind soul that disciplining pupils didn't come easy to her. She had started her career as a single young teacher in Maidstone and became a legend during her long service to the school over several generations of pupils who all remember her fondly. Midway through my Standard 5 year, headmaster Nic Strydom retired. Following an interim head, Mrs Brown, for a few months, a new headmaster, Eric Reid, moved into the school house on the property with his wife and only child, Neville. Mr Reid was an excellent teacher, firm but fair and in manner and

---

[32] thick soured milk

background as English as Nic Strydom was Afrikaans. As pupils are wont to do, we summed up our principal's moods by the suits he wore, and woe betide anyone who stepped out of line on the day Mr Reid wore his mustard suit!

Eric Reid possessed a spirit of encouragement and keen enthusiasm to see his pupils succeed. At one of our English lessons he threw me the challenge of presenting an impromptu radio programme of Aunty Midge's BBC 'Children's Hour' to the class. From a microphone set up outside with an extension cord leading to the speaker in the scout hall, I had great fun presenting my lesson to the class. I scored a high mark with encouragement from Mr Reid to pursue my dream of becoming a teacher, as he believed I would do well in the profession.

Many years later while sorting through my possessions, I discovered all my school reports from the year 1942 when I started school in Class 1 to the end of my matriculation high school days in 1953, plus Durban Speech and Drama Festival certificates and Training College Teacher's Diploma. From all my reports it is clear that I enjoyed primary school, but disruptive boarding problems in my high school years were reflected in less favourable matriculation results. However, I scraped through and moved into my chosen career as a teacher.

Spiritual Awakenings

My heart responded to God's love at a very early age. For me His character as a loving Father in heaven was epitomised in my own Dad, and Christian faith was lived out practically in our home. With Mother's faith firmly grounded as a missionary's daughter, her daily example of positive trust in God laid a firm foundation of faith for all her children. Our illustrated Bible story books held tales of the men and women of Old Testament days whose obedience to God brought great blessing and sad consequences of disobedience in turning to false gods.

We lived too far from Maidstone village to go to Sunday school but on Friday afternoons after school we attended Bible classes in the Anglican Church next door. My imagination was captured and my young heart reached out to God as I listened intently to the Rev. Truscott bringing stories of the Bible to life. I loved to sing well-known old hymns and every week treasured the little Bible memory verse with pretty flower decoration that I stuck carefully into a tiny notebook.

Every school morning began with Assembly and the words of the hymns we learnt in those days were firmly imprinted on my memory. 'Abide with Me' reminds me of Cedric Melsetter, one of the boys in my Standard 6 class who died suddenly at twelve years of age. He was the only young person I knew to die in childhood, so his death left a deeply sobering impression on me. Growing up in an age of lingering post-Victorian traditions, funerals were generally attended only by men. In that day there was real respect for human life, so whenever a funeral procession of hearse and cars passed on route to the cemetery, everyone along the road stopped and hats were raised to show respect for the deceased. How different things are today, when life appears to have little or no value for so many!

As a fifteen-year-old member of the West Street Methodist Youth Guild in Durban, I attended my first Easter Youth Camp at Bothas Hill in 1951. The weekend teachings on the life of the Son of God, Jesus Christ and his sacrificial death were from the Bible passage in John's Gospel: "If we claim to be without sin, we deceive ourselves and the truth is not in us. If we confess our sins, he is faithful and just and will forgive us our sins and purify us from all unrighteousness."

With hundreds of other young people, I enjoyed daily times of worship and praise to God in song, group discussions around the Bible, prayer, and time for relaxed fun-filled team games. At the closing service in the chapel on Easter Sunday, an invitation was given to all who wished to receive Jesus Christ as Saviour to come forward. My heart was broken by the revelation that Jesus had gone to the Cross for *my* sin, and fighting my shyness I began the long walk up the aisle to the front of the chapel in tears of repentance, to declare my personal commitment to Jesus Christ.

One of the camp counsellors, Marjorie Tarbett, took me aside to pray and guide me in the first steps of my Christian walk, before we prepared to leave for home.

I had just made the most important decision of my life, because it brought me into relationship with God as my Heavenly Father. My heart was filled to overflowing with a wonderful sense of peace, joy and freedom from guilt I had never experienced before. As a child in God's family, my lifelong journey of faith had now begun! Jesus became very real to me and with simple childlike trust I asked him to help me overcome shyness as I stood on the Bible promise in Philippians 4 verse 13: "I can do all things through Christ Jesus who strengthens me." Finding victory in small challenges, my faith and trust in God grew steadily from there on.

At high school my quiet stand for Jesus brought gentle mocking from friends when during our break-times I plucked up courage to ask them not to take His name in vain in conversation. Even at home I faced some teasing for being a goody-goody if I withdrew from listening to risqué jokes, but I was taking my faith seriously. Many years later I was amazed and humbled to hear from my dear friend Norma Riley that she had secretly admired my stand for Jesus in our high school days, and shared how after searching for truth down many spiritual paths the memory of my faith in Jesus had inspired her to find the answer in Jesus Christ, the Son of God.

High School Challenges

When I finished primary education in 1949, I followed sisters Enid and Coral in a four-year Commercial Course at Mitchell High School in Greyville, Durban. Enid had moved on and for one year I boarded with Coral in the home of Bill Windsor, an old friend of Mum's before he remarried and I was asked to find alternative accommodation.

This presented a serious problem and Standard 8 became a very turbulent year for me, moving house four times within the year. I started with a couple of months in the home of Granddad's friends, the Gough family in Bellair, followed by a short time with Coral's kind work associate Grace Sadler in Cowey Road. My next brief stopover was sharing a bedroom with Helen Dykes in St. Thomas Road, after which I was hosted for the remainder of the year by compassionate friends Denny and Gladys Thomas in Montpelier Road. We were grateful to all these kind friends but the constant moving was most disruptive to my studies.

In Standard 9 I had no alternative but to live at home with Mum and Dad, who had recently moved from the farm to live at Tongaat Beach. My prayers for transport were answered when God provided morning lifts with Mr Frank Elliot who worked in Durban, and I returned on the school train leaving Greyville Station at 2.30pm. Dad had started a new job with changing shifts at the Masonite factory in Canelands, so when he was on night duty I took up the offer of a lift home by the driver of the local Tsampiras Bakery in Tongaat. When Daddy was ill, Helen Tsampiras, manager of their family business, had told Mum that if ever we needed help with transport her driver and vehicle were available. Dad's pride found it hard to accept what he saw as charity but I persuaded him that he was robbing others of the pleasure that he enjoyed in helping people, and I continued to accept their gracious offer of lifts when I was stranded in the village.

Aware that I was in my final matriculation year, my sister Lorna and her husband Brian Christian kindly offered to board me so that I could focus on my studies. With their little Meryl just two and baby Colin only a few months old, I was tremendously grateful for their sacrifice of space and privacy that enabled me to study and pass the important exam at the end of the year which opened the door to my teaching career.

I've never been a sporty person and because of my unsettled boarding arrangements wasn't able to take part in extra-mural activities at Mitchell High School. Knowing that I was not a strong swimmer, I panicked when told that I'd been chosen for our school relay team at the Inter High School Swimming Gala. My strong

My Childhood Home

protests were dismissed by our gym instructor who told me there was no-one else! My fears were realized when I was left behind by the other competitors in my race, to finish almost the entire length of the Durban beach baths on my own while all proceedings were held up. I struggled to the finish, watched to the last exhausted stroke by hundreds of high school scholars, feeling deeply humiliated at the time but later consoling myself that there was merit in persevering to the end!

My interests and talents lay more in the line of literature and the arts in my high school years, and good results at Speech and Drama Eisteddfods for four years led to winning a bursary from the ASPRO Company for private tuition. I began individual lessons with Phyllis Goudge, one of the best Speech and Drama teachers in Durban. When I moved to training college in Pietermaritzburg, I transferred to the only private Speech teacher in town to complete the remaining sessions. I've never forgotten the sense of spiritual foreboding I felt every time I stepped into the eerie darkness of her musty house in Longmarket Street, and was most relieved when the lessons came to an end.

In my high school days Granddad was a great strength to Mum when Daddy was in Addington Hospital for three months suffering from mysterious symptoms, which after many tests was diagnosed as Malta Fever. At the age of eighty our Granddad, Frederick Long, suffered a heart attack and under doctor's orders was persuaded to move from his lodgings in the Durban YMCA into our family home where Mum was able to care for him. He later moved with them to Ocean View, where he passed away peacefully in his sleep on 3rd July 1953 and was buried with Granny Frances in Stellawood Cemetry, Durban.

In December 1954 at the close of my school days, there was an anxious wait through the long holidays until the matriculation results arrived by mail in the recognizably "Official" brown envelope. With pounding heart, I dashed into the garden privy to read the contents in private, releasing loud whoops of joy and relief at the news that I'd scraped through with matriculation exemption in spite of a very low Mathematics result. I sent

101

application forms off at once to the Department of Education with personal references, in the hope that the Mathematics mark would not scupper my chances of acceptance to training college.

To my delight I was accepted at Natal Teachers' Training College in Pietermaritzburg, and thanked God as my dream became reality with a two-year loan from the Education Department to be repaid in service over four years. To cover my annual travelling costs to and from college, Granddad Fred applied to the Methodist Trust for a small grant, which covered the Pullman Coach fares between Durban and Pietermaritzburg.

On the day I was due to register at training college I set off in the car with my parents, filled with a mixture of excitement and nervous apprehension about the unknown. The journey went well until the outskirts of the city near Cato Ridge, where our car broke down. "My girl, I'm sorry, I'm going to have to ask someone to give you a lift to college," said Dad, anxious that I should get there in time for registration. He flagged down a passing motorist who kindly delivered me to the door, while he and Mum got help from a nearby garage and sadly returned home without seeing me into my new abode. Once again I saw God's faithful intervention in providing help when it was needed, both for me and for Dad who found garage help close by.

The Joys of College Days

Arriving amidst hundreds of other new students was quite overwhelming to this 'country bumpkin' but it wasn't long before I met five friendly girls assigned to my dormitory. In the old Residential Block I settled in for two years of great fun with these new friends who shared my Christian faith – Elaine Gibson from Dannhauser; Eileen Seeby, a missionary's daughter from Nongoma (Zululand); Diana Stott, a doctor's daughter from Hillcrest, Durban; Gill Baker from Rhodesia; Winnie Drew; and Mary McKenzie from Pietermaritzburg.

When items for our Freshers' Concert were discussed, my friends badgered me into singing a solo because I was always singing in the dorm. I'll never know how I plucked up courage to stand before parents and important guests to sing the old favourite 'Mother' which Mummy played often on the piano, but I did.

> *M is for the many smiles she gave me,*
> *O is only that she's growing old,*
> *T is for the tears she shed to save me,*
> *H is for her heart of purest gold,*
> *E is for her eyes with love-light shining,*
> *R is right, and right she'll always be,*
> *Put them all together, they spell MOTHER,*
>   *the sweetest name of all to me.*

After the concert I was astonished when Miss Gordon, a Music lecturer, offered to give me free singing and piano lessons in her spare time! Unfortunately, her schedule with music students was very full so I didn't have time to make much headway. However, when I started teaching, I enrolled for piano lessons with the village music teacher, and was making good progress until she left and put a sad end to my piano playing for life, but not to my appreciation of the instrument.

The Blight of Shyness Overcome

My early years were spent on the farm in the company of sisters, without opportunity to mix socially with boys and discover their interests, which left me feeling very shy and awkward in boys' company during my high school years. Provided with blind dates by friends for both the Matriculation Dance at the end of high school and the Student First Year Freshers' Ball, I wasn't relaxed enough to enjoy the occasions, but as I settled into college life things began to change in the relaxed company of fellow students. It was good to feel confidence growing as I emerged from the cocoon of shyness.

Envious of the confidence of other girls at training college, I decided to ask God to help me overcome my inhibitions. I took the plunge and volunteered to address the whole first year student group in the last session of our weekly Tutorial period. Using every ounce of courage to stand up with quaking knees, I presented my talk on the life of Lewis Carol, author of 'Alice in Wonderland'. At the finish, knowing full well that my presentation had been faltering from a muddled set of notes, I nevertheless felt a significant sense of achievement in having stood before the whole class to do it!

In my first year at training college, 1954, I joined the Dramatic Society and enjoyed my role as Hero in Shakespeare's 'Much Ado about Nothing' produced by Eileen Macdonald. The male parts were played by Wouter de Vos, Frikkie Kleynhans, Swithin Stride, Alwyn Grové, Paul Lotter, Francois le Roux, Peter Randal, Neville Nuttall, Neil Chapman, Peter Kelsall, George Pattison, tom Metcalf, Wallis Wells and Andrew Myburgh. The other ladies were played by Anne Dorfling, Wendy Hurd, Bregda le Grange and Eileen Seeby. Lesser roles were played by Isobel Hickman, Ruth Woodhouse, Ricky Lubbe, Eve Slabbert, Johannes Lombard, Stoffel Viljoen, Charl du Plessis, Jean Buchan-smith and Eileen Halstead.

Taking part in this production helped my transition from shy country girl to confident young woman in social gatherings. But what remained an ongoing ordeal for me was having a lecturer sit at the back of the classroom to assess my teaching skills throughout the weekly 'prac' lessons in front of a class. It never got any easier and my disappointing marks reflected my lack of confidence.

In spite of this I wanted to get as much experience as I could in different mediums, so in trepidation chose to do a term in the Afrikaans-Medium Voortrekker Infant School. To teach in Afrikaans was a big challenge, taking me outside my comfort zone, but I persevered. My other choice was to spend a term at Alston Coloured School for children of mixed race, where the class teacher, Miss Penny Antobus, was kind and encouraging. Ten years later, to my surprise, when Peter and I moved to live in Armstrong Drive, Wembley, I discovered that we were living

My Childhood Home

across the road from Miss Antrobus and her aged mother. I visited Penny on several occasions and was able to thank her for the kindness she had shown me in my student days.

Entertainment the Christian Way

Many students could afford to buy clothing, go to the movies and treat themselves to hot French fries from the nearby café, but without pocket money to spend my Christian friends and I found joy in different pleasures that didn't cost a penny. Our entertainment after church on Sunday afternoons was to gather around the piano at Tom Metcalf's home for a happy singalong of favourite Methodist hymns, followed by tea and his mother's delicious home-made scones!

We shared the true joy of born-again believers and within our dormitory there was always fun and laughter. Coming from the warm east coast of Natal, my wardrobe was minimal and summery, so in the freezing cold of my first winter in Pietermaritzburg I discovered that a coat was a real necessity. With a very limited budget of £10 I went shopping at one of the Indian stores near college, hardly the place for designer clothes but I was delighted to find a long, charcoal grey, woollen coat on sale for £10! A selection of pretty, bright scarves added a cheery lift and I felt very grand in my first winter coat.

Throwing myself with enthusiasm into training for a Lifesaver's Bronze medal, on freezing winter mornings I was found at the edge of the pool at 5am ready to brave the icy water with half a dozen others. Quite apart from the reward of a bronze medal, we arrived for breakfast feeling alert, warm as toast and ready for the day while others trundled in half asleep with tracksuits pulled hastily over their pyjamas.

In my second year at training college, now aged eighteen, I attended the Chapel Street Methodist Church and joined Confirmation classes with the Rev. W. I. C. Shipley. It meant a lot to me that Mummy made the journey to be at this significant service confirming my commitment to Jesus Christ, wearing the white frock and bolero she had made for me. I could never have guessed that within six years I would be married in this church and become part of the same congregation.

My Career Begins at Maidstone

At the end of 1954 I received official notification from the Natal Education Department that I had qualified as a Primary School Teacher, and applied at once for a post at my own village school in Maidstone. There happened to be a vacancy at the time and I joined the staff with three teachers who had taught me – Rhona Kean, Eileen Coleman and Eric Reid – with the addition of John Schoeman and a Woodwork master, Tony Weare, who came from Durban to give lessons once a week.

What a joy it was to teach unsophisticated country children who were eager to learn. Despite feelings of nervousness in my earliest days I thoroughly enjoyed nurturing them all and giving special attention to those who came from difficult home situations. Of course some boys tested the 'rookie' teacher's ability to maintain discipline in the classroom, but soon realized I was not to be trifled with and settled with respect into the pattern of our schooldays.

Zululand Mission Trips in ELLA

Every July holiday during my college years and five years of teaching at Maidstone, I joined a group of young Methodist volunteers helping on mission sites in Zululand. Our transport was an old ex-Army truck from the 'CONGELLA' Regiment, affectionately named 'ELLA' from the remaining four letters still visible on the cab door. Our main objective over the years was to help the poor local population who existed on a meagre diet of fish from the lake, home-brewed wine from the sap of the lala-palm and ground nuts, the only crop that thrived in the poor sandy soil. The projects included repairing the manse for the black minister at Threllfall Mission overlooking Kosi Bay; repair church buildings at Ubombo and Bethesda; build wards at the Manguzi Mission Hospital and erect simple corrugated iron churches at Mazambane and Mahlabatini.

On all these mission trips the girls prepared and cooked meals over open camp fires, but at times were asked to help on the construction site when I could put to good use our brother Stanley's brick-laying advice to his little sisters years before. We slept in tents and mission buildings, learned to bathe in a basin of water and used temporary long-drop loos which were rustically screened from view. These mission trips provided us with rich experiences in the friendships forged, interaction with black Christian brothers and sister, and opportunity to enjoy the outdoors and learn keys to simple living.

The Joys of Scooter Travel

Living with Mum and Dad in their idyllically peaceful life at the beach was a great joy, but having no transport to get to school presented a challenge. As my modest income wouldn't stretch to buying a car, the only alternative was a motorised scooter. My enquiries revealed that 'DKW' was the only scooter being imported at that time, though 'Vespa's and 'Lambretta's would follow soon after. Having arranged a viewing with the DKW dealers in the city, my colleague John Schoeman kindly offered to give me a lift to Durban on his motorbike and the deal was swiftly completed. After a quick lesson on the mechanics of this single-gear engine I took it for a quick spin up the street and set off on the long journey home with John following patiently behind.

It is hard to believe but there was no legal requirement of crash helmets, so a headscarf and sunglasses sufficed. During the next few weeks I took a simple driving test at the Verulam Licensing Department and secured a licence. On my journeys along the main road I received many smiles and friendly waves from passing strangers, all surprised by the novel sight of a young lady on a motor scooter in 1956.

Riding High with Jesus

In light showers during the rainy season I wore a plastic apron under my raincoat to catch the pool of water that gathered in my lap. But in torrential downpours it made sense to travel barefoot and warm my frozen feet in the staffroom hand-basin before changing into dry clothes and shoes from a waterproof bag. These minor inconveniences were more than compensated for by the sheer joy of spinning along the deserted beach road in the beauty of early summer mornings, with clear blue sky overhead and birdsong greeting me from the hedgerows as I passed.

After school on humid summer afternoons I kicked off my shoes and walked along the beach with the wind in my hair, cooling my feet in the waves that swished up the shore. Feeling wonderfully refreshed, I set about marking books and preparing lessons for the next day. These were halcyon days of simple pleasures with Mum and Dad that lasted for almost five years before being brought to an abrupt close by the Education Department.

During my years at Maidstone School I enjoyed the friendship of William Jooste, who was working as a clerk in the mill offices. An accomplished ballroom dancer, Will invited me on Saturday nights to 'dance the night away' at the well-known 'Roadhouse Hotel' in Durban to the music of live bands. Ever the thoughtful gentleman, he always had a bag of apples in the car to munch as we drove home along the old road past the 'White House Hotel' at Avoca in the early hours of the morning. I valued our friendship deeply and could not have wished for a finer friend, but was not in love with Will and found it extremely hard to turn down his proposal of marriage.

Listening to my happy accounts of days in the classroom and the sense of fulfilment I derived from my career, Will was inspired to resign from his desk job and become a teacher too. Being a lot older than his student peers had its advantages, and after graduating from training college it wasn't long before he was appointed Headmaster of a school in Durban. He enjoyed his teaching career immensely but tragically died of a heart attack not many years later, leaving a young wife and little son.

My Childhood Home

Prince Charming Appears

Every year Peter and Doreen Hackland, Methodist friends in the Umhlali district, held an Easter camp on their beach property and in 1959 I rode up on my scooter. Approaching the large meeting tent, the first person I met was a handsome young stranger in an eye-catching grey, red and black bunny jacket. He introduced himself as Peter Hurd and I felt immediately attracted to him with his tawny hazel eyes and dark hair. That evening I was asked to read the Scripture passage during devotions, and sitting among friends in the group from Pietermaritzburg felt very conscious of Peter's close attention. Later he teasingly confessed that he'd fallen in love with my voice, and I responded that it was his colourful bunny jacket that did it for me!

Over the long weekend our mutual attraction deepened, and at the close of camp Peter told me he'd been invited by the Hacklands to spend the night and invited me to do the same. We enjoyed a happy evening with our friends and early next morning Pete set off for Pietermaritzburg by car while I rode home on my scooter, with the tingling sense in my heart that I had met my Prince Charming – in his red 'Vauxhall Victor'. Our romance blossomed over the next nine months by letters, phone calls and Peter's weekend visits, with our Hackland friends claiming undisputed credit for the success of their matchmaking plans!

Engagement

When Peter proposed to me the following year, I wasn't sure that I was ready for the serious commitment of marriage, but driving together to Tongaat Beach for Christmas with Mum and Dad, I felt a deep reassurance that God had brought us together. To Peter's surprise I told him I was happy to accept his proposal and suggested that we surprise everyone with an engagement announcement on Christmas Day. Peter was delighted but raised the question of a ring at such short notice. My quick solution was to call at Greenacres Departmental Store in West Street, Durban, where Mum was a longstanding customer. From their Jewellery Department I phoned Mummy to ask permission to purchase a ring on her account! We found a beautiful diamond in simple white gold setting for £50.00 and shared the surprise news with our family the following morning at the Christmas service in the scout hall.

I'd always dreamed of being a winter bride wearing white velvet, but practical sense prevailed and we decided on a summertime wedding early in January so I could settle into our new home during the long school holiday. My plan was to finish the year at Maidstone School and transfer to a school in Pietermaritzburg in the New Year. But in the third quarter I received shocking notice from the Natal Education Department that I was to transfer immediately to Howick Senior Primary School for the last term! I was bitterly disappointed and contested the untimely transfer but was told that a vacancy was needed for a teacher about to marry a local man, and being the only single teacher, move I did.

During the October school holiday Peter helped me move clothing and essential items to the home of Granddad's elderly friends Grandpa and Gargie Rycroft in Howick, who kindly agreed to host me for the term. Their old two-storey home 'Bowdon' on Clarendon Drive was conveniently close to the school. Ironically, I was only there a couple of weeks when I fell ill with measles for the first time in my life. For a whole month I was seriously ill with extreme nausea and very painful eyes, unable to do anything to pass the time in the darkened room except listen on Peter's portable radio to music and the morning book-reading, the highlight of my day.

Throughout the day dear old Gargie made trips up the stairs to bring me glasses of warm ginger ale, the only thing I could face. Not only was the timing disastrous with my wedding six weeks away, but I had to abandon to other teachers all the year-end school duties including the children's reports. The advantage of being closer to Maritzburg was that Peter could visit, discuss last minute wedding details and, once my eyes could focus, prepare our wedding invitations for late posting.

When Peter was just a boy, his father Cecil Hurd was killed in a tragic accident in the town of Barberton, South Africa, where he was Town Clerk. Cecil's parents, Herbert and Lily Hurd, became guardians of the three grandchildren and their Grandfather established a Trust Fund for Peter and his young sisters Wendy and Gillian, conditional on their inheritance being held in trust until they reached the age of thirty. In time their ageing grandfather transferred legal guardianship of the children to his daughter Ruth Morris with Power of Attorney over the Trust Fund.

Within months of Peter turning thirty, Aunt Ruth was able to authorise the early release of a deposit for us to purchase a little house in the new suburb of Northern Park, Pietermaritzburg. I had been saving for a ticket on a Union Castle liner to England with my friend Elaine Gibson with the intention of finding teaching posts over there, but once we'd met our prospective husbands we changed plans and I invested my savings of £350 in our new home. I chose pretty curtaining in lovely floral designs and soon had curtains hanging at the windows ready for our return from honeymoon.

Wedding Dress Magic

When my sister Enid heard of our plans for a summer wedding, she offered me the use of her wedding gown. Her original bodice of ivory Guipure lace with long sleeves and Chinese collar had been modified, so she sent the straight pieces of fabric from the sleeves with the bodice attached to the full tulle skirt. Being so ill with measles, I had lost ten pounds in weight and the dress fitted perfectly. Our gifted little mother created a new bodice top with short sleeves from the pieces, using satin binding to complete the new creation, and Enid's circlet of pearls held my shoulder length veil in place. Madeline and I had been bridesmaids to Enid, so it was very special for me to have them as my Matrons of Honour. They looked charming in long sunshine-yellow crystalline frocks with full-blown golden roses in their hair. A friend of Aunt Ruth's made our beautiful crescent-shaped bouquets of cream and gold frangipani blossoms, with tiny touches of blue delphiniums and miniature pink rosebuds.

In the old tradition of brides wearing a 'going away' outfit, my plan had been to shop for a navy skirt and a jacket with sailor-suit collar, but measles put paid to that! Mum came to my rescue by bringing a selection of frocks 'on approval' from a departmental store in Durban. With spinning head, I could barely stand long enough to try on dresses, battling to see in the mirror through blurred, painful eyes, so Mum and I were both very relieved to find an attractive cotton shirtwaister frock that filled perfectly. The search over, I crawled back into bed utterly spent, while my darling Mum took the long journey home to Dad.

Our Wedding Day

Peter and I were married by the Rev. Arnold Walker on a gloriously sunny morning at ten o'clock on 7th January 1961 in the Chapel Street Methodist Church. Aunt Ruth and Uncle Edwin Morris had invited Mum, Dad, Enid, Madeline and me to spend the previous night on their farm 'Drumclog' in Pentrich, Pietermaritzburg. When the young photographer from AV Farren Studio heard I had no hairdresser appointment in the morning, he asked to come early and try out his new flash on indoor shots before we left for the church. We were all dressed in good time for the photo shoot and the result was a lovely selection of intimate family photos taken inside and on the farmhouse verandah.

On the fifteen-minute drive from the farm in brother-in-law Doug's smart 'Mercedes' I felt so relaxed chatting to Daddy that at the church door I was asked to lower my voice! There at the altar stood Peter; his Best Man, Daryl Hackland; and Groomsman, brother-in-law Harry Cockerill; who had all dressed at Peter's 'Raldor' flat in Loop Street. As I walked down the aisle on Dad's arm, my heart overflowed with thanksgiving to God for restoring my strength in time for this wonderful moment.

At the completion of the moving ceremony of promises made to one another before God and the signing of the Register, our bridal party drove up the hill to the new Wylie Park in Athlone for the photos while our guests made their way to the reception. By kind favour of Peter's golfing associates at the elite Pietermaritzburg Country Club, we were given privileged access to the front verandah for our reception tea overlooking the beautiful valley and green hills of Montrose. Aunt Ruth and her gifted Richmond Garden Club friends blessed us at the church and the reception with beautiful floral arrangements of dahlias, delphiniums and roses from their own gardens.

With the picture-taking complete we were more than ready for tea served with delicious home-made treats, while our friend Dave Donaldson kept everyone entertained with his speech of light-hearted humour. Peter responded with simple thanks to all who had made our day a happy event and we cut our wedding cake, a wedding gift baked and iced by friend Daphne Coleman. After circulating among our guests I tossed my bouquet in the old tradition, with all the single young ladies jostling to catch it in the hope of being the next bride!

As noon approached I changed into my white cotton frock and stood on a chair to toss the garter to the single young men fighting to catch it. As our guests gathered to wave goodbye, Peter felt really smug driving off in his clean little blue 'Austin A40'. Having outwitted his pals by parking the car in a secret location safe from decorating hands, we'd escaped tell-tale signs of "Newly Married" lettering, confetti and tin cans on string rattling behind as we set off for our honeymoon in the mountains. But we hadn't escaped a thick layer of red dust from the country road covering our luggage, as we discovered when we opened the boot a few hours later at the Drakensberg Gardens Hotel.

Our two-week honeymoon in the glorious splendour of the mountains was a very happy, relaxed time – just what the doctor ordered. I hadn't yet built up stamina for strenuous exercise so

Riding High with Jesus

while I read, knitted and chatted to guests, Peter joined mountain-climbing parties and together we enjoyed the less demanding walks and swam in the refreshing river pools and waterfalls.

My Childhood Home

Colleen's Baby Days, 1936

Lorna, Stan and Enid on the farm

Marjorie Enid and William Collin Eckersley and family, 1937

With cousin Sheila and Auntie Hilda, 1937

Lorna, Stan, Enid and Coral, 1935

Eckersley family, 1937

115

Riding High with Jesus

My Childhood Home

Childhood Life on the Farm

Our farmhouse, south view

Granny's painting of the sugar mill from the farm

Colleen's childhood farmhouse

Annual fancy dress in Maidstone, about 1938

Riding High with Jesus

Colleen at Lorna's wedding

Fancy dress as Zulu maiden at 11 years

Colleen with puppy

Little fishermen Colleen, Beth and Madeline

Colleen and little sister Beth on our farm, 1944

My Childhood Home

Beach Holidays

Enid's painting of the front of The Shack

Enid's painting of The Shack from the back

Early days at The Shack

At The Shack cottage in the bush at Tongaat Beach

Fishermen at The Shack

The Shack beach cottage

The brown rock at Tongaat Beach below Gran's cottage

On Mum and Dad's cottage lawn at Tongaat Beach

View of Tongaat Beach toward the river mouth from Mum's cottage

Our beach cottage, Tongaat

Dad and Stan with their catch

One view of Tongaat Beach from Ocean View

My Childhood Home

Colleen's High School Years and Single Days

A prefect in my final school year, 1953

Taken by a street photographer, 1952

Colleen's 21st key

Confirmation dress, 1957

Sports Day at Maidstone School

Maidstone School

Friend William in centre, Peter on left, at Easter Camp

Riding High with Jesus

Colleen as a single teacher

Peter Graham Hurd

Colleen on her scooter with friend Elaine

My Childhood Home

Zululand Mission, 1955-1959

Riding High with Jesus

Mum and Dad

Mum, Dad and Granddad Fred on our farm

Dad and Mum's 25th Anniversary, 1948

Granddad Fred Long with Dad, Mum, Doreen and Sid Smith, and all his grandchildren on our farm, 1946

3

Marriage and Parenthood

Both eager to get back to our little home we found several "Welcome to your New Home" cards waiting on the mat, and like two excited children we went straight into the back garden to explore every inch up to the fence on Sanctuary Road. We found everything flourishing in the sunshine and rain, and Peter, a keen gardener, had itchy fingers to start tidying the flowerbeds and mowing the lawn. As we meandered through the garden, our hearts overflowed with thanks to God for the enormous privilege of having a home of our own at the start of our marriage.

Coming in from the garden, Peter switched on the electric geyser[33] while I set a tray with the dainty polka-dot porcelain tea set from Cousin Alfred Dore in Tongaat. Filling the pot with boiling water from my new kettle, I felt as if I was 'playing house'. After tea we unpacked our cases and set about making up the old wooden-framed double bed inherited from Aunt Ruth, which had been stored in the outbuildings on the farm for years.

After the long, hot drive back and the excitement of coming home, we looked forward to a good night's sleep but no sooner was the light out than we began to feel fierce burning all over our bodies. We put the light on but could see nothing and the mysterious burning continued well into the night as soon as the

---

[33] boiler

light was switched off. In desperation we made up the twin beds in the spare room to catch a couple of hours' sleep before daybreak.

The next day Peter and I turned the old wooden bedstead over and were horrified to discover a thriving mass of bedbugs hiding in the woodwork! Neither of us had ever seen these horrid little creatures before, and with the discovery came a sense of shame because I'd always associated bedbugs with squalor. Peter went straight out and bought exterminating smoke bombs which he lit and placed in the sealed room for twenty-four hours. These did the trick of killing the bugs, so we took the bed out into the sunshine to clean it thoroughly and get rid of the smoky smell. Despite knowing that the problem was solved I could still feel an imaginary bite for a few nights. Sharing the story with family and friends brought lots of laughter and a sincere apology from Aunt Ruth for not checking the bed herself.

New Teaching Post at Athlone School

At the end of January 1961 Peter returned to work, but I still had a few days of school holiday to settle into being wife and homemaker before taking up my new post at Athlone Primary School close by. When the term began, I immediately felt the contrast between the simple homeliness of the village school I'd been in for years and the attitudes in this city school in an affluent suburb – and I wasn't happy.

Athlone School had been chosen by the Natal Education Department to be the 'guinea-pig' school where new teaching methods in Reading, Writing and Arithmetic (now called Maths) would be modelled before being introduced in all schools. We regularly had teachers from other schools coming to observe the new techniques, and being under scrutiny while trying to adapt to the high standard expected of us wasn't easy or enjoyable for me. A new 'Marion Richardson' script of mixed print and cursive letters was being launched, which teachers had to master first. I've never seen any virtue in the change to this script which ruined my own cursive handwriting for ever.

Marriage and Parenthood

I was most grateful to find another new young teacher who felt as unsettled as I did. Afrikaans-speaking Bettie Truter and I developed a friendship that was a blessing to both of us and made my year at Athlone School more bearable. Bettie's husband, Kobus, and Peter struck up a firm friendship and the four of us shared many happy times together in the years that followed, long after we had both left the school.

First Pregnancy

As Peter and I had hoped to start our family soon, I was very excited to discover mid-year that I was pregnant, but coping with morning sickness in the classroom was not the most comfortable experience. I managed to see the year out and thankfully handed in my notice a month before term end, only too happy to be released from the 'fishbowl' pressure to perform.

How wonderful it was to be an expectant mum with time to plan and prepare for our first baby, scanning the 'For Sale' columns in the paper to set up our nursery. To help with housework we engaged a Zulu maid, Norah Dladla from Mphophomeni Township outside Howick, and provided her with a kia[34] in the garden with adjoining ablutions. Her children visited frequently and became good playmates with ours.

Determined to learn to drive before our baby arrived, I sold my DKW motor scooter and enrolled with OHMS Driving School. Peter drove me to meet the instructor at the city hall and having had no previous experience before, I was very nervous. I felt really alarmed when I was told to take the wheel because I would be driving along the winding road to Richmond village! To my huge relief he then explained that there were dual controls and I would only have to steer the car. I soon felt at home behind the wheel which helped me to pass my test with ease after eight lessons. Peter had a company car so his Austin A40 was available for getting to the clinic weekly once our baby arrived.

---

[34] home

Riding High with Jesus

The months leading up to the baby's arrival sped by with our sense of wonder growing at every stage of development in the womb. Both of us chose to wait in eager anticipation for the surprise – a boy or a girl? I joined the prenatal classes for expectant mums at Greys Hospital and kept extremely fit throughout the pregnancy.

D-day Arrives for Andy's Birth

Having passed my estimated due date by two weeks, Dr Tibbit decided to induce labour, so I spent the night of June 29th in hospital and started the procedure at 5am the following morning. The sisters on duty instructed me to keep walking the passages to help bring on labour and by three o'clock it was time to call Peter for the delivery. He wasn't confident about attending the birth but on arrival, without discussion, was given a mask and gown by the staff and swept with me into the Theatre. Finding himself placed at the top of the bed, he held my hand and encouraged me while I worked hard at delivering our baby. Unspeakable joy, relief and thankfulness to God flooded my exhausted body as our little boy, Andrew Graham, made his entrance into the world. He was held up for us to see his perfect little body weighing in at 7lb 9oz, and Peter and I embraced with tears of joy coursing down our cheeks as we beheld our first little miracle.

Dr Tibbit insisted that I remain in hospital for nine days to rest, and when at last I was discharged with our precious gift, Norah was waiting to welcome us and the nursery embraced its little occupant. I was grateful to Dad for sparing Mum to come and initiate me into settling the baby into a routine. After a week she left and it was hands-on experience for us, coping with sleepless nights and enjoying the daily growth and development of our little boy.

He was the cutest wee lad in stature and our pride knew no bounds when he took his first steps at ten months. Before Andy was born Peter had bought a full-grown boxer / bull mastiff dog

Marriage and Parenthood

called 'Pindar' by his owner, a former British Army officer who had served in India. We changed his aristocratic name to 'Pindy' and he took to lying as faithful protector next to Andy's pram in the sunshine, and later beside the rug on the lawn when his little charge learned to sit up.

For me those early years of enjoying simple chores and fulfilling tasks of motherhood were the happiest time imaginable. This was what I had been created for and my heart brimmed over with gratitude to God for my husband Peter, our home and the start of our family. Just an hour's drive away from us in Cowies Hill, my sister Madeline had given birth to Andy's little cousin Karen six weeks before, and these two were an absolute delight as we watched them grow apace. Many were the happy visits we shared at Granny and Grandpa's Tongaat Beach cottage. Andy was a contented baby whose smooth progress brought us such joy that by the time he was a year old we were planning a companion for him.

Saying Goodbye to our First Home

During our first year at Clydesdale Ave the level of noise in our developing suburb rose considerably. Right outside our bedroom window every morning at 4am we were woken by the departure of our neighbours who owned a Cafe, so it didn't take much for Peter to be enticed into a deal by Frank Smith, an Estate Agent who already had a buyer lined up for our house. Totally unaware of the potential deal I was devastated when Peter told me that he had been approached by an Agent to sell our property. I felt betrayed and it fell to my visiting sister Lorna to console me when I sobbed at the prospect of leaving my lovely little home. Peter assured me that he had not committed us to a sale, but asked me just to view the property which Frank was offering.

New Home in Wembley

I agreed and was driven up the hill to the suburb of Wembley, neighbourhood of the wealthy elite. To my amazement the Agent turned into the driveway of a large property with an attractive house surrounded by the homes of Medical doctors, Specialists, Dentists and Accountants. The house was built on the side of the hill above a double garage, with a vast expanse of open green lawns, flower beds and shrubs. The Agent's remark as we drove up was: "This house is structurally very sound and the only reason the asking price has been set below its true value, is because the house needs love. I think you two are just the people to give it that." Walking up the steps into the house I noted superficial signs of neglect, and moving from room to room felt a quickening inside me as I visualized the walls transformed with pretty wallpapers. Peter was delighted when I told him that I would consider the deal if he was sure it was financially within our means, and very soon we had begun to pack for our first move!

Transformation began as Peter and I chose a selection of beautiful wallpapers for the passage and bedrooms, and had great fun on our first wall-papering experience. The effect was stunning and a credit to our hard work. I introduced myself to our immediate neighbours and found the Doctors' wives friendly and accepting of this young mother from a different social league. Peter hired a quaint black labourer called "Doo" to build supporting shale walls around the flower beds and with his love of gardening, soon had the beds filled with flowering seedlings. With Norah our maid and "Pindy" the Boxer we soon settled into our new home at 36 Armstrong Drive, continuing to live by our simple standards while surrounded by 'the Joneses' on every side!

Stephen Bradley's Birth

I was delighted to discover that I was pregnant with our second baby soon after we had moved to Armstrong Drive. Blossoming again throughout the nine months, I chose to have this

Marriage and Parenthood

baby at the private St Anne's Hospital which had a more personal atmosphere. I needed no induction with this baby as he surprised me by arriving ten days before due date! During the evening of the 20th February I told Peter that I had begun to feel very mild contractions. Being one who couldn't keep his eyes open after 8pm, he said, "I'm sorry, Honey. Please wake me if you need to." I fell into a light doze myself and woke an hour later to find that the contractions had settled into a strong, regular pattern.

At 9pm I rang the sister at St Anne's who advised me to come in immediately, so I woke Peter: "Darling, my contractions are strong and I need to leave right away." With ready-packed case we hastened to the hospital, leaving our maid Norah in the house to keep little Andy company. Peter left me in the capable hands of the sister who promised to call him in good time, but this time, things moved so fast he had hardly got home when he had to return as the baby's arrival was imminent. He raced down the hill just in time to witness the delivery of another bonny little son, Stephen Bradley, on the stroke of midnight – our second beautiful miracle from God with dark brown eyes and brown hair!

Steve arrived with a touch of jaundice which had lifted by the time Dr Tibbit allowed us to go home. From the start he was a very robust little fellow, nicknamed 'Chubby Checker' after the pop singer of the day. In no time he became a playmate for Andy and not yet two years old, was found climbing up behind his brother on the tall wooden trellis which Peter had built for a garden creeper! The two little lads played happily together for hours, indoors or in the sandpit which Pete built for them outside the kitchen. By eighteen months little Stevie had developed his own unique way of showing a 'paddy' – jumping up and down on the spot wailing loudly, then sitting down hard on his bottom.

Third Home – The Glades

Estate Agent Frank Smith knew he was on to a good thing when he met Peter Hurd! In spite of being in the process of adding a laundry and playroom to our Wembley home, Peter was once again enticed by another proposition out of the city. By now I had developed a spirit of adventure in Real Estate matters, so when Pete said, "Honey, Frank has a six-acre property in Hilton he wants to show us," I was intrigued by the description of 'The Glades' which sounded most inviting. Following Frank's directions, Peter and I took a drive up the hill from Pietermaritzburg and found the charming home on the country lane beside the Hilton Hotel.

We drove through the gate and I stepped from the car into a storybook picture. The old white-walled homestead with black roof was set back against the hedge bordering the lane, while rolling green lawns stretched down to a small Blackwood forest where I could hear the faint tinkle of a running stream. The small grove was fringed by towering swamp cypress trees in russet winter dress beside massive plane trees with spreading branches and sturdy, peeling trunks.

Exploring the perimeter of the garden along the Hilton Hotel border fence, I came across large gardenia and magnolia bushes full of magnificent blossoms that glowed with luminous beauty. Suddenly we were enveloped in the thick Hilton mist which descended on the whole garden giving it an atmosphere of instant mystery. In a thatched cottage to the right of the drive lived a diminutive tenant, Mrs Fitzgerald, who had requested that she be allowed to remain.

Set beside the house the previous owner had built a long modern hall for entertaining his business friends, with a kidney-shaped swimming pool against the terrace wall covered in cascading periwinkle creeper. Looking at the pool I called out, "Oh, Pete, can't you imagine our little boys enjoying this pool and the freedom to explore this wonderful space!" We meandered around the whole garden, falling more and more under the spell of its charm. Turning our thoughts to the practical matter of distance from town, we decided it wasn't of immediate concern as the boys weren't at school yet. Driving home in a tingle of excitement, Peter worked out the financial implications and with that done, it wasn't

Marriage and Parenthood

long before we were packing up to make our second move. And planning our third baby!

Heart-breaking News of Dad's Death

I was already six months pregnant in our Hilton home in June 1966 when my sister Coral phoned me with the shocking news that our beloved Dad had died very suddenly from a severe heart attack. She explained that he'd been feeling unwell and had gone to the kitchen to tell Mum who was making a batch of scones. She suggested he lie down in the back room while she popped the scones in the oven but suddenly heard a terrible crash. Rushing to the bedroom, she tried frantically to open the door but Daddy had fallen against it. Finally, with servant Moti's help she managed to push the door open only to find that Daddy had died instantly.

Coming so soon after the recent joy of Mum and Dad's visit to our new Hilton home, the shock of his death was agonizing. I stood silently holding the phone for a few minutes, which made Coral anxious that the shock might bring on premature labour, but I reassured her that I was alright before replacing the phone and breaking into heaving sobs.

Dad's Cremation service took place at Dove's funeral parlour in Moore Road, with Stan representing Mum and the girls. Unfortunately, our brother had the most traumatic day. Delayed in leaving work he drove at speed to get to Durban on time, but went to the wrong funeral parlour in Greyville and had to be redirected to Moore Road. In the days before mobile phones he couldn't let anyone know what had happened and proceedings were held up till he arrived, quite distraught. Coral, Enid and Madeline met with Mummy for an intimate time of thanksgiving at her cottage, while I spent time at home quietly reflecting on what a wonderful father Daddy had been to us. Mummy later scattered Dad's ashes in a beautiful rose garden.

Murray Brenton

By the time of our third baby's due date we had settled happily into The Glades and Mum came a few days early to help with Andy and Steve while I was in hospital. On the evening of 8th September 1966 I was feeling very uncomfortable with low backache, and the sister at St Anne's Hospital advised me to come in. Peter saw me admitted to the labour ward and drove home to wait for the phone call. Missing the urgency in the sister's call he had a cup of tea with Mum before returning to discover that he had missed the arrival of his third little son by minutes. Murray Brenton weighed in at 8lbs with blue eyes and light brown hair.

Two months later we celebrated his Christening at The Glades with a family lunch after the ceremony, very conscious of Dad's absence but blessed to have Mummy and many of our family and special friends with us on this happy occasion.

Our dear friends Terry and Elaine McKenzie had bought the farm 'Glentworth' in the Baynesfield Valley and on one of our visits Terry proudly showed us a new litter of beautiful German Shephard puppies, also known as Alsatians. Peter was very keen to buy one but for the year I boarded with my sister and brother-in-law, I'd had to run the gauntlet every afternoon past their growling, cantankerous old Alsatian 'Blackie' when I came from high school. I had also heard disturbing stories of people being attacked by German Shepherds.

However, Terry assured me he had traced the pedigree of their dogs and they were not of a vicious temperament. He explained that German Shepherds are often trained to be vicious guard dogs but by nature they are not aggressive. I relented so Peter chose two identical pups which we named 'Romulus' and 'Remus'. They grew into very handsome animals, excellent watchdogs yet gentle with our children for the ten years of their lives.

Marriage and Parenthood

Peter's Work Experience

After leaving high school at the age of eighteen, Peter had spent a year at agricultural college. He enjoyed practical outdoor farming activities but struggled with the academic studies, so left to find work as a dairy hand on the farm of Mr Foster in the Ixopo district. From there he moved into Pietermaritzburg to work as Junior Salesman in the Motor Spares Department of G. North and Son. When I met Peter, he had moved into the precarious job of second-hand car salesman in a time of recession, but as a Christian Peter refused to do business by 'bending the truth' to clients to secure a sale. As a result, he came under pressure from his bosses for failing to meet targets.

Once married, he applied for a position as Sales Representative with Moshal Gevisser, the Jewish firm of General Wholesalers based in Durban. He was given an African driver and a truck loaded with samples of every commodity used in the native trade. His five-day business trip began on Monday mornings and took him to trading stores spread across a vast area, so he and his driver slept in local hotels along the way and returned on Thursday evenings. The Zulu driver, Robert, was fluent in English, efficient at his job of drawing out specific cases of samples requested by storekeepers and the two men developed a good working relationship of mutual respect.

Dreams of Trading

After some time Peter began to dream of owning his own business. In conversation with friends Garnet and Joan Venn, he discovered that Joan's father Mr McKenzie was an estate agent dealing in the sale of country trading stores. When Peter heard that Joan's sister Mary and her husband Ian Smith were running their 'Sibudeni Store' near Nkhandla in Zululand, his appetite was whetted by stories of their lifestyle so Mr Mackenzie offered to drive us up to meet the Smiths.

135

After a long journey into northern Zululand we had a fascinating experience exploring Ian and Mary's store, with the wide range of stock and different aromas from ground meal, brown beans, and bolts of fabric, to cakes of soap. Far from the city their store catered for every need of the black community, from sewing needles to three-legged cast-iron cooking pots, raw leaf tobacco, freshly milled maize meal and recently slaughtered cuts of beef. By the time we left, most of Peter's questions had been answered and I could see he was very keen to make serious enquiries about a store Mr McKenzie told him was for sale in the hills of lower Zululand just beyond the Tugela River.

Mr Mackenzie arranged to drive us up to view 'Ndulinde Trading Station' and we set off early one morning with a sense of eager anticipation. Taking the Nyoni Village turnoff we followed the dirt road into the small village community of post office, butchery, railway siding and health clinic run by Swedish missionaries. Mr McKenzie stopped the car outside Colin Foxon's butchery and introduced us to the blockman Dan McDonald. He was living next door with his wife Maureen, young daughter Vicki and little handicapped son Maurice. Encouraged by the friendly spirit of this family who made it clear that they would welcome us as neighbours, we left Nyoni and climbed for seven miles on the dusty ribbon of dirt road up into the rolling hills.

Passing many local huts en route, we arrived at last at the rustic setting of 'Ndulinde Store' with the old homestead standing close beside it. The property was surrounded by tall rustling gum trees which reminded me of our childhood farm, and I felt immediately at home standing in the cool breeze. The store itself was a plain, unimposing rectangular building with open verandah, that had a mailbox fixed to the wall. Inside, a long concrete counter separated customers from staff, and the back wall covered with shelves now displayed only a meagre selection of basic items in groceries, toiletries, sweets, matches and tobacco.

At the rear of the store a large open quad was bordered by rusting old outbuildings, one of which housed the gristing mill used to grind local customers' dried maize. In the front of the store

Marriage and Parenthood

a little distance away, I could make out the simple structure of a cattle dip where, as a protection against disease-bearing ticks, local cattle were periodically driven through a deep trough of disinfectant under supervision of the government inspector.

Peter's interest lay primarily inside the store, while I was keen to explore the old homestead, so while the men got down to business I wandered on my own across the driveway into the vast garden surrounding the house. Through the wooden latch gate, I made my way up the narrow concrete path to the back door which opened into a narrow enclosed passage. Facing me in the kitchen stood an old anthracite-burning Esse stove, a few basic kitchen cupboards, a sink with chipped enamel draining board and a wooden table. Next to the kitchen was the bathroom, with hand basin and free standing bath on a concrete floor.

The kitchen led into a large square dining room and out on to a wide red-polished verandah which ran round the front of the house to the toilet. A second door from the dining room opened into the lounge, and beyond that a passage led off to the bedrooms – two medium sized, one large main and a small room leading off which had a strong musty smell. A couple of holes in the wooden floorboards suggested the presence of rats, not at all surprising in this rural setting. I had proof of this later when I was woken from sleep one night by something tugging at my hair. In the morning there was a small tuft of my hair on the pillow, nibbled off to line a nest, no doubt.

Stepping out on to the front verandah I looked across the gently rolling hills to a distant glimpse of the sea. An enormous wild fig tree dominated the front garden with its branches spreading like a huge umbrella over the scrubby lawn beneath, part of its gigantic root system visible above ground. The front garden had once been totally enclosed by a bougainvillea hedge, which now had large gaps like missing teeth, and the stone-edged flower beds were filled with hardy daisy plants that had survived without any attention since the last occupants had left many months before. As I explored around the back of the house, I found a huge underground concrete tank, which stored the only drinkable water from life-giving summer rains. Beside the tank were some old corrugated iron outbuildings which later served as cowshed, goat enclosure and duck pen.

Beyond the house on the lawn I could see a magnificent cycad plant with spiked leaves, an endangered species which can only be possessed with a licence. Mr Mackenzie explained that these cycads only bloom once every seven to ten years, so we felt very privileged a couple of years later to witness this stunning spectacle, when the giant pineapple seedcase at its centre broke open to reveal brilliant, fiery orange and red segments glistening in the sunlight. Truly a magnificent sight!

We drove home to Hilton that evening, bubbling with excited thoughts of how different country life would be on this trading station. We'd asked questions about schooling prospects for the boys and were assured that in the town of Eshowe, an hour's drive away, there was a high school and a choice between a government primary school and Catholic convent which both had boarding hostels. After this trip Peter was totally inspired and I agreed it was a good time to take the plunge while the boys were still young. So he immediately began the process of applying to the Government to purchase Ndulinde Store on the '99-year Lease Plan' which had for many years permitted white traders to run businesses in the tribal homelands of the Zulu people. We understood that we may have to wait some time to get a reply because the wheels of Government turned slowly, so we settled back into life at The Glades, enjoying the beauty and relaxed atmosphere of our lovely property.

Sale of The Glades

In anticipation of the potential move to Zululand, Peter felt he should test the property market by putting The Glades on the market in 1967. A buyer was found almost immediately but we explained we couldn't move as we were waiting for official Government notification. Eventually the buyers were pressing for date of occupation and, not wanting to lose the sale, in faith we set

Marriage and Parenthood

a date based on what seemed a reasonable time in which to have received a reply.

Hard Lessons Learned

Some lessons are learned the hard way as we discovered when we realized that we'd clearly run ahead of God without seeking his direction in our premature decision which led to unbelievable complications and financial loss. After months of waiting without word from the Pretoria Office of the Bantu Trust Department, we concluded that we'd not been successful in our application and faced a serious dilemma! Bound by the agreement with the new owners to move, we began the search for interim rented accommodation in Pietermaritzburg but the property market was in a severe slump and, unbelievably, there was nothing to rent for our sized family.

What a pickle we had landed ourselves in! Under pressure to move out of The Glades and mindful that if we were unsuccessful in getting the trading licence we would need another home in Pietermaritzburg, our only option was to buy again. We chose a lovely home facing indigenous bush at 3 Iona Place in Boughton, packed most of our possessions for storage and moved with the bare necessities. Early in the morning at first light when I opened the lounge curtains to enjoy the early freshness and beauty of our garden, to my delight I caught sight of a slender little deer grazing peacefully on the lawn. Many times I watched these graceful creatures grazing quietly in the early morning mist, until a neighbouring dog barked and sent them leaping back across the stream into the cover of the bush.

Ironically, we had barely taken ownership of Iona Place when, in June 1967, we received word that we had been granted the licence to trade at Ndulinde with immediate effect! We were now in an even greater pickle, having invested in our house the capital that would have been the down-payment on the business. We put our new home in the hands of an estate agent who told us confidently that he had a trustworthy buyer in the new partner of the city's most popular GP. The sale was subject to his raising a small shortfall from his father-in-law and all seemed positively on track when we packed up and with the removal trucks left for our new life in Zululand.

Zululand Trading Days Begin

As we wound our way up the dusty road from Nyoni village to Ndulinde, we received a warm welcome from local black residents who greeted us with cheery waves and broad smiles, the men raising their hands to 'khuleka'[35] respectfully. The removal truck ground its way up the steep incline on to the property and with lots of willing hands, the rooms were soon filled with furniture and piles of assorted boxes.

In July 1967 we began rural life at Ndulinde Store. Once it became known that we had taken over the business, sales reps began to call and take orders for every conceivable item needed to meet our customers' needs. Two of our staff members, Eunice Mhlongo and Hamilton Sithole, who had worked in the store before, were able to advise Peter in what products sold well in that area and within weeks the shelves began to fill as consignments of goods arrived at Nyoni Station.

Five-year-old Andy and three-year-old Steve explored their vast new garden and it wasn't long before they began to make their way across the path into the store. They made daily calls to see Daddy, but we soon discovered that the real draw was a row of boxes with loose four-a-penny sweets under the counter. The boys stole the hearts of our patient and indulgent Zulu staff who couldn't bear to see them being disciplined. In the store room the boys loved to climb up to the top of the sacks of beans to watch Aaron, Victor (an epileptic) and fellow workers weighing and bagging raw groundnuts, dried sugar beans, rice and brown sugar or making up packs of raw leaf tobacco dripping with the thick brown nicotine liquid that kept it moist.

---

[35] salute

Behind the counter the shelves to the left held bolts of bright cotton fabric in primary colours for young Zulu maidens' wraps; fabric with traditional designs for skirts, dresses and matching headscarves; reels of sewing cotton of every colour; multi-coloured glass beads from Eastern Europe sold in packets by weight; sewing needles from long, fine ones for beading to thick, strong ones for stitching leather; scissors; nail files and clippers; balls of inexpensive, brightly coloured wool and knitting needles; braiding; elastic; simple household medicines; writing pads, pencils and ball pens; blankets; pillows; clothing; stockings and underwear.

Tucked into a corner of the counter was the post office lock-up safe in which all registered mail was kept until claimed. Attached to the back wall was an old-fashioned telephone, connected by an extension line to a callbox on the verandah. Here customers could pick up calls from family members working in the towns, which we had made on their behalf and transferred to the callbox.

On the right the shelves were stocked with toiletries, food and household items: deodorants; cakes of 'Lux' and other perfumed soaps; skin-lightening creams; Johnson's baby talc; Vaseline; combs; nail clippers; tinned baby formulas; packets of raw peanuts; dried white and speckled sugar beans; samp[36]; maize meal; tins of pilchards in tomato sauce and curried fish; tinned fruit; tinned jams; tea; coffee; sugar; salt; pepper; flour; baking powder; dried yeast; torches and torch batteries; packets of wrapped sweets; biscuits; washing powders; bars of green 'Sunlight' soap for washing clothes; disinfectant Jeyes fluid; paraffin for lamps; candles; packets of matches; crockery; cutlery and sharp knives; moist leaf tobacco and packets of cigarettes.

Under the counter on a shelf lay open boxes of four-a-penny 'Conversation' sweets in different shapes with printed love messages, nutty toffees and apricots. To the side stood a refrigerator filled with bottled cool drinks and cans of Coca cola, while a large chest freezer held frozen packs of chicken portions,

---

[36] crushed maize

chicken heads and feet, chicken livers and packs of beef brisket from the butchery.

Shopping is regarded in rural Zulu custom as the woman's job and when finished, the bags or boxes of goods are lifted on to her head to carry back to the kraal[37]. Black women develop amazingly strong neck muscles from a young age when little girls fetch water from the river in large tin cans balanced perfectly on their heads. Things have changed a lot since then, but traditional Zulu customs are still very different from the white man's culture. A husband is not involved in the details of shopping for groceries or carrying the goods, but if he accompanies his wife on a shopping trip she might consult him on the spending and he pays the bill. As his forbears have done for generations, he walks ahead of his wife, which in the past had the purpose of protection in case they were confronted by wild animals on the walk home.

Our one-year-old Murray was immediately taken under the wing of Ma Dlamini, a dedicated, hardworking old Zulu woman who helped me with housework and proved the most faithful of nannies. Our young Zulu gardener, Bonginkosi[38], enjoyed the company of the two older boys and won their childlike admiration by holding a live coal from the outside boiler between his teeth! Little Murray was soon found toddling to the gate, trying to lift the heavy chain which held it secure. Our rural black customers and neighbours were curious about all the antics of these white children who had moved into their community, and as the months passed our little lads settled into the freedom and enjoyment of country life.

Great excitement was spread abroad among the locals when one of our best loved staff members, Eunice Mhlongo, was married in all the traditional wedding finery of Mlungus[39] with white bridal gown, gloves and veil. Peter and I were among the honoured guests at the ceremony which was followed by a feast in true Zulu style. A slaughtered beast was roasted on a huge spit

---

[37] hut
[38] meaning 'Praise God'
[39] white people

over an open fire and a generous supply of sweet cakes and cool drinks made up the wedding fare shared by the community well into the afternoon.

Our life took on interesting, unfamiliar dimensions as we helped to meet the needs of our rural customers in their tribal setting. We lived at the gentle pace of the people we served, enjoying the quality of life which is lost in the hustle and bustle of the city. Our children were blessed with the gift of a simple upbringing, learning about the treasures of nature and respect for their Zulu neighbours in the same way that my siblings and I had learnt from our parents.

First Year Challenges

The first year at Ndulinde Store from 1967 to the end of 1968 held severe challenges we could never have foreseen, which tested our faith to the limit in unexpected ways. After six months our estate agent in Pietermaritzburg telephoned to say that the young doctor could not raise the full price and had withdrawn his offer to purchase our house. The news was devastating as we had been waiting for the proceeds from the sale to put down as deposit on the business.

Peter was suddenly faced with the daunting task of finding another source of income – and fast! He approached other traders who advised him to start buying and selling goats which have significance in the tribal life of African people as live 'currency'. He began to order regular batches of goats by rail from the Transkei, Eastern Cape. Among them were pregnant nanny goats that gave birth to the cutest little kids which we sometimes had to bottle-feed, much to the delight of our boys. The income from the goats kept us afloat for a few months until finally we received the good news that a new buyer had been found. This sale went through smoothly and all was well, but the trade in goats continued by request of our Zulu customers.

In the rainy season the dirt road from the village became very slippery with a surface slick of mud, and in heavy summer storms the rain washed deep ruts across the road accentuated by the constant flow of vehicles. It became necessary every year for the Natal Roads Department to bring large graders to scrape the surface and fill in the 'dongas'[40] to keep the roads open. It soon became clear that we'd have to invest in a vehicle that could cope with the situation and bought a French 'Citroen' which had the advantage of a chasse that could be jacked up high enough to negotiate the terrain. What a great asset that vehicle proved to be, tailor-made for the purpose!

Andy and Steve enjoyed the wonderful freedom of those carefree days at Ndulinde with their own pets, ducklings and newborn kids. We invested in two old horses which they learned to ride, and bought a gentle little Jersey cow from a farmer at Tugela Mouth, named 'Poleesh' by Zulu staff for her boot-polish mahogany colouring. She was tethered at night in an old shed beside the house and milked daily by our faithful old night watchman, Nyoni.

Life was simple with none of the electrical amenities of town life. We had our own diesel-driven lighting plant, which was started up at dusk and switched off at dawn, except on dull, rainy days. Our rainwater supply was stored in the massive underground tank and saw us through to the next rainy season if we were careful. However, one year the drought was so severe that our tank ran dry and Peter had to fetch water for drinking and household purposes from the village in large drums, while Ma Dlamini took our clothes to the river to wash. It was here that we learned to value God's gift of rain.

Illnesses

The next crisis we faced in 1968 was five-year-old Andrew falling ill in the summer with a mystery fever. Our local GP Dr Alan Curzon referred him to Addington Hospital in Durban, a three-hour journey away, and I spent a month with Andy while

---

[40] deep ruts

extensive tests were done. I had to use my imagination to think of ways to keep the little lad occupied in bed during this long spell. One idea that worked was French knitting, using a cotton reel with four tacks to make a square frame at one end. With a crochet hook and different colours of wool we made a very long Wiggly Worm and then a multi-coloured striped jersey to slip over him. The eventual diagnosis was paratyphoid virus which Andy had in all probability picked up from our own milk supply. He was successfully treated and we returned home, but from then on we boiled our milk or used bottled long-life milk.

The next blow came later in the same year when the three boys contracted mumps. I was very alarmed when one-year-old Murray woke one morning with his little head swollen like a rugby ball on one side. I drove in great haste to Dr Curzon in Mandini, who diagnosed a mastoid infection in the bone behind his left ear and booked him at once into Entabeni Hospital in Durban for an emergency operation to scrape the infected bone. After packing hurriedly for the two of us Murray and I drove to the hospital where I stayed with him for ten days, until he was discharged with a drainage pipe behind his ear. It wasn't long before antibiotics cleared the infection and he was as 'right as rain' again.

Various Services to Customers

Surrounded by the tribal kraals on the rolling green hills of Zululand, we became our neighbours' link with the outside world. All able-bodied young men of age and some young women went off to the cities to find work, leaving parents, grandparents, sisters and young brothers at home. Though still only in our mid-thirties, Peter and I earned great respect from our old customers, who referred to us as 'Mama' and 'Baba'[41] out of gratitude for the help we gave them in many practical ways.

The most vital service we ran was the Government Postal Agency, which entailed collecting the large padlocked canvass

---

[41] 'Mother' and 'Father'

mailbag from the nearest post office at Nyoni. Every month-end there were several registered envelopes containing cash, sent home to parents by their working sons or daughters in the city. These we receipted officially and locked in the safe until the recipients arrived to collect. With a staff member present as witness, we opened the envelopes and checked the amounts before they signed the post office register with a cross or thumb-print, as these old people could neither read nor write. After spending the cash on essential supplies for another month they set off on foot to their kraals.

Another greatly appreciated service was Peter's role as undertaker, driving his low-bed truck to kraals that were off the beaten track to collect deceased relatives for identification at the nearest police station before burial. The only other option was for relatives to hire taxis from their own people, who charged outrageous prices for the service if they agreed at all because of superstitions about transporting the dead.

Pension Paydays

Twice a year an official team from the Government Department of Pensions drove up to our store in a rugged 'Land Rover' to pay Old-Age Pensions. On these occasions hundreds of old folk made their way across the hills to wait, some able to walk very slowly, others crippled with arthritis being pushed in wheelbarrows, and the blind often led by little children. Those living closest would arrive at dawn, and by mid-morning the open quad behind the store was filled with old people sitting on the grass, waiting with quiet resignation to receive their meagre pension.

Those days were turned into socially festive occasions by women who set up stalls selling pre-cooked meals of boiled mealies, amadumbes[42], sweet potatoes, amagwinye[43], amasi[44],

---

[42] a root crop
[43] deep-fried dumplings
[44] soured milk

Marriage and Parenthood

cooked chicken pieces, fresh fruit in season, dried herbal medicines, live chickens and live goats. In addition, they sold indigenous craft work of beautiful beadwork, hand-woven grass baskets, mats, brooms and hand-made clay bowls, all sought after in the towns by tourists to our country.

We had our own gristing mill which ran noisily throughout pension days, grinding the dried maize kernels which customers brought in bags and carried home in the form of maize meal, their staple diet. The black staff members Victor and Aaron who had the task of running the mill were a source of great amusement to our little boys at the end of the day because their peppercorn hair, eyebrows and eyelashes were frosted white with the flying corn dust! Zulu people have a wonderful sense of humour with ability to laugh at life's more serious adversities – and our little sons' teasing.

The Swedish Lutheran missionary sisters from Nyoni timed their weekly visits to coincide with pension days, to give advice to mothers about feeding and care of their infants and to treat old folk with minor ailments in the small brick clinic on our property.

Looking for different ways to help our customers we hired Constance, a very pleasant young Zulu seamstress, and set her up on the verandah of the store with a hand-operated Singer sewing machine. She used her own initiative in designing and making dresses, skirts, full aprons and headscarves from a range of popular imported cotton-print fabrics. Brightly coloured bias binding trims added distinctive patterns, and these fashionable garments of the day sold like hotcakes. She also hemmed lengths of brightly coloured strong fabric worn as tribal 'wraps'[45] by young girls, and her presence at the front of the store stimulated a buzz of animated conversation among the women all talking at full volume!

There was a real buzz of activity on Saturday mornings when locals came to shop or just meet up with friends for timeless socializing. Zulu women are renowned for their magnificent

---

[45] skirts

beadwork, using brilliantly coloured glass beads which we imported. The beads arrived from the Eastern Bloc countries in strong, wooden crates which became invaluable to us as packing cases for breakables during our many house moves to come. There came a time during the apartheid era of government discrimination when countries placed an embargo on the importing of glass beads and we were forced to buy locally made plastic beads, which were a very poor substitute by comparison. The bead workers were very disgruntled with the inferior product but for a few years had no choice.

They amazed us with their skill at producing intricate patterns incorporating coded messages in their designs for necklaces, headbands, bracelets, wide beaded belts stitched on to fabric, decorative handles on hand-carved wooden spears, knives, forks and spoons. Peter bought a generous selection of articles from our own customers and mounted these on reed mats to make striking wall hangings in the house, which generated lots of interest among our guests. A newly introduced skill was weaving attractive baskets and bowls from plastic-coated copper wire extracted from cables. This brightly coloured medium known by children as 'Scooby Dooby' wire produced articles which were both strong and useful.

School Begins for the Boys

The months passed swiftly and soon Andy was in his sixth year and it was time to register him for school. Being too far from the nearest town of Eshowe for daily commute, we registered him as a weekly boarder at the Roman Catholic Holy Childhood Convent under the mothering care of the nuns, in January 1968. It wasn't easy for me to leave our little lad there on the first Monday morning, but the week passed quickly and soon it was time to fetch him home for the weekend. He adapted well to the routine thanks to the care of the sisters, especially Sister Carina and Sister Kunhilde who were very kind.

Marriage and Parenthood

The following year Hostel Sister Kunhilde was a special blessing to Stephen, as he had to cope with the frustration of wearing spectacles and suffered from severe growing pains in his ankles, which the doctor said he would grow out of. Being there together made it easier for both boys, and they coped very well with their lessons. Little brother Murray, now on his own at Ndulinde, played under the watchful eye of Ma Dlamini, his faithful companion, and looked forward eagerly to the return of his big brothers every weekend.

It was best for Peter as the authority figure to be in the store most days to keep his eye on the business, so I took over the responsibility of delivering heavy loads of meal or boxes of goods over the hills to customers on our little flat-bed truck. Trips to fetch supplies from the village station or wholesalers in Eshowe were scheduled to fit in with Monday and Friday school trips, with occasional extras in between if necessary.

Some friends felt anxious about the safety of my driving the seven-mile journey to Nyoni on my own, but I assured them that living among our customers I was absolutely safe. I treated our neighbours with great respect and repaid strong helpers who changed a flat tyre for me along the way, by giving them a lift all the way to the village. Because their only means of travel was on foot, it was our pleasure to give them lifts on the back of the truck whenever there was space.

Our Family Grows

Peter and I had always dreamt of having four children so our next baby was planned two years after Murray, but I failed to conceive during the busy year of our move to Zululand. Our local GP, Dr Alan Curzon, found me to be in perfect health, so advised me to wait six months and return if nothing had happened by then. To my great delight, the day before my booked appointment I felt the familiar symptom of nausea confirming that baby four was on the way. I was extremely fit throughout this pregnancy, monitored regularly by Dr Curzon. Of course my life was very

Riding High with Jesus

busy raising our three little boys, running our home and helping Peter in the business, but I was never happier than in this immensely fulfilling role. Looking back years later we concluded that God in His gracious wisdom had supernaturally intervened to block the fourth pregnancy because He knew all the unforeseen stresses that I would be facing during the coming year.

Having grown up in the company of five sisters, I was enjoying the novelty of raising little boys and would have been content to round off our family with another son. I chose to deliver this baby at Mothers' Hospital in Durban because it would be convenient for family members to pop in between Peter's visits. Sister Madeline had spoken so highly of her Durban gynaecologist, Mr Batchelor, that I decided to consult him.

On due date, when Mr Batchelor examined me he recommended that I remain close at hand in Durban, and with a smile asked if I was hoping for a girl this time. I told him I didn't mind, to which he responded with a bet that the baby was a girl based on his theory that girls have a faster heartbeat than boys. I left in high spirits, excitedly considering seriously for the very first time that the boys might have a little sister.

Sister Lorna invited me to stay with them in Durban North and as the next day progressed I began to feel very uncomfortable with low backache. Recognising the onset of labour, I phoned the sister at Mothers' Hospital who suggested I come in at once. By 3.30pm on the 30th May 1969 our petite little Princess Shelley Anne was born sucking her weeny thumb! 'Batchy' had won the bet and our adorable little daughter made her entrance weighing 6lb 3oz. Peter and I were elated as we studied her tiny features, cap of dark, wavy hair and deep violet eyes, which later changed to hazel.

When Peter brought the three boys to visit us there was much vying to get closest to the crib to see their baby sister, so Peter lifted them all up on to the high bed beside me. I placed Shelley between them and opened the blanket so they could see her tiny body and feel the grip of her teeny fingers. As each had a turn to hold her they were amazed at how small she was. Seeing our older

Marriage and Parenthood

children for the first time after the birth of each new baby was always a surprise, because they looked *so* much bigger than when I'd left home just a week before!

Knowing the demands of my busy life, Mr Batchelor was adamant that I stay in hospital for a full nine days to rest. It was wonderful to have Mum and my sisters pop in during visiting hours, to share the joy of our baby girl. Looking ahead to going home I tried the new white jacket I'd knitted on Shelley, but she was so tiny that her little frame was lost in it. So with fine baby wool I knitted a diminutive first size jacket which fitted her perfectly. She looked as cute as a doll when Peter came to fetch us, to the delight of her brothers and all our Ndulinde staff and Zulu customers. Being a placid baby, Shelley fitted quickly into the pattern of my daily activities, even coming with me to the monthly meetings of the Amatikulu Methodist Women's Meetings where I was President at the time.

Having to make frequent trips into town I employed Esther, a young Zulu maid, to keep an eye on Murray and Shelley while I was away. She was a cheerful, resourceful and loyal servant who enjoyed her work and was loved by the 'kiddies'. Living so close to nature, we kept our eyes open for snakes in the vicinity of the house, especially lazy venomous puff adders which were well camouflaged by their markings as they sunned themselves on the warm cement pathways.

On one occasion Esther showed great courage and presence of mind in the face of potential danger. I had gone into the bathroom to fill a basin of hot water from the bath tap and as I turned was shocked to see a puff adder curled up beneath the hand basin just a few inches from my feet! Reacting out of a deep-seated fear of snakes, my instinct was to scream and rush out of the bathroom with the basin of water past little Murray who had followed me. Esther put me to shame by running in to sweep little Murray to safety before disposing of the snake without a hint of fear. She was treated as one of the family and proved a valuable help to me with our growing brood at home, on holidays and frequent weekend trips to Granny at Tongaat Beach.

Little Shelley grew quickly under the adoring, protective watch of her three brothers. I nicknamed her 'Topsy' for her mop of soft, brown curls, a special love-name that has followed her into adulthood although her curls have long since been replaced by an elegant short style. She was soon taking her first steps and exploring the outdoors within the fenced garden.

As I looked to the future when her three brothers would all go away to school, I imagined that Shelley would be lonely so suggested to Peter that we extend our family with a little companion for her. My pregnancy sixteen months later was as joyful as the others, once again under the watchful care of our local GP, Alan Curson, and Mr. Batchelor at Mothers' Hospital.

On the stroke of midnight, 22nd September 1970, our bonny little son Justin Peter was born at Mothers' Hospital, making our quiver full. From the start he was a handsome, robust little boy with dark hair and dark brown eyes like his brother Steve. He and Shelley were inseparable companions and he soon caught up to her in height. Ironically, soon after the arrival of 'Justy' we were forced by Government decree to leave Ndulinde Trading Station and move into town, so the reason for providing Shelley with a playmate was no longer a pressing issue! Nevertheless, none of us could imagine our family without the special joy that Justin has brought.

Forced to Sell Ndulinde

After many years of white storekeepers trading within the tribal lands under the 99 Year Lease Agreement, the Government decided that stores should be returned to black traders. Much to our disappointment we faced the inevitable prospect of moving from Ndulinde. Some storekeepers in northern Zululand sold their businesses immediately but we were so enjoying our country life that in good faith we decided to hold out to the last, little knowing the problems we would incur as a result.

We prayed as Peter began to look for another viable business to purchase, then we heard that Tony and Sue Geyer had put their

Eshowe business 'Gureff Store' up for sale. Due to Tony's ill health this Christian couple were willing to sign a Sale Agreement subject to the release of the secure finance that was due to us from Government coffers from the sale of Ndulinde Store. Peter began sale negotiations with the Bantu Trust Department, and when months had gone by without any progress, he flew to Pretoria to ask for answers. He met with a Mr Hitge who assured him that our file was in his hands and we would be paid in four to six months' time.

Peter assumed that we would be paid a fair price and decided to go ahead with the purchase of Gureff Store. He appointed an experienced manager, Mr van Rooyen, and his wife Marie to manage Ndulinde Store for what was meant to be a brief interim period, and took over the running of Gureff Store in 1972. Peter renamed the store 'Kwa Isilevan' after his Zulu nickname 'Isilevu' given to him by our Ndulinde staff because of his prominent chin.

New Home in Riddell Lane

Our search for an affordable property for our growing brood led us to a large, comfortable old home just around the corner from Gureff Store in Riddell Lane, with a spacious garden and three huge jacaranda trees. Peter transported furniture and personal possessions to our new home and we were soon settled in the country town of Eshowe.

Our immediate neighbours, Ron and Marilyn Wilkinson, had three children – Lynne, Keith and Darryl – of similar ages to our young ones. Next to them in the lane lived an elderly lady, Mrs Howse, with a gaggle of twelve fierce geese, which sometimes wandered out of her garden and blocked the path from our gate into the lane. Mrs Howse admitted that her geese even gave her a sharp bite at times, but assured us that if they tried, we could just give them a sharp whack on the beak. Our boys put me to shame by bravely running the gauntlet to get past them, but I confess to being so intimidated I wasn't willing to risk a bite and waited until they'd gone back into their garden before daring to venture out on foot!

Social Interests Develop

Life in town offered new and interesting opportunities. Andy and Steve become day scholars at Eshowe Primary School down the road and family life took on a different pattern altogether. Peter was able to indulge his passion for golf on Saturday afternoons after closing the store. His play improved steadily and he was popular with his golfing peers, so the day came when he was voted Captain of the Eshowe Golf Club. Because captaincy required a greater commitment of Peter's time at weekends, I decided to enter into his sporting world to be near him. Not being a golfer myself, the perfect solution was to join the catering group of other wives who prepared and served meals to the golfers. Later I even had the honour of presenting the prizes as the Captain's wife. It meant a lot to Peter that I had made the effort to support him in the sport he enjoyed so much, and I developed a widening circle of friends among the ladies.

Round Table

Peter was invited to join Round Table, and we had a lot of fun at their social events – ballroom dances, relaxed family picnics in the sunshine and art exhibitions. Annual fancy dress balls on given themes were great fun, dressed in costumes which I made at minimal cost. Photographs have us on record as Red Indian Chief and squaw for the ARTSA Festival; a Middle Eastern sheik and belly dancer; a Hawaaian couple in sarongs and garlands. For the last event our staff dressed us authentically as a young Zulu couple in tribal costume from our own stocks, a maiden adorned with beadwork and her young warrior suitor armed with spear and shield.

The Eshowe Table Chapter hosted annual variety shows and art exhibitions which drew support from the wide farming community. At one exhibition I was browsing among the paintings when I came upon an oil painting of a South African farm by a rising South African artist, Gerrit Roon. Gazing at the old weathered sheds and gum trees in the background so reminiscent of our childhood farm, I was suddenly overcome by a rush of nostalgic memories so intense that I was choked with emotion. It was all there – the slate-blue corrugated-iron roofs, the tall gum trees behind the buildings and the rutted farm road.

Peter found me standing transfixed before the painting with tears brimming. He had never seen our farm and wondered at the cause of my tears, so I explained the deep emotional impact to him. After studying the picture, he asked, "Would you like to have it, Honey?" I stared at him speechless, as we'd never bought an original painting before and the cost was R230. Before I could reply he went on to say, "Last week I sold an old safe from the store for that exact amount, so we can buy it if you would like it!" When the art dealer saw our interest he suggested we take it home on an overnight trial, and needless to say it graced our lounge wall for many years, admired by everyone who saw it. After Peter died and I moved to the UK I gave it into the safekeeping of Andy and Lynne, where it continues to give me joy on every visit.

Children's Hobbies

In our garden at Riddell Lane the children romped with a litter of new puppies, whose needle-sharp teeth caused many tears. Murray asked for a cockatiel for one of his birthdays and we trimmed its wing feathers to stop it flying away. But the wings grew undetected and one day his pet escaped through the cage door and flew into our neighbour's tall jacaranda tree. His teenage brothers climbed on to their garage roof over the next few days to coax it out of the tree with food, but sadly their efforts were unsuccessful.

Andy became interested in the hobby of his friend Craig Pettit, a snake collector, and asked if he could start his own collection at home. With my dread of snakes, I shuddered to think of having snakes anywhere near my family. But his dad agreed when Andy promised to be responsible and learn all he needed to know about the potential danger and procedure if bitten, so Peter sank a small water tank into the lawn and the collection grew to several different varieties. The only time we had a scare was when the fang of his tiny poisonous ruby herald accidentally scratched Andy's thumb while he was handling it. His thumb swelled up severely so our doctor suggested he spend a night in hospital for observation. Andy was amused to find he knew far more about the antidote to the poison than the doctor did, and by morning he was discharged none the worse for wear!

Crisis at Nkhandla

One weekend in 1972 we visited our friends Ian and Mary Smith at their Sibudeni Trading Store in Zululand. Little Shelley who had inherited her dad's asthmatic tendencies had a bad cough when we left, so I went prepared with cough mixture and a small friar's balsam lamp to burn through the night to ease her breathing. During the day Mary and Ian took us for a walk in the Nkhandla forest to see a magnificent display of red hot pokers growing wild in the glade. The kiddies had great fun running in and out of the tall blooms, but by the time we returned to the house our little three-year-old Shelley was suffering with a severe asthma attack. I put her to bed with a dose of cough mixture and lit the friar's balsam lamp for the vapour to help clear her chest.

However, I felt anxious when she was still struggling to breathe in the early hours of morning and by the dim candlelight gave her a full spoon of what I thought was cough mixture. By the first light of day I was horrified to realize that I'd given her a spoonful of friar's balsam by mistake! She was as white as a sheet and feeling nauseous which terrified me in case I had poisoned her! We decided to rush her back to our doctor so packed the children into the car at once and left in haste for Eshowe. En route Shelley needed to throw up so we stopped the car at the side of the road and thankfully most of the mixture was expelled. When we reached the doctor's rooms we were hugely relieved to hear that friar's balsam was not poisonous but had in the old days been taken in moderation. The asthma attack subsided and little Shelley Bells was none the worse for my mistake.

Many were the happy kiddies' birthday celebrations in our garden with neighbours and friends during those years in Eshowe. We made friends with an American missionary couple, Sandy and Charlotte Sinclair, with five children identical in age and order to ours: three boys, Michael, Richard, Wayne; a daughter, Michelle; and little Johnny. Television had just arrived in South Africa and we enjoyed many Friday night hotdog suppers with the ten children lined up on the carpet to watch family 'telly'. Years later we still think fondly of our favourites: local South African Afrikaans programmes, 'Liewe Heksie', 'Wielie Walie', 'Haas Das' (the Bugs Bunny news reader) and English programmes from the USA like 'Little House on the Prairie', 'The Brady Bunch' and many others.

Living in town enabled Andy, Murray and Shelley to take piano lessons with a very patient music teacher, Helga Solberg. These early lessons were to be of great value later in life when they all learned to play the guitar and lead worship in church.

Writing on the Wall for our Business

The months dragged on into years as we waited for the Government's settlement on Ndulinde Store. To our dismay when at last the offer came, the figure of R22,000 was R13,000 less than we had paid for the business six years before! Peter had increased the turnover considerably and in addition my brother Stan had constructed a large new corrugated iron shed worth R6000. No government official or valuator had ever been to Ndulinde to take stock of the business, so Peter lodged a strong objection and informed them that we would not accept this totally inadequate figure. Our refusal forced the correct procedure and local assessor Leo Vermaak came up to do a proper stock-take which was sent off to Pretoria.

This was a very tense time in 1972 because inflation had hit our country as we had never known it in our lifetime. Banks froze their overdraft facilities and our new business came under severe strain. Gureff Store had been a flourishing business with a dependable core of regular customers earning good wages on the railway, who settled their account without fail every month. But this changed in the recession when the local ADAMS supermarket built a separate section for black trade, and our regular railway workers began to alternate between the two stores. Without the injection of the expected capital from the Government for Ndulinde Store, and no loan available from rich relatives or the banks, we had absolutely no means of keeping our business afloat. The delay caused by poor Government handling of our case extended the crippling wait to three-and-a-half years, and Peter watched helplessly as sales declined alarmingly.

Drakensberg Boys' Choir School

At ten years of age Andy sang a solo 'Good King Wenceslas' at the school concert. His clear, sweet soprano voice impressed everyone and after the concert a local couple, Barry and Eileen Warren, approached us with a surprise proposition. Their twin sons had recently attended the Drakensberg Boys' Choir School in the South African Drakensberg (Dragon-Mountain) range and they encouraged us to enrol Andrew at the school. The boys' choir was soon to hold a concert in our town, so it was arranged that we meet with choirmaster Lionel van Zyl at the pre-concert practice. Andy passed a brief audition and we made an appointment to meet the principal at the school. During the December school holidays, we set off with great excitement on what was to be the first of many trips to the 'Drakies' School.

In those early years the school had the informal character of a small farm school run by its founders Ron and Gwen Tungay. On arrival we were met by a bustling, elderly lady in grubby trousers and Crimplene blouse who introduced herself as the principal, Gwen Tungay! She shook hands, apologising for her

Marriage and Parenthood

dishevelled state and hastened to explain that a dirty handkerchief tied around one hand was covering a cut she'd just got from a barbed wire fence as she chased her goat to tether it. What a novel introduction to our son's place of learning!

We were given a tour of the simple classroom and hostel complex, all the while absorbing the history of the school which 'Mother' Tungay imparted as we walked. There was a lovely atmosphere of tranquility around the grounds and we could hear the fast-flowing mountain stream splashing its way over boulders through the trees below the school. The soccer field was nothing more than a grassy patch with wooden posts, and we both felt that this would be a wonderful place in which Andy would thrive – singing, pursuing his lessons in line with the Government curriculum and having lots of fun with other boys from around the country. We went home with all the information we needed about fees, school curriculum, fund-raising concerts around South Africa, tours abroad and the practical uniform of black T-shirt and shorts.

So in January 1973 our firstborn left home at eleven years for boarding school in the mountains. It was hard to drive away and leave him there so far from home, but all the boys were encouraged to write weekly letters home and I kept Andy regularly posted with family news. Because the pupils came from far and wide, there wasn't time to travel home for free weekends so parent weekends were held at the school.

In his first year Andy's choir was invited to sing at the opening of the prestigious new Nico Malan Theatre in Cape Town. The day after the choir had left, Peter and I were chatting at the breakfast table, imagining what the boys might be doing at that moment. Suddenly Peter threw me a beaming smile with a question that took my breath away: "Honey, how would you like to fly down to Cape Town, to surprise our boy?" Wow, what a question! I had never flown before and riding on the wave of his exciting idea, Peter booked our flight with the local travel agent. Our close friend Mavis Getkate offered to host our two younger boys, and with minimal packing for four days we were ready to leave from Durban Airport the following day.

Riding High with Jesus

Nico Malan Theatre Visit

We arrived in Cape Town around lunchtime and booked into a small, furnished flat in Tulbach Square in the centre of the city. I felt heady with excitement at being in the beautiful 'Mother City' for the first time, and the call of the seagulls wheeling overhead made me feel I was in a magical bubble.

Leaving our luggage in the weekend hideaway we asked directions to the theatre and set off to get our bearings in the square. We discovered that our flat was within walking distance of the theatre so wasted no time in crossing over in search of the boys. We found the lads backstage taking a break in the middle of their rehearsal, and Andy's expression of shocked delight was a picture! The show was sold out but we were given permission to stand in the wings and enjoy their very polished performance to an erudite audience from the fields of politics, music, art and culture.

We were given special permission by his choirmaster, Lionel van Zyl, to keep Andy with us for the weekend if we promised to get him back promptly for rehearsals. We started by taking the cable-car up to the top of Table Mountain to enjoy the spectacular view of the beautiful coastline and the city of Cape Town spread out in a wide arc around the foot of the mountain. Peter hired a car and drove us to the picturesque fishing village of Hout Bay with colourful scenes of the people of Cape Malays with their sturdy, colourful little wooden fishing boats and tiny whitewashed cottages. Having grown up in the Eastern Cape, Peter had acquired a taste for locally caught snoek and treated himself to a box of the smoked fish to take home.

Another memorable drive took us out to the world-renowned 'Kirstenbosch Gardens' for tea, where an amazing collection of indigenous South African trees, shrubs and plants are carefully protected and the extensive lawns are kept in pristine condition. Our spontaneous adventure in Cape Town remains in my mind as one of the happiest experiences of our lives.

Marriage and Parenthood

Parent Weekends

For the parent weekends many families towed private caravans to the Dragon Peaks Caravan Park alongside the school property, others hired local caravans, while those who could afford it stayed in hotels or chalets in the area. The choirboys were allowed to sleep out with their families, so the cost-effective option for our family of seven was to invest in our first second-hand caravan, bought through an advertisement in the newspaper. With great excitement Peter towed it home and started to open it up. Only when the roof was lifted to standing height and the four striped canvass sides were lowered did we realize how small it was – like a canvass matchbox on wheels! There was a double bunk at one end, minimal storage area and just enough space at night for three little bodies in sleeping bags to fit side by side on the floor like sardines.

With snow on the mountains and minus degree temperatures, it only took one winter sleeping in all the warm clothes we possessed to convince us that we needed a bigger caravan with more protective insulation against the bitter cold. So we sold the little one and invested in a new model with semi-solid sides that provided much more warmth, sleeping bunks, living space and generous storage space. When travelling, the roof lowered over the folded canvass sides to a height below the minibus roof, making it easier to tow in the slipstream of our Kombi minibus with less wind resistance.

Gathered around our barbecue fires in the summer sunshine and warming campfires in winter, we made friends very quickly with lots of other parents in the caravan park. We far preferred the relaxed, friendly atmosphere of camping to hotel formality, which was just as well since that suited our pocket better. Children's birthdays were celebrated with lots of home-baked goodies and special treats for each absentee son in turn, and there was generally a wonderfully happy spirit throughout the weekends.

On the Saturday night of the parent weekends, the choirs put on a free concert in the caravan park hall for families. Peter treated me to a battery-operated tape recorder for my birthday to record the concerts, so through the afternoon I felt a mounting sense of excited tension as I waited to slip into the hall to secure good front row seats with rugs spread out on the chairs. In winter we dressed snugly and the rugs helped to keep out the icy chill rising from the concrete floor throughout the long evenings. There was a crackling air of excitement in the hubbub of conversations as parents, siblings, grandparents, aunties and uncles gathered in the hall. Our hearts swelled with fierce pride as our little lads took their places on stage in grey longs, blue waistcoats and white jabots to delight us with their angelic voices.

Stephen Goes to DBCS

We became aware when Stephen about nine that he was tone deaf and asked music teacher Miss Solberg for her advice. She suggested we buy him a recorder and in no time his musical ear had been perfectly tuned. During Andy's first year Stephen auditioned with the head choirmaster and was instantly accepted into David Matheson's choir. So for one year we had two boys at the choir school. At that time the academic limit was Standard 5 so Andy left at the end of his second year in 1974 to enter Eshowe High School.

In his second year Steve became a soloist and when the academic level was raised by another year to Standard 6, the school asked us to leave him for a third year as one of their soloists. Facing the devastating loss of our business, we explained our financial crisis to the board, who offered Stephen a bursary. The clear bell-like quality of Steve's high soprano voice added a special dimension to his choir, and he made his mark with the beautiful solo 'Kokowiet' in 1976. Andy, Steve and later Murray were all privileged to be chosen in their second year for the international choir to represent the school at the 'Zimriya Choir Festival' in Tel Aviv, Israel, which was an amazing experience for them.

Novelty of a Girl in the House

We enrolled Shelley in ballet classes for tots, and seeing our little girlie developing the feminine graces in her tiny pink tutu and soft pink ballet shoes was quite emotional for me. She was every bit a girl, playing happily with my high-heeled shoes, hats and handbags in her own make-believe games, and her brothers had to be taught to respect the difference between her games and theirs. Andy and Steve were amused when she started playing preacher to her dolls, but the brotherly teasing turned to mockery because of her plump little figure. When their nickname 'The Reverend Pork Sausage' reduced her to tears, it was time for me to intervene! As the only girl in the family, Shelley was adored by everyone because Peter and I avoided the mistake of indulging her just because she was a girl.

My Job at Eshowe Home for the Aged

In 1974 when Gureff Store turnover was declining at an alarming rate, an old Club friend, Doug Vanderwagen, popped into the store for a chat with Peter. Doug, who was Chairman of the 'Eshowe Home for the Aged' committee, was bemoaning the fact that the secretary/treasurer of many years had just resigned. She had walked out of the job without notice, leaving them in a flat spin because she'd guarded her role jealously and no-one else had a clue about keeping the books. They were desperate for someone to step in and knowing I had worked as a receptionist, Peter told Doug he was sure I could help. Viewing the opportunity of a salary to help with our personal expenses, he came home to break the news with a beaming smile. "Honey, Doug Vanderwagen came into the store today, and I've got you a bookkeeping job at the old age home!"

I stared at him in stunned disbelief! "Pete, how could you do that? I know *nothing* about bookkeeping! I did Geography instead of Bookkeeping at school and wouldn't know where to begin!"

"I'm sure you can work it out, Love," was his confident reply.

When I'd got over the shock, I agreed to take on the challenge with the Lord's help. Over the next few weeks I studied the previous 'Income & Expenditure' entries with a fine toothcomb, applying common sense as I went and making numerous phone calls to the Department of Social Services in Durban to ask for guidance concerning Government rulings and conditions governing homes for the aged. To my great delight, faith and common sense prevailed and I earned the committee's profound gratitude by bringing the books up-to-date within the next few months, in readiness to hand over to someone qualified when they found a new secretary. In the process I had won my husband's deep admiration and pride over a challenge well rewarded.

Frail Age Home and a Sprained Ankle

The committee had been involved for months in the process of adding a Frail Section to the Home and soon after I took on the job as secretary the plan began to take shape. A private home was purchased across the road from the rest home, carpenters were soon busy making alterations, and painters were bringing the old building to life. Part of the garage at the back of the property was turned into an office and once the telephone line was installed and workers had left, I was given the go-ahead to move in.

Having collected all the files and office equipment from the old office, I drove our Kombi minibus on to the lawn at the side of the house and opened the door. With both arms cradling a tray full of files, I slid down from the height of the driver's seat on to the uncut grass, not knowing that the long growth was covering a deep hole. My right ankle twisted so badly that the ligament was torn from the bone and I almost fainted from the excruciating pain.

When I could muster enough sound through the agony, I called out to the only other person on the large property, the black

Marriage and Parenthood

painter on top of the roof. I asked him in Zulu to bring me a bucket of cold water to soak my foot, and when the pain had subsided sufficiently, I crawled to the office on all fours and rang the matron. She came quickly with strong painkillers and a bandage to bind my swelling foot firmly. I thanked God for the fact that the painter had been on the roof and that the new telephone had just been installed. On examining my foot our doctor gave me the disappointing news that nothing could be done to reattach the ligament. She prescribed a course of painkillers, lent me a pair of crutches and I worked at my desk with my tightly strapped foot resting rather awkwardly on a chair for the next few weeks.

At Gureff Store I could see that the mounting tension of company sales reps calling on Peter for outstanding payments was taking a severe toll on my husband, so I enrolled four-year-old Shelley and three-year-old Justin in playschool and went into the store daily to intercept the callers and explain our financial difficulty.

As the situation worsened, Peter was clearly on the verge of a nervous breakdown, waking at night out of nightmares in cold sweats. Night after night I made tea and sat up with him, reminding him of God's promise in the Bible that he would never leave nor forsake His children, and quoted my parents' experience of God's faithfulness in desperate times throughout my childhood. The scale of our debt seemed insurmountable to Peter, so I told him that even if he couldn't believe that God would find a solution, I had enough faith for both of us, and urged him to rest and leave it with God! He desperately needed spiritual encouragement and support, but sadly our elderly Methodist Minister had emotional struggles of his own and was not in a place to offer any help to his flock.

Assemblies of God Church

As a result, we began to reach out for spiritual encouragement and uplift from the newly opened Assemblies of God (AOG) church in Eshowe. Being traditional Methodists, we'd never been taught that the Holy Spirit baptism of power experienced by the disciples at Pentecost was available to believers today. We were as yet totally ignorant about the 'charismatic' form of worship in the Assemblies Church, so on our first visit didn't know what to expect and were a little apprehensive. The stories we had heard about 'strange goings on' in the church services were totally dispelled once we entered into worship with this Christian congregation and sensed the powerful presence and peace of God as we'd never done before. One of the elders, Heinz Bartels, and his lovely wife, Stella, had heard of our plight and began to pray for us.

Heinz had already sold his sugar farm in the area and was about to view prospective farms in the midlands of Natal. To lift Peter out of the stressful environment in the store he invited him on a couple of trips while I held the fort. In time he and Stella decided to purchase a farm called 'Buckstone' in the Karkloof Valley near Howick, which had a dairy herd and agricultural lands. After praying for God's confirmation they offered the position of Dairy Manager to Peter who'd had experience on a dairy farm as a young man. This amazing answer to our prayers was the first of a series of absolute miracles from God!

Faith is a gift from God to all who believe and I give all the glory to God for my unshakeable faith throughout the challenges we were facing. I know that the seed of faith was planted in my heart as a child by seeing God honouring our parents' faith in very practical ways. But I recognize that in nurturing my faith from the time of my salvation I opened the door to experiencing personally the evidence of God's amazing faithfulness by the power of his Holy Spirit.

Faith Honoured by God

At the time of our family crisis in Eshowe, I was President of the Methodist Women's Auxilliary (WA) and our small band of twelve ladies offered to host the Annual District Meetings in our town in 1975. With more than a hundred delegates coming, we were fully aware of the organizational challenge before us and laid the massive undertaking on a solid foundation of prayer.

The delegates arrived to a warm country welcome before being shown to their prepared accommodation in private homes, bed and breakfasts and the local hotel. The sessions flowed seamlessly through the days and our home-baked teas and tasty meals were served to very appreciative guests. When the three-day meetings were over, the visitors remarked on the awesome sense of God's presence throughout the week, and our weary but triumphant little team was filled with thanksgiving for His divine help. That evening I had the privilege of sharing a very positive report at the church leaders' meeting, giving all the glory to God. I went home to bed with my heart bubbling over with joy and gratitude to God for His presence and anointing on every part of the proceedings.

My Personal 'Pentecost'

The next morning, I woke with the same bubbling lightness in my spirit, eager to record in my prayer journal the happenings of the past week. After breakfast Peter left the house to walk to the store and I sat down at my desk to write. Suddenly I felt a surge of power through my whole being as if I had been plugged into a power socket! An overpowering feeling of elation, of praise and thanksgiving, was coupled with the desire to run into the streets of Eshowe and shout, "JESUS CHRIST IS LORD!" to the town. This was followed by a compelling sense in my spirit that I should go to the church, where I knew that the elderly members of our congregation would be meeting with our minister for their short weekly service.

Sensing the prompting was from God, my first presumptuous response was to question, "Why, Lord? You know I don't go to that meeting," but His insistent "GO!" sent me scurrying to the car. I drove to the church not knowing what to expect. Walking into the building, I found the group of old folk sitting silently in the pews waiting for our minister. Taking my place in a pew near the back, I glanced across at Granny Makkink playing quietly on the organ and smiled at the bright sunbeams streaming through the window and dancing off the fine dusting of face powder on her spectacles!

The previous day, Rev. John Rist and his wife Bobs had gone to visit parishioners in the northern Melmoth area of the circuit, fully intending to be back by nightfall. Minutes ticked by and there was no sign of John so we sang a couple of favourite hymns. As we sat down I felt as if a giant hand had scooped me from the pew on to my feet and I found myself propelled up the aisle to the front of the church without knowing why. Only when I reached the front did I sense the inner voice of God tell me what He wanted me to do.

Many of the older folk didn't know about the struggle that Peter and I were going through with the loss of our business. God directed me to share how He had begun to answer our prayers, giving us hope for the future through the offer of a job for Peter. When I had finished, others came up one by one to tell their stories of God's faithfulness and the hour slipped quickly by. We sang a closing hymn, repeated the Benediction blessing together and in joyful spirit filed out of the building just as our minister and his wife Bobs drove in through the gate. They apologised for their absence, explaining that they'd been marooned in Melmoth because the newly-graded dirt road had turned into an impassable mud bath after heavy rain.

I knew that John and Bobs had both been filled with the Holy Spirit, and greeted them with the exciting news of my Holy Spirit anointing with the release of His power in my bedroom. When I explained how He'd sent me to lead the unexpected glory-session, we rejoiced together at God's surprising ways of glorifying His Son when we're obedient to His promptings.

Marriage and Parenthood

Sad Closure of Kwa Isilevan Store

In spite of everyone suffering the financial constraints of recession in 1975, Peter had no option but to try to sell our Eshowe business. He arranged for an auction to be held in the store and on the morning of the sale a dozen people gathered, but there was no way of knowing whether they were potential buyers or just idle onlookers. The auctioneer, Leo Vermaak, began proceedings by calling for bids on the business as a whole.

From inside our glassed office I watched and prayed, hardly able to believe there wasn't a single bid. Leo then separated the building from the stocks and offered them individually, but there were still no bids. After waiting a while he closed the sale, the casual onlookers drifted out and Leo approached Peter with reassurance: "Don't worry, Pete. From my experience this often happens. It's possible that someone will come to me with an offer and I'll get back to you as soon as they do."

In fact, no-one ever came forward with an offer to purchase and, sadly, the store ceased to trade. The clerk of the court sealed the building with stock intact and Peter left town empty-handed with a heavy heart, owing his creditors over R60,000. Our Kombi minibus was returned to the hire company and in the final hour one of our fellow traders graciously took possession of our lovely old home in Riddell Lane for what was outstanding on the mortgage.

On moving day in June 1976, with our kiddies sandwiched in among personal possessions, we followed the removal truck out of town in our leaky old green 'El Camino' truck packed to the hilt. As we headed to the Bartels' new farm in the Karkloof Valley, our hearts were overwhelmed by God's merciful provision which included a full tank of fuel paid for by our benefactor Heinz.

In delivering Peter from the pit of despair and sense of failure, God impressed on him a foundational truth: "Peter, *you* are not the source of supply for your family. *I am!*" This revelation began to bring Peter into much closer relationship with his Heavenly Father, setting him on a path of trust infinitely deeper than he'd had before. Losing the business had left him with a heavy conscience about unpaid debts, but six months after we left town the building was bought by the Bantu Handcraft Trust, the stocks were sold to pay the creditors and by God's merciful intervention Peter's integrity was restored!

Karkloof – Buckstone Farm

On Buckstone Farm Heinz brought builders and painters in to repair the second homestead while we lived for the first month in their large home. With their four teenagers – Egmund, Adrian, Mark, Michelle – and little five-year-old Pierre, plus our five children, the Bartels' home was stretched to the seams with fourteen under one roof!

What excitement reigned when our family was able to move across the garden to our own space in July 1976. Heinz and Stella's generosity extended to advancing us money for food and second-hand school uniforms for Murray, Shelley and Justin at Howick Junior Primary and Andy and Steve at Howick High. It was delightful to be living in a farm atmosphere, and Peter was in his element working with dairy cattle again.

We joined the Howick Methodist Church under the leadership of the Rev. Lindsay Hayward, a newly ordained young minister, but were also warmly welcomed as guests of the Bartels family at the love-feasts of the Howick Assemblies of God fellowship. There we formed deeply significant friendships with folk and began to attend their midweek bible study in the hall beneath the Catholic Church known as 'The Catacombs'. Pastor Bill Winter and his successor Tony Balcomb brought the Word of God to life, expanding our spiritual growth with teaching and revelation about parts of the Bible we'd never had before.

South African Christian Leadership Assembly

In 1978 a hugely significant spiritual event took place in South Africa in the city of Pretoria, the political heart of our

Marriage and Parenthood

country. The South African Christian Leadership Assembly (SACLA) was the first Christian multiracial gathering of its kind to defy the apartheid racial segregation laws by having white, Indian and black church leaders sharing the platform.

Peter and I had built close links with a group of believers in the Howick Methodist Church who, like us, were all hungry to experience more of God in their lives. We and our friends Dave and Aileen Goodenough, Garth and Janet Holden, Ted and Ann Webster, Don and Barbie Richards and Gordon and Jackie Turner felt called by God to attend the rally, in spite of strict petrol rationing and a ban on carrying extra fuel in containers. Our faith level was so high that we decided to make the journey in faith, trusting God for a miracle because we knew that the petrol tank of the minibus could only hold enough fuel to get us to Heidelburg, 50km short of our destination.

Much prayer went into the planning of the journey and when the day arrived, twelve of us set out in the minibus praising God with hymns, choruses and prayer as the kilometres sped by. We watched the needle gauge dropping steadily until it registered empty, and continued to praise and thank God in faith, tears of joy and exaltation streaming down our cheeks as we completed the last fifty kilometres on a dry tank! By the miraculous power of God, we arrived at the conference venue, pulled up and went in to register. When the men tried to start the vehicle to fill up with petrol, it was bone dry, which confirmed the miracle and the minibus had to be pushed to the nearest garage. There were many other delegates who arrived with similar stories of God's miraculous intervention, so the conference began on an amazing spiritual high. To have black and Indian brothers sharing the platform with whites after thirty years of racial discrimination was a deeply emotional experience for everyone, and God was able to move in power throughout the week-long sessions bringing reconciliation, restoration and healing to many hearts across the country.

My heart was ready to embrace more of God's Holy Spirit in this season, so I was eager to be baptized by full immersion, but our Methodist church did not embrace water baptism as part of the church doctrine. So a large group of believers from the Assemblies of God fellowship gathered one very chilly winter day on the bank of Arthur and Zoe Duncan's farm dam for the occasion. The spiritual significance of water baptism is experienced by those who follow the Lord Jesus in obedience and receive the full blessing of His power and unwavering assurance of salvation. Peter was not yet ready to take this step of commitment with me, but later did so with his Aunt Ruth Morris, Uncle Edwin and Tom Gemmel's wife, Margaret, in the swimming pool on her Richmond farm 'Ivanhoe'.

Murray at DBCS

In the year that Stephen left the choir school, Murray auditioned and was accepted from January 1977. Thanks to the bursary passed on from his brother, the family tradition and our visits to the school continued to bring much joy. Murray was chosen for the Zimriya Choir Festival in Tel Aviv as his older brothers had been and his flight took him via Switzerland to Israel. Arriving into the intense heat of July in the Middle East was an experience the lads would never forget. Little did Peter and I know then that we too would have the privilege of visiting the Holy Land in years to come.

Unexpected Change on the Horizon

Christians aren't perfect and even among believers there are differences of opinion, culture and lifestyle. Very soon it became evident that some of the things our sons were doing were an irritation to our employer, and tensions began to creep in. Stella and I had a wonderfully close and loving relationship as sisters in the Lord. We met weekly to pray for the farm, for our husbands and families, and it was my pleasure to cut her hair for her every month.

Marriage and Parenthood

Sadly, in the farmyard our husbands didn't share the same communication skills. Peter became more and more frustrated by criticism of his work and often came home dispirited at lunchtime, asking me to pray for him. I will never know what brought things to a head, but one day in June I skipped home across the garden from my prayer time with Stella, to find Peter standing ashen-faced in the lounge. He handed me a cheque he'd just been given in lieu of a month's salary, and in a state of complete shock told me that he had just been given notice! The news was like a bad dream which neither of us could comprehend.

My immediate reaction was to offer Peter comfort and encourage him to trust God for his help in finding another job. I reassured him that at least we had a roof over our heads for a month while he explored job possibilities, but the following day while he was in Howick on farm business, something happened that brought a sudden change in my attitude. Our employer came to the kitchen door and with icy coldness announced that he had forbidden his wife to come to me for her haircut! Enraged by such pettiness, I was bubbling over with anger when Peter returned. I hurried out to tell him I couldn't spend another day on the farm under that mean spirit.

Meanwhile he had come home with good news that he'd called on our friends Garth and Janet Holden in town, and they had offered us the use of the unfinished shell of a house they were building on a plot on the Bulwer road just outside Howick. Eager to move out, we began to pack bare essentials to take with us and left the rest in the house for a month.

In July 1977 we moved into the little haven we called 'The Little House on the Prairie'. Murray was away at the choir school so Peter towed our caravan to the plot for the older boys to sleep in and the two little ones slept on a bunkbed in one of two bedrooms. For lighting we used our gas lamp and I cooked our hot evening meals in the pressure cooker on the portable gas ring. Here we relaxed in camping mode, with solid walls and a roof over our heads to keep out the weather! How grateful I was to the Holy Spirit for giving me the grace to maintain a positive spirit which turned times of inconvenience into a family adventure. The nearest shop for emergency supplies of milk, sugar, bread and matches for the gas stove was a small Indian store within walking distance across the grassy field.

By God's mercy, within days Peter found temporary employment with Basil Crookes, another dairy farmer in the Bulwer area. He invested in a noisy old second-hand motorcycle which carried him to early milking at 4am every morning and brought him home at nightfall, leaving me with the use of the old El Camino truck to take the children to school and back. Life was simple and the living was good, thanks to God's gracious provision.

But my heart was not at peace about the broken relationship, and weeks after leaving the farm I felt compelled to go and be reconciled with Heinz by apologising for anything we had done to upset him. Peter was still carrying hurt but agreed reluctantly to come to the farm with me, where we found Heinz unwell in bed. Having made my apology and shaken his hand, I felt free in my heart, but it took a few more weeks before a reconciling handshake set Peter free too.

Heart Attack from Prolonged Stress

In October 1978 we spent the long weekend with Mum at Tongaat Beach, celebrating with the nation the memory of Paul Kruger, one of the early Dutch Fathers of the Afrikaner nation. Our Cockerill cousins were there too and the mood was relaxed and happy until the last day when Peter began to feel discomfort in his chest. What appeared to be heartburn wasn't eased by home remedies, and by mid-afternoon Peter began to complain of pain. He urged me to pack up for an early return home as he didn't feel well so we gathered our children and friends, Sonja Keyser and Justin's little buddy Alistair Pepper, and set off for home soon after lunch.

Crossing the wide Umgeni Bridge on the outskirts of Durban, Peter pulled the minibus off the road saying that he couldn't

Marriage and Parenthood

continue as the pain was too severe. This being the age before mobile phones, I saw that he was in urgent need of help and frantically tried to think of the nearest source of a telephone. Knowing that we'd left Madeline and her family at the beach, I took the slip road at Westville hoping to call on her neighbour to phone a doctor.

As we approached the emergency pharmacy I saw with huge relief that it was open, so pulled up and ran inside to phone the first GP on their emergency list. Peter followed me in writhing in pain. When I described the severity of Peter's chest pain with pins and needles in his fingertips, I was horrified when the doctor told me my husband was having a heart attack and needed to get to the Intensive Care Unit (ICU) at hospital immediately!

Desperate for help, I rang Mum in tears. She told me that Harry and Madeline had left immediately after us so I dialled their home, willing them to be there. Harry heard the phone ringing as he unlocked the front door and told me to wait there as he was coming. Hastily unpacking their minibus, he laid down the back seat to make a bed and sped back to meet me at the pharmacy. Settling Peter in the back he rushed him to the ICU of Addington Hospital in Durban, waited to see him admitted to the ward and connected to a drip, then phoned to tell me that they had done all they could. I learned later that the damage to his heart was so severe, the head sister did not expect Peter to survive the night.

When Harry had left for the hospital, I drove to their home where Madeline prepared a quick scrambled egg supper while I phoned ahead to Alistair's mum, Althea, to explain what had happened. She immediately started a prayer chain for Peter among our friends, which spread rapidly around the country and beyond.

After Harry's reassuring call that Peter was settled in the ICU I drove the children home to Howick, dropping the young friends en route. When our children had gone to bed, I packed myself a case of necessities and a bag for each of them. Next morning after dropping them at school I delivered Shelley's and Justin's bags to Gordon and Jackie Turner, and Andy's and Steve's bags to Dave and Aileen Goodenough before heading back to be near Peter.

Harry and Madeline opened their home to me and I spent five days from 9am to 5pm at Pete's bedside in the ICU. In spite of Peter's faint heartbeat, I felt hope in my spirit that as God had enabled him to reach the hospital in time, it was possible that he might pull through. We know the power of prayer to be awesome, and while I sat beside Peter's bed listening to the faint bleeping of his monitor, God's divine peace that passes understanding held me every day in quiet trust. From Tuesday to Sunday, while Peter's life was hanging on a thread, I experienced gentle reassurance in my heart that whether Peter lived or died I could trust our Father in heaven to take care of me and our family.

On Sunday afternoon, 15th October 1978, the fifth day in Intensive Care with no change in his condition, I left Peter at five o'clock with his once-bronzed skin now the colour of putty, too weak to sit up on his own, supported by one sister while another spooned soup into his mouth.

The Miracle

The following morning, I walked into the ICU ward and the sight that greeted me was utterly astonishing! Peter was sitting up in bed joking with the sisters on duty, his healthy tan restored and the sparkle back in his eyes for all to see. It was quite clear that a miracle had taken place during the night. His amazing recovery confounded the doctors and staff, opening the way for me to give God the undisputed credit for Peter's divine healing. The X-rays revealed scars where his heart muscles had been torn by the massive cardiac infarction but all was now completely healed.

1978-79 Brucillosis

After two days of observation in a general ward Peter was discharged with great rejoicing among our praying family and friends. However, within days of coming out of hospital he developed a high fever and disturbing pains in his chest. Doctors presumed that his heart was the problem but thankfully that was

Marriage and Parenthood

not the case. He was admitted to Greys Hospital in Pietermaritzburg for a series of blood tests to identify the mystery fever and sent home with a course of antibiotics. As soon as the course finished, the puzzling symptoms flared up again, and the pattern of returning to hospital for more and more blood tests was repeated over the next three months.

Christmas 1978 arrived and we went down to stay with Mum, hopeful of putting the problems behind us with a relaxing seaside holiday. All went well until the third course of antibiotics came to an end and, unbelievably, on New Year's Day the pain in his chest returned. I rang Greys Hospital and by God's grace the call was taken by the Hospital Superintendent himself, a fine doctor who had begun to take a personal interest in Peter's puzzling case. He advised me to bring him straight in, so disappointedly the children and I packed up our holiday luggage and left. True to his promise, the doctor was waiting for us. "I promise you, Mrs Hurd, that I will personally do all I can to get to the bottom of this mystery condition."

While doing many more tests over the next few days with a panel of young doctors, one of them remembered reading about a virus known as 'Brucillosis' which fitted Peter's symptoms. Unbeknown to us the herd at Buckstone Farm carried the virus which causes 'contageous abortion' in cattle and Brucillosis in humans, which Peter had picked up while artificially inseminating cows. The virus had attacked his lungs causing the high fever and excruciating pain from inflammation of the pleural lining. Sure enough, the test for this virus proved positive, so two combined antibiotics were prescribed which finally brought the long battle to an end and, with immense relief, Peter was free of all pain!

During the months that he was undergoing the prolonged treatment and needed bedrest, we were still living in what we called The Little House on the Prairie. Realizing it would be impossible for Peter to get quiet rest in the confines of that tiny house, a Methodist friend, Una Longmead, made a generous offer of the free use of her old family home 'Bowdon' which had been on the market for a couple of years. By coincidence this was the very house in which I'd been ill with measles while boarding with Una's parents, Gargie and Grandpa Rycroft, as a young teacher! Upstairs in the large bedroom of this charming old house, Peter found the quiet he needed to sleep, while downstairs our teenagers could invite their friends for coffee after school and the little ones had freedom to play with their pals.

In addition to prayer, our wonderful Howick friends opened a bank account for us and their donations kept our family in food and essentials through the coming months when we had no other income. I applied to companies to do in-store supermarket promotions of their products in Pietermaritzburg, and my first assignment with Lever Brothers earned me R150 a month. Later I was approached by the Baynesfield Bacon Factory to promote their bacon rolls and Rustlers sausages at a tasting table, which went very well.

This was a chapter in our life when we saw God perform one miracle after another to meet our family's basic needs. We had no substantial income but my small efforts combined with the gift fund enabled us to live frugally with basic needs met. Generous friends Dave and Aileen Goodenough gifted us with an old car to use or sell, and farmer friends within our church kept us supplied with fresh produce. On the school front, knowing of Peter's long-standing illness, the headmasters at both schools sympathetically waived the payment of school funds, which was a great asset.

I recall with deep joy and humility the different ways in which our Heavenly Father provided in 1979 and 1980. One afternoon all I had in the pantry for supper was an onion, but having seen God Almighty's hand at work, I was trusting in faith for him to provide for our evening meal. At 3.30pm there was a knock at the door and Eileen Matheson from the Karkloof Valley stood with a large basket brim full of fresh vegetables which made several tasty suppers that week. Perfect timing of the wonderful supply through other people's giving confirmed God's faithfulness in awesome and surprising ways.

Sarmcol Rubber Job

Fully recovered from Brucillosis by January 1980, Peter was nevertheless as weak as a kitten from the repeated high fevers he had suffered for three months. So I was surprised when he said to me, "Honey, please buy the paper so I can check the adverts. I must find a job."

My immediate response was, "Pete, you've hardly got strength to stand, so how are you going to cope with a job?"

He was adamant and began to scour the job columns.

One day he saw that the 'Sarmcol' rubber factory in our town was advertising for a shift foreman, and though he had no experience of factory work, we prayed for favour and he put in an application which was successful. He coped with supervising workers on the production line which required minimal physical effort and, as he gained strength, applied for promotions when vacancies opened up in the factory. As Peter moved up the ladder, his income increased to the point where we were now in a financial position to offer Una a modest rental.

With a steady income, albeit modest, Peter and I stepped out in faith to trust the Lord for a home of our own. We loved old Bowdon and had dreams of restoring it and enjoying it for many years to come, so approached Una eagerly with a request to purchase. Our disappointment was deep when she took the advice of her lawyer, a mutual friend, to accept a higher figure than we could afford. The decision went against her heart judgement and she regretted it bitterly when the new buyers sold it within the year at a large profit.

House Search in Howick

We had moved on in our search for a home in 1980, having worked out the maximum purchase price we could afford was R20,000. While Peter was at work our estate agent friend Althea Pepper began to show me what was on offer in our price range. It soon became evident that properties in that range were old and in very poor condition, with the exception of two brand new little houses priced at R22,000 each. The owner had told all the agents emphatically that he was not open to offers below the asking price but Althea took me to view them anyway.

The first was at 75 Ridge Road on a subdivisible one-acre plot of land. On first viewing the rooms seemed far too small for our family of seven but having seen everything else, I decided to return a couple of days later for a second look. This time I felt faith rising in me and saw possibilities through different eyes. There were three bedrooms inside, but an outside laundry within an enclosed courtyard had potential as a bedroom for our teenage sons Andy and Steve.

Althea and I both had faith to present an offer of R20,000 so we went back to Bowdon to tell Peter and fill in the necessary forms. As a security for me and our family, Peter put our homes in my name so I signed the offer and Althea left, intending to deliver it to the owner first thing in the morning. However, on her way home she felt a strong prompting not to wait, so taking a chance on finding the farmer out of bed, she drove out to his farm. Half expecting it to be in darkness, she was surprised to find the house ablaze with light. When the door opened, Althea discovered that the family was celebrating the son's return after two years of National Army Call-Up.

Althea quickly explained the reason for her visit and gave the farmer details of Peter's illness, our family's plight and personal reference of Peter's integrity as a prospective buyer. After brief consideration of these facts he agreed to accept our offer! She pushed for yet another concession of grace, explaining that we had no deposit and to her delight he agreed to provide collateral security of R600 which enabled the deal to go through. Another miracle of God on our behalf! We were ecstatic when she phoned with the good news early the following morning, and with deep gratitude to our friend Una for the year at Bowdon, we moved into our own little home in Ridge Road.

During this chapter ten-year-old Justin was accepted as a chorister in the famous Drakensburg Choir School. By his acceptance, in 1980 the Hurds made 'Drakie' history by being the first family to have four sons in succession at the school.

Roodepoort

Grateful as Peter was for the opportunities he had embraced in the Sarmcol rubber factory, within eighteen months he became restless to return to marketing. On applying for transfer to the Sarmcol sales department he was told that all deals concerning the sale of the rubber hosing and products used in the mining industry were negotiated on the Reef where the mines were, so he would have to relocate from Natal to the Transvaal.

We placed this important decision prayerfully into God's hands and put our house on the market, asking the Lord to lead us in his will by finding a buyer at a figure that would enable us to afford another home in the more expensive part of the country. Within a short time, prices had risen and we received an offer of R42,000 – twice what we'd paid for it! Taking this as positive confirmation from God, we prepared with great anticipation for the move from small-town living to the challenging life of working in the fast lane.

New Jobs and New Schools on the Reef

Contrary to schools opening in Natal in mid-January, Shelley and Murray had to register for Highveld schools on 3rd January 1981. So while Peter worked his month's notice in Howick, the children and I were hosted by my sister Enid and her husband Douglas in their Northcliff home. We had decided to settle on the West Rand so enrolled both teenagers at Westridge High, and at the end of January Peter brought our caravan which we booked into the Florida Park caravan site.

We began our search for a house in the old suburbs of Roodepoort, and it was soon evident that even modestly priced houses were beyond our pocket. In the tiny suburb of Selwyn, Roodepoort we found a comfortable old brick house with real appeal but it was priced R11,000 over our budget at R53,000. Praying once again for God's intervention, Peter approached his Sarmcol bosses for a loan but they refused outright saying it was not their policy to lend to employees. However, to Peter's amazement, within a week they called him back to say they were making an exception to their rule! This enabled us to purchase the property at 10 Pioneer Avenue, yet another occasion to give God praise for his amazing grace on our behalf! Murray was well settled at West Ridge High for the remainder of his high school years, but Shelley chose to move to Florida High School within walking distance of our new home.

Roodepoort Assembly

Our next important mission was to find a spiritual home, so we began to search for an Assemblies of God church we'd heard about from Ted and Ann Webster in Howick. They had attended the opening of the new church in our town, and were very impressed by the address from the guest speaker, Sam Ennis, pastor of the Roodepoort Assembly. So one Sunday afternoon Peter and I set off from the caravan park to begin our search having only the street name to guide us. After driving around for some time without success, we gave up and were heading for home when suddenly I spotted the elusive street name on the corner of the pavement: "Peter! Peter! There it is!"

Tracing back along the street, we came to a church building without any identifying board. However, at the back of the building we could hear voices and laughter coming from an adjoining flat. I knocked at the door and enquired of a tall, smiling gentleman, "We are looking for Sam Ennis's church. Is this it?"

"Yes, it is," he confirmed. "You are at the Roodepoort Assembly." Bun Heaton introduced himself as one of the church elders and apologised for the absence of the church board, which was being repainted. He drew us inside with a warm welcome to meet his wife Joy and their guests, and after a brief chat invited us

Marriage and Parenthood

to return for the evening service, promising to reserve seats for us. We drove back to our caravan with a sense of eager anticipation.

From that very first service Peter and I knew we had found our spiritual home. Irish pastor Sam, his wife Louisa and her Afrikaans parents Ike and Issie Liebenberg all made us feel instantly welcome. We were to be in close fellowship with these loving folk and the congregation of born-again believers for the next six years until we moved back to Natal.

I have always loved singing, especially opening my heart in songs of worship to God in church, and was blessed at our evening services when a soloist in the fellowship brought an item in song. One Sunday morning I was in for a shock when Peter and I chose to sit on the other side of the church for a change, a couple of rows behind our pastor's wife Louisa. At the close of the service Louisa came up to me and said, "Colleen, I've been listening to you singing. I didn't know you had such a lovely voice. You should be singing solo for us at evening services." I was instantly thrown into a state of panic at the thought of singing solo before hundreds of people, but my efforts to resist were brushed aside as Louise insisted that I arrange with the church pianist André Naude to prepare a song for an evening service.

It was Andre's encouragement and vocal training that slowly helped me to overcome my deep sense of inadequacy, to be able to glorify the Lord with beautiful songs composed by the blind worship leader Marilyn Baker. Little did I know that I would have opportunity twenty years later to thank Marilyn for her anointed music when I met her in England. By breaking the barrier of self-consciousness, God was preparing me to lead others in worship in the years to come.

When our daughter Shelley showed an interest in learning to play the guitar, we surprised her with her own instrument for her twelfth birthday and she joined a group of young girls in the church receiving free lessons from Ruth Naude. Shelley had a natural aptitude for the guitar and was soon playing well-known choruses and singing with other girls in their youth worship group. As the years passed, it became clear that from these early beginnings that she too was being prepared by God for future ministry in leading worship.

Our six years in the fellowship of the Roodepoort Assembly was an extraordinarily rich time for us. Spiritually Peter and I grew amazingly through the anointed preaching of God's Word, and through fellowship with a great band of friends studying the Bible midweek, praying together and having fun socially. While Murray and Shelley were completing their schooling, Andy and Steve completed their National Service training during this period and found work on the East Rand at the large AECI chemical plant for a short time.

Our New Jobs in Sales

In our new Highveld environment Peter settled into sales with Sarmcol but by 1984 the company policies had changed, and he moved into a position as Sales Rep with Moshall Gevisser, a wholesale company based in Durban. I became a sales rep with 'Easifit Covers' in Pretoria, marketing custom-made washable stretch furniture covers. I followed up on telephone enquiries to the office in Orange Grove, Johannesburg, and called on clients in homes across a vast area to give on-the-spot quotations. If the quote was accepted, my exact measurements would be sent to the factory in Pretoria. The completed orders were sent to the office, and delivered and fitted for clients by a team of strong African men. I was with the company for six years, during which time the business changed hands. The factory was moved to Cape Town and, sadly, the spirit of the company under the original owners was lost. Our happy working conditions changed radically and business declined significantly due in some measure to competition from cheap new suites flooding the market.

As my commission from Easifit Covers dwindled, I was offered another part-time job by our friend Anita Geyer, consultant with 'MAPP' a Christian firm of Medical Aid brokers. I found the challenge as consultant in this very competitive market both stimulating and expanding, not least because I had to brush up on my Afrikaans to conduct business in a dual-language province. The calls I made to present 100% Medical Aid cover to company directors dovetailed with my Easifit appointments across the Reef from Vanderbyl Park in the west to Benoni in the east, Alberton in the south to Sandton in the north.

Working totally on a commission basis in both jobs, I prayed every month for favour with prospective clients in order to generate my income. I upheld God's standards of honesty and integrity in all my dealings with clients and trusted him for the release of R2000 monthly to supplement Peter's salary, so we could meet the increased expenses of our children's education. My testimony at the end of six years was that though I sometimes waited until the twelfth hour, my earnings never failed to reach that total every month, confirming that God is faithful to those who put their trust in Him!

First Tour of Israel

At a Sunday morning church service in 1983 guest speaker Faans Klopper, Director of the International Christian Embassy in Jerusalem, shared briefly about the embassy's work, which fired an instant spark of interest within me about the Holy Land. Little wonder that I was excited at the end of the service when Issie Liebenberg stopped me in the aisle to ask if Peter and I would join their tour to Israel in February the following year!

As she spoke, I felt a sudden surge of joy so powerful that I could hardly breathe and felt it was the Holy Spirit confirming that we would go. I hurried out to the car to tell Peter the exciting news but was met with a deflating response of total disinterest. He reasoned that at that time of year, having just returned from the annual Christmas / New Year shutdown, there was no way he would be allowed to take an extra two weeks' leave. I was disappointed but knew that the conviction had to come from God, so I prayed and held my peace in the quiet belief that we would be going.

Riding High with Jesus

Months went by and when the deposits were due to be paid, Peter could see I was of the same mind. I asked him simply to write a letter to his Jewish bosses at Moshal Gervisser requesting leave to visit the Holy Land, and promised to accept their answer as final. To my delight he wrote the letter without coercion and posted it the next morning before he left on his country round of calls.

During the four days he was away I waited with eager anticipation for their postal reply. Imagine my surprise when I received a phone call at my place of work, asking Peter to ring his Durban boss when he came home. I knew it was in connection with his letter and could hardly wait for Peter's return. The next morning, he called the Main Office and was told by his Jewish bosses that they gave their blessing on his visit to Israel and arranged to send a replacement sales rep to do his calls. Now Peter believed it was God's will and with great enthusiasm arranged payment of air tickets through his bank credit card and cashed in an insurance policy worth R600 to cover land arrangements.

With great excitement we set off with a group of thirty members of our church, led by tour organizers Ike and Issie Liebenberg, to enjoy a life-changing experience in Israel. In anticipation of possible reactions to unfamiliar spicy foods in the Middle East, I went prepared with a good supply of Kaomagma medicine and dosed several appreciative members of our group who had come unprepared. The joy that Peter and I had, and our unbridled enjoyment of everything we saw and did on this fantastic trip, drew warm appreciation from our group.

We developed friendship with our Christian Arab guide, Farah Salem, that lasted for years. It was an awesome privilege to be in the land where Jesus had lived, preached, ministered healing and life to multitudes, was crucified and rose again. We both felt deeply inspired spiritually as passages of the Bible came to life while we travelled the land. Peter, who had never learnt as a child to read for pleasure, became hungry to read the Bible, which over coming days transformed his relationship with God.

Marriage and Parenthood

Our mutual love for Israel had been awakened, creating a deep desire to return and work there one day. We wanted to feel the true heartbeat of the country through contact with the local people, which isn't possible as a visitor being shepherded round tourist sites in an air-conditioned coach. We asked God to grant us this desire if it was in His will and settled back into our life of commitment to jobs and family, not knowing if this would ever happen.

Our Home in Pioneer Avenue

In our back garden at Pioneer Avenue three gnarled old apple trees, two apricots, and a flourishing young fig tree were all bearing fruit in season. Coming from the tropical coast of Natal, I had grown up with pawpaws, oranges, guavas, grapefruits, lemons and pineapples, so it was a novelty to have our own crops of deciduous fruit. Every garden on the Highveld had its own fruit trees so with the abundance of fruit we couldn't give away, Peter and I turned our hands to the delights of jam-making. In our large farmhouse kitchen, we set to work in a joint effort which filled the pantry shelves and gave us a lot of fun in the process. Pete loved jam on bread, his favourite jam being whole apricot, so he was more than happy to prepare the fruit while I did the measuring, cooking and bottling. As a child I had tasted crystallized figs in Christmas gift boxes but never picked fresh figs off a tree before. So it was a treat in the summer to stand with bare feet in the early morning dew and eat my fill of the luscious cool fruit from our own tree.

Our New Swimming Pool

Having experienced the intense heat of the dry highveld summer, Peter came home one day and declared, "Honey, I think we should put in a swimming pool." Comparing prices and maintenance costs of gunnited pools and fibreglass moulds, he was advised that fibreglass was cheaper and easier to maintain. With the choice made, excavators arrived with a massive digger to begin gouging out huge chunks of rich red earth and dumping it on a growing mound in the garden.

At last the day arrived when a huge low-bed trailer carrying the fibreglass pool drew up in front of our house. Watching the driver in conversation with the workmen, I sensed there was trouble and went out to meet them. They had just realized there was no access to the back of the house for the enormous crane because of our narrow gate and brick walls enclosing the whole property! With quick thinking, I suggested we ask our friendly neighbour Ethel for permission to bring the crane up her wide driveway, and with her consent, the plan was carefully executed. Swaying precariously overhead, the pool was lowered slowly over the fence into the hole and levelled on its bed of sand – a breathtaking feat safely accomplished! With our patience tried to the limit, we had to wait weeks for slate paving to be laid and the lawn to be replaced by a contractor before the pool was ready to fill.

It was a great investment for family and friends who shared many a barbeque with us around the pool. Peter and I swam daily through every summer and continued well into winter, when we came inside glowing and warm. It reminded me of my college days when I trained for the Lifesaving badge, getting up at five o'clock in the middle of winter for an invigorating plunge into the freezing water with the team!

After living with our pool for a couple of years, both working hard to make ends meet, Peter began to wonder what it might be like to live in a townhouse free of maintenance chores. He had the novel idea that we should let our house and try renting, and I agreed to the plan because I could see he wouldn't rest until he'd tried it. So we let our house for a year and moved into an attractive townhouse complex 'Jedidiah' just up the road. As expected, it wasn't long before Peter began to feel the claustrophobic effect of living 'cheek by jowl' with neighbours, overlooked and overheard, and was more than happy to move back to our spacious family home.

Marriage and Parenthood

To celebrate my fiftieth birthday in June 1986 we arranged a simple party in our home for close friends from our church fellowship. Shortly before the day, Peter and I accepted a dinner invitation from Vic Jacobs and his wife, and on arrival discovered that Vic ran his own photographic business from home. He surprised us with a smiling confession that he'd had a hidden motive for inviting us: to take a series of studio photos as a fiftieth birthday present for me! The results were lovely and I placed an order for twelve copies of the best for all my siblings and our children, but when I came to pay, Vic insisted on giving me the whole order as a gift, and they have been a special treasure to all of us, especially since Peter died.

Mum Springs a Wonderful Surprise

After Daddy's death in 1966 Mum had lived on her own at Ocean View for years with servant Moti as her constant companion and helper. During that time her lifelong widowed friend Saxon Groom had often brought bunches of flowers from his large garden on the farm to several lady friends along the beach road. But in time it became quietly apparent that Saxon's visits to Mum had turned to courtship, and one day she asked us all rather shyly, "Girls, what do you think? Saxon has asked me to marry him." Our unanimous response was one of absolute delight, having known Uncle Saxon, his late wife Trina and their three children all our lives.

With joyful celebration, at the age of sixty-two years, our precious mother became a bride again! Leaving her cottage in Moti's safe hands, she moved to Saxon's farm near Maidstone village, where they shared four blessed and wonderfully happy years together before his sudden death from a cardiac asthma attack. How tragic that Mummy lost both Dad and Saxon with the same shocking suddenness.

She returned bravely to single life in her little beach cottage and spent her days tending her garden, knitting, crocheting, keeping up her diary entries and blessing her few remaining beach friends with love and encouragement. Unbeknown to us, for some time she had been recording the memoirs we would discover after her death. We visited her often with our children but she shared with us the sense of loneliness she'd begun to feel as her circle of close friends diminished one by one. As the years passed, Coral invited Mum to spend the nights in her home and cared for her needs.

Mummy's Death

In July 1987 our beloved Mum and Gran, who had survived many challenges in her lifetime, was admitted to Addington Hospital for an operation to repair an aneurism in her aorta. The afternoon before the operation, Peter and I travelled down with our children to visit her. In a private ward we found her sitting up in bed in her cosy blue dressing gown, bright as a button and positive as ever. Surgery was planned for eight o'clock the following morning, so after a short chat we wished her well and promised to visit again soon.

Very early the next day our sister Madeline received a call from the sister on duty with the crushing news that the aneurism had burst before Mummy had got to the theatre and she had died at 4am that morning! The sudden loss of our precious, courageous mother stunned us all, but our heartbreak and deep grief were eased by the peace of knowing that she had gone straight into the presence of the Lord whom she loved.

In a moving Thanksgiving Service at the little Westbrook Methodist Church at Tongaat Beach, we celebrated Mum's life, giving praise and thanks for her devotion to Jesus and family, and her spirit of love, joy, courage and resilience in the face of severe trials. Mum had played the organ and worshiped for years in this church, which was full to overflowing with family and many friends gathered to honour her. After the friendship tea a few of her closest friends met with our family at her little seaside cottage, Ocean View, to reminisce with tears and laughter over the many happy memories of her imprinted on all our hearts. She had been the strong rock for our beloved dad, her seven children and spouses, and twenty-eight of her grandchildren already born. She would be deeply missed for the rest of our lives.

Faithful Moti, who had remained with Mum until her death at the age of eighty-eight, returned home to his wife Constance and their family.

The Changes of Time

The character of Tongaat Beach had changed forever when the area was incorporated into the township of Tongaat. After generations of families had enjoyed beach holidays in the cluster of modest holiday cottages along the seafront, the owners were now required to pay heavy rates on their properties. Many were forced to sell to new owners who wished to build fancy residences there, sadly pushing up the values beyond the reach of all but the wealthy.

Stan, being the only son, had inherited the Shack property, half of which Coral's husband Andrew Porter bought from him and Peter and I bought the other half. However, when our business failed, we were unable to keep up our payments and it broke my heart to have to sell our portion. Ocean View had been left to all six girls to share but the rates on the property became too heavy for us to afford, unless we leased the cottage throughout all peak holiday times. This meant, in effect, that we couldn't enjoy it in season ourselves and were simply keeping it for the benefit of others. None of us was in a financial position to buy the others out, and the cost of someone managing it as a shared holiday cottage made it an unviable solution. We agonised over the decision to sell before eventually accepting that it had to go. After Mummy died, when Coral sold and moved to her retirement cottage in Durban North, our strong ties with Tongaat Beach were broken – but our wonderful memories live on forever.

Riding High with Jesus

Return to Natal and New Challenges

I note that most of the significant moves that Peter and I made took place mid-year, and the next change came after six years of working in the fast lane of marketing on the West Rand, in July 1987. Peter was approached by his cousin Anthony Morris to become Dairy Manager on his farm 'Maywood' in the Richmond district of Natal. By now we were both ready to return to a slower pace of life so the prospect of farm life was most appealing. We resigned our jobs, said a fond farewell to our wonderful friends at the Roodepoort Assembly and packed up to return to Natal.

During Andy and Stephen's senior years at high school, Peter and I faced a challenge we were totally unprepared for. Unbeknown to us, both our sons had started to smoke dagga[46] with friends, but Peter and I were quite ignorant of the tell-tale signs. However, things changed on one family occasion when I observed very uncharacteristic behaviour and discovered the truth. In tears I begged them to give up. Moved by my sobbing, Steve promised to do so but Andy assured me that he was not addicted and saw no reason to stop. Distraught with anxiety, I cried out to God who spoke words of reassurance into my spirit: *"Step aside, Mother. You've done all you can; now leave him to me."* These words held such powerful promise that I was set free from anxious fears and able to place Andrew in God's hands, which saw me through challenging times yet to come.

Andy's Story of God's Grace

Having passed his matriculation examinations during the previous year, in 1981 Andy was drafted for his two-year National Service into the South African Army at TEMPE Base in the Orange Free State. During the week before he was due to leave he had stripped the 'Buzz Bike' he was handing on to Steve, and his dad

---

[46] cannabis

Marriage and Parenthood

gave him strict instructions to put it together in running order before he left for camp on the afternoon troop train. Andy disappeared for the whole morning and came back with barely enough time to complete the task, leaving no time to clean up before we rushed him down to the station with hands and jeans covered in grease! Tension had been building up in all of us during his absence and I was choked with anger at his rebellious attitude. We sped down to Pietermaritzburg, arriving on the platform as the train was pulling out and Andy had to run to jump aboard as it gathered speed. I stood with tears running down my cheeks, uncharacteristically *not* tears of sadness but of emotional relief that this boy was now under Army discipline for two years!

Tempe Camp was the largest and most dreaded camp in the country for the conditions there. On arrival Andrew applied to go into the Dog Unit, but by the time the shortlist came out and he hadn't made it, his second choice had been filled and he was left as a driver in camp which he found terribly boring.

Sometime before leaving home Andy had told me in a rebellious mood that he didn't want to learn from our mistakes, and his journey of choices with their consequences was about to begin here in the Army. One day he was caught with a small cannabis butt on his person and was given the choice between paying a R50 fine or attending a Rehabilitation Course. To escape the boredom of camp he chose the latter and spent several weeks tending the vegetable gardens in the sunshine. His letters home at this time expressed pleasure at being constructively occupied out of doors, and referred to the counselling sessions as a positive time of conversation with the counsellor in which he could express his thoughts.

Following his discharge from National Service in 1983, Andy found a job at the AECI Chemical Plant for a year, before moving to Durban in 1984 to share a flat in 'Sheraton Court' with his girlfriend Lynne Robertson. He started a course at university but after six months decided to try selling Encyclopaedia Britannica to earn enough to cover his fees for the second half of the year. Lynne took a waitressing job in West Street to support them both for that

Riding High with Jesus

year, an admirable sacrifice in her challenging job situation. Encyclopaedia Britannica sales were slow and unpredictable so Andrew applied to the South African Railways to drive their articulated trucks commuting between Durban and the Reef. Life on the road began and many of his meals consisted of baked beans heated over a gas flame on the roadside, with sleepovers at the SAR depot to await his return the following day. This job held great responsibility, requiring a full knowledge of every working part of the vehicle including tyre pressures in order to handle problems on the road. Andy proved to be an excellent driver and the job paid his wage, but the lifestyle was by no means desirable in the long term.

He continued to smoke cannabis with friends who visited their flat opposite the Durban yacht mole. But he and Lynne had a couple of friends from school days who were born-again Christians and wanted to share the joy of their faith with them. In spite of Andy's lack of response to the Gospel, they continued to visit, show unconditional love and lend them Christian tapes. One evening while Andy was downstairs with friends, Lynne went upstairs to their bedroom to listen to a testimony tape. As she heard the story of how God's power had transformed a life, her heart was deeply moved by the Holy Spirit. She felt God's love drawing her to repent of her sins and invite Jesus into her life. Her life-changing decision opened the door to personal relationship with Jesus from whom she could draw comfort and strength through the severely stressful years that lay ahead.

Peter, Justin and I had settled at Maywood Farm by the time Andy and Lynne were married in the little Greys Chapel in Pietermaritzburg on 10th January 1987. A new season of hope and prospects for Andy and his family was about to begin when Lynne's friend Terri Coughlin urged her father, Managing Director of 'Unitrans'[47], to take Andrew on as a driver. After much persuasion, Mr Coughlin agreed to give him a chance and they made plans to move to Empangeni. Needing to look for

---

[47] a large transport company

accommodation but not having a vehicle of their own they accepted my offer to drive them to Zululand. Our youngest son Justin accompanied me as far as their flat in Durban and the three of us set off early in the morning in heavy rain.

An Unforgettably Scary Trip

It had been raining heavily for several days and while crossing the bridge over the very wide Tongaat River I was alarmed to see how high the river had already risen. Noting this, I said to the children, "We'd better be quick in Empangeni if we want to get back safely," and carried on toward Mtunzini. Heading downhill at one point we had a miraculous escape from certain death when our car aquaplaned on a deep sheet of water into the direct path of an oncoming truck travelling at high speed with a long line of cars behind it. Utterly helpless to control the vehicle, I cried out to God for mercy and immediately felt the car being pushed back to safety on the left side of the road out of the line of imminent danger. We knew without doubt that God had sent His angels to save us within seconds of a collision and we drove on in awed silence and shock.

Close to the Mtunzini Bridge the police stopped us with the bad news that the huge structure had been completely washed away. Determined to find a way, I turned the car round and headed for Eshowe and a short cut to Empangeni that I knew of. We hadn't gone far along that route when we were faced by a deep fast-flowing stream of water across the road. I knew that even if we got through, the level was rising so fast that we'd be marooned on the other side so I manoeuvred a quick U-turn in the road and headed back toward Eshowe.

At Melmoth I called in at the police station for a road report and was told the shattering news that the mighty Tongaat Bridge we had crossed barely two hours ago had been washed away too! I thanked God in my heart that we had crossed safely. Now our only option to get back to Durban was to make a very wide detour journey via Ladysmith on the old road. At Inchanga, just outside

Pietermaritzburg, a major landslide from the rocky krantz[48] had blocked the road completely so we climbed up over the ridge on to the old road and inched our way to Durban in the pouring rain.

On arrival at Andy and Lynne's flat the sight that met our eyes as we opened the door left us speechless. Their wooden-framed windows facing the sea were tightly shut, but the gale force wind behind, lashing rain, was forcing water through the frames like a waterfall on to the lounge floor, already three quarters covered!

Having tried and failed to reach Peter by phone at Maywood Farm to reassure him that we were safe, I phoned the nearest police station at Baynesfield and was told that all the electricity power and telephone lines were down. The road to Richmond was impassable as the small bridge over the swollen stream at Baynesfield was under water, so Justin and I had no option but to spend the night and wait until it had subsided sufficiently for us to get through the next day. He and I spent the night huddled on couches at the dry end of the lounge, and next morning another call to the police established that the road had opened so we set off for Richmond.

On the farm we discovered that the shallow stream crossing the driveway had risen to a rushing torrent, so I parked the car high up on the pasture slopes and linking arms to brace against the flow, Justin and I waded up to our waists through the freezing water. At the top of the hill in dismal dusk light Peter waited anxiously for our return, and was overjoyed when the dogs alerted him to the arrival of two drowned rats at the back door. Justy and I lost no time in stripping off our sodden clothes to warm our chilled bodies in winter woollies and blankets. With no electricity, we boiled water on a gas ring for a hot cup of tea, while I related to Peter the extraordinary saga of the previous day's events and together we gave thanks to God for our safe return. By candlelight we made packet soup for supper and headed to bed warmly wrapped to sleep off the shock to mind and body.

---

[48] cliff

Marriage and Parenthood

Our First Grandchild

Andy and Lynne succeeded in finding a house in Empangeni and to our great delight our first little grandchild Jonathan Peter was born on 26th July 1988 in the local hospital. He was a most gorgeous baby boy with blue eyes, blonde curly hair and a gentle, placid temperament. We spent a weekend with the little family, rejoicing at both the safe arrival of 'Jonty' and the good news that Andy had been appointed Depot Manager at Unitrans. Having driven for South African Railways, he was the perfect choice to monitor the performance of drivers and vehicles with his experience and knowledge.

Thursday, 13th July 1989 marked a very dark day for all of us when Andrew almost lost his life in a freak accident on duty. As Depot Manager he had gone out to the timber forests to check on the progress of workers trying to extricate a truck and trailer from deep mud. Standing well back in a group with others, he watched as they placed a massive hook around a tree trunk serving as crossbar and attempted to pull the vehicle back with a steel cable.

The immense pressure on the log caused it to snap in two, sending one half spinning at great speed toward the group. It struck Andrew with terrific force on the side of his head, knocking his left eye out of the socket on to his cheek and cracking his skull, causing a blood clot to form on the brain. The bones in his temple, cheek and jaws were crushed, and teeth were knocked out of both gums. The medics who arrived on the scene put his eye back in its socket and rushed him to the Empangeni Hospital, not expecting him to live long enough for an ambulance journey of three hours to Durban. However, doctors were able to stabilize him and he was rushed to Entabeni Hospital on the Berea.

At home in Richmond, Peter and I received the shocking news of the accident in a call from Lynne, but all she could tell us was that Andy was on his way to Entabeni Hospital. I called the hospital but the ambulance hadn't arrived so I put a call through to his boss, Bernard Coughlin, to find out the details of the accident and the extent of his injury.

Immediately on arrival at hospital, Andy underwent surgery by the skilled neurosurgeon Mr Fuller, to drain the brain clot under the fracture in his skull. When I rang the ICU in the evening, they reassured me that the procedure had been successful and by 8.30pm Andy was in the ICU, heavily sedated but conscious and able to respond. The following afternoon Peter and I drove straight to the hospital where Lynne and Jonty were waiting. Together we went to the ICU and found Andy still heavily sedated but lucid for brief moments. Peter and I spent the night at my sister Madeline's home and the next day Lynne and I visited Andy again.

On Sunday morning in a four-hour operation, two plastic surgeons, Mr Beaumont and Mr Lalbahadur, did an amazingly intricate operation, reconstructing Andrew's face. They pieced together fragments of his left cheekbone with seventeen screws, inserted a metal plate over his temple, removed broken teeth and wired his jaws together so that he was limited to drinking liquids through a straw while the bones healed.

When we visited later, Andy was under very heavy sedation and his bandaged head looked like a huge wasp's nest, the only part of his face visible around his eyes now dark purple from bruising. The fact that he had survived the accident and reached the hands of the highly skilled surgeons at Entabeni Hospital was a miracle in itself, and gave us hope that he would make a good recovery. But we knew that he was in a very serious condition with possible brain damage, and only God could mend what had been so badly broken. So we thanked all the medical staff for their wonderful skill and put our trust in God to heal our precious son.

Having done all that they could, the doctors estimated that Andy would be in hospital for six weeks, so Lynne accepted her friend Terri Coughlin's invitation to move with Jonty into her Durban flat. Her brother Craig drove them down from Empangeni, but without transport Lynne couldn't easily get to the hospital, so I fetched them and booked them into a bed and breakfast across the road from the hospital.

Marriage and Parenthood

Our prayers were being answered rapidly as Andy was moved from the ICU to another ward (FIN1) a week later. On Monday 19th, only eight days after being admitted, Lynne and I met a nurse in the passage and were astonished to be told that Andy was ready to be discharged! With the doctor's confirmation, the following morning the company paid for the little family to be booked into a hotel within reach of the hospital for check-ups and dressing changes.

On 26th July 1989 little Jonty celebrated his first birthday in their hotel room. In spite of the circumstances I felt we needed to mark this special day for the little man, so I bought a big chocolate muffin and stuck one lighted candle in the middle. Lynne and I sang to the little darling, while his poor Daddy lay on the bed unable to lift his head due to the excruciating pain. However, Andy's rapid improvement was evident when he asked if we could liquidize a steak for him as a change from the tasteless liquidized meals he'd been drinking through a straw!

Noting his remarkable progress, the doctors agreed that Andy was fit to return home, but although he appeared well enough to work after a few weeks, the damage to his brain had caused disturbing changes. As well as suffering complete loss of memory, Andy was alarmed by sudden uncharacteristic bouts of uncontrollable anger. He approached his boss for permission to see a clinical psychologist and arrangements were made to send him to Durban with a driver two or three times a week.

He consulted a wonderfully gracious lady, Shirley Tolman, who, with her partner Anne, began to help Andy understand his mood swings and trained his active brain cells to take over the work of those that had been damaged. With infinite patience and compassion, both ladies helped him to move forward to the place where he felt in control of his emotions. In the workplace he used a small tape recorder to keep track of daily tasks and responsibilities throughout the day while his memory was slowly being restored.

On April 9th 1990 Jonty's baby brother Dominic Andrew was born, the dearest little fellow imaginable, with dark hair and hazel eyes. Peter and I visited the family in their Empangeni home and rejoiced at the safe arrival of a second beautiful, healthy baby boy. When little Dominic was six months old, the amazing healing progress that Andy had made was confirmed by his transfer as Depot Manager to the Unitrans Branch in Manzini, Swaziland.

Manzini – Swaziland

Their move was made to a lovely company house with a large garden. On the work front Andy continued to cope but sadly had not stopped smoking cannabis and was now dependant on the drugs which had seen him through the unbearable pain of his accident. He fell into a pattern of meeting with friends straight after work, coming home in the early hours of the morning. This was very hard on Lynne and the boys, who hardly saw their daddy. When Peter and I visited over Easter, we could see that Lynne was under tremendous strain in a new town with no support system of family or friends and we returned home very disturbed.

Soon after our visit Lynne phoned to say she couldn't take any more and was considering leaving Andy. While praying for them next morning I felt God clearly tell me to go and do spiritual warfare in prayer to release him from the bondage of drugs. Taking authority in prayer over spirits of addiction was something I'd never done before, but I was willing to be obedient to God. Peter agreed so we asked the Unitrans manager in Durban for permission to travel up in one of their transport vehicles. He agreed as long as I signed an indemnity form, so on 1st November I set off from the Durban Depot on this adventure. Seated high up in the cab beside the Zulu driver Thomas Ndwandwe, I chatted to him about my experience of God's faithfulness and found in Thomas a man of integrity with great respect for God and my faith. After stopping in Empangeni for fuel and refreshment and a brief delay at the Border Post into Swaziland, we arrived in Manzini at 11.30pm where Lynne was expecting me. She knew the purpose of my coming but I hardly saw Andy and gave him no reason for my visit. He continued with his usual after-work smoking routine while Lynne and I prayed quietly at home through the day.

Back home in Richmond some Christian ladies had given me contact details of friends in Manzini and told me about a Ladies' Retreat to be held in the capital Mbabane. Keen to find avenues of spiritual and emotional encouragement for Lynne, I phoned the local ladies who arranged a lift for us to the uplifting meetings.

I explored the proximity of a church for Lynne and found a black Pentecostal fellowship within walking distance, so we set out on Sunday morning with both little boys in the large old pram. Being the height of summer, the sunshine was fiercely hot as the two of us struggled up the steep hill with the heavy load of pram and boys, little Jonty's fair complexion flushed bright pink in the heat. The pastor of the church was sympathetic to Lynne's situation and later came round to pray with her at home.

Andy Set Free by the Power of God

Over the weekend when Andy was at home, he went into the empty playroom to prepare a pipe to smoke. The unconditional love of God in my heart for my boy was so deep that although everything in me rebelled against his drug habit, I felt relaxed and able to talk heart to heart. Later Andy would say that what he felt in that time was the accepting love of Jesus, which I knew was due to the presence of God's Holy Spirit.

One day he came home from work and asked, "Are you praying for me, Mum?"

"Yes," I answered briefly, to which he replied, "I can feel it."

A couple of days later he said, "Mum, please will you pray for God to help me give up."

Sending a quick prayer up to God for Holy Spirit help, I invited Andy to sit on a dining room chair, and Lynne and I laid hands on him. In a simple prayer of faith, I bound the spirit of addiction in Jesus' Name and asked God to set Andy free from the bondage. Without any visible demonstration of the spiritual deliverance, the power of God touched Andy deeply and for the remaining days I was there, my boy came home every day straight after work and began to enjoy what he had been missing of family life. Having done what God sent me to do, I left a couple of days later trusting that Andy would surrender to the Lordship of Jesus and begin to build relationships with other Christians in the church together with Lynne. But that was to come later.

God's hand of protection was surely on Andy, because one day in Manzini he blacked out in the company car, which left the road and wrapped around a tree. A business colleague driving past recognised the car, a total write-off, and headed straight for the local hospital expecting to find Andy's body in the morgue. Instead he found him sitting up in bed with a clean cut down his chin and nothing more to give a clue to the seriousness of yet another accident that he had survived!

While I had experienced the grace and unconditional love of God in my heart for Andy, I could see that his dad and brothers were battling to forgive him for hurting Lynne and robbing his little boys of love and attention. I reminded them that God has forgiven *all* of us for *our* sin and challenged them to let go of their anger and do the same for Andy. Holy Spirit conviction followed with a change of attitude and family unity was restored.

Stephen's Story

Stephen was drafted into the Air Force for his two-year National Service and stationed at the remote Hoedspruit Airforce Base near Pretoria. He had suffered severe pain in his spine at high school from a condition diagnosed as Scheuermann's disease in which there is abnormal development of the cartilage plates and discs of the vertebrae. In spite of a doctor's certificate confirming the painful condition, Steve was made to do all the physical rigours of army training, which placed huge stress on his spine and he suffered with unrelenting pain until his death at forty-three years of age.

An Awesome 'Sixth Sense'

We were living in Roodepoort while Steve was based at Hoedspruit. On the way home from a family weekend at Gran's cottage at Tongaat, I had an experience of God-given discernment that was truly extraordinary. Steve had secured a weekend pass from duty and was due back at base by 11pm so he left early in the afternoon to hitch back. We left much later and by the time we arrived near the town of Harrismith it was pitch dark without a star in the sky. We'd talked about Steve on our journey knowing that his camp was off the beaten track for public transport, and hoped that he'd had good lifts to get him back to camp before curfew.

As we sped along the freeway at 120 km/h, I glanced out of my side window into the inky blackness and for a split second caught the faintest hint of a gleam in the dark. I suddenly had the compelling sense that it was our Stephen standing there and it was the glint of his spectacles that I'd seen! Peter thought I was bonkers: "Don't be ridiculous! You couldn't have seen anything in this darkness! It's just your imagination." But in my spirit I knew that the Holy Spirit had alerted me, so I begged him to stop and go back, which he did most reluctantly.

We had to reverse some distance before the rear lights eventually picked up the vague outline of a figure at the roadside. The car stopped and I wound down my window as the figure loomed out of the darkness and approached my passenger window. Irrepressible joy filled my heart as I looked into the face of our beloved son, who was speechless with shock at finding it was his own family who had stopped! Everyone started to jabber with surprise and joy at the amazing thing that had just happened, and the little miracle is etched in my memory as an illustration of untold blessings when we hear Father God's intimate whispers and obey His promptings.

We drove home rejoicing in a state of awe and I made Steve a sandwich and hot drink before his Dad drove him back to camp in the nick of time. Without a doubt, had God not spoken to me,

Steve would never have got a lift in that pitch darkness and would have been punished. For me the incident remains a simple yet powerful illustration of God's intimate concern for His children!

An Artist's Heart

After his National Service, Steve worked with Andy at AECI on the Reef for a year before registering for a Diploma in Art at the Johannesburg Technicon. In his first six months he learned a lot but was concerned about the heavy drain on our limited finances from the cost of art materials. True to his considerate nature, without telling us, Steve moved out of the hostel and took up secret residence within the Technicon building, sleeping on the model's couch at night and showering every morning in the ablution block before the students arrived! He kept his personal possessions in a locker and made friends with the black night watchman, who appreciated his company and made sure he was awake early in the morning! Once I heard of his ingenious plan I bought him a kettle with supplies of tea, coffee, sugar and powdered milk to keep in his locker, and he had access to a midday meal at the cafeteria.

As the cost of materials mounted towards the end of the first year, Steve established that he was a fine artist and would never work in Advertising. His reasoning was that for him the Diploma qualification would be irrelevant, so in spite of my pleas for him to continue with his studies, he left the college. Moving down to Durban he worked for a season as a waiter in a restaurant on the seafront, before securing the position of fulltime sign writer for Coca Cola, painting new ads and keeping their billboard advertisements in good condition.

After a couple of years, the lack of stimulation in the job drove him to start using his artistic skills in the building trade, refurbishing homes and bringing his eye for colour to bear in matching wall and floor tiles, paint and fabrics. On one occasion Steve showed me the home of a friend in Durban which he had redecorated with the help of one unskilled black labourer. I was so proud of the excellence of his workmanship, his choice of toning colours for the decor in every room, and the scale of the job he had accomplished with minimal help on the construction side.

Steve was a man gifted with a rare spirit of contentment with few worldly possessions, and continued to earn his living in house renovation up to the day he died in 2007. In the back garden of his partner Annie Webber's home in Manor Gardens, surrounded by the lush indigenous trees and shrubs, Steve built a beautiful circular swimming pool with wide red brick surround. Painted black on the interior, it captured beautiful reflections of overhanging Tibouchina blossoms by day, and the moon and stars at night. Sharing Annie's home and friendship circle of talented musicians and art lovers, he drew her into his close friendship circle with high school friends Sonja and Carl Keyser and their partners, Brett and Sandy. His death was a devastating loss to Annie.

Murray's Story

Murray was drafted into the Airforce for his two-year National Service, based first at Hoedspruit before being sent to Epping in Cape Town. At the close of his two years' training he returned to Pietermaritzburg and started work with Reid's Removal Company. Sharing a flat with his sister Shelley, he met a beautiful young colleague, Michelle Lewis, at the building society. He and Michelle became engaged in 1992 and married in Pietermaritzburg a year later. After four years Murray accepted a job with Magna International Removals based in Cape Town.

He and Michelle bought a home in Table View in 1997 and attended 'Life Changers Church' where Murray was later ordained as an elder. Their beautiful baby girl, Jemma Louise, was born in November 2000, followed two years later by a handsome little brother, Jethro James, on 12th September 2002.

In 2008 Murray and Michelle felt God's call to plant a church in Jeffreys Bay, where they're in ministry at 'Face to Face Church' at the time of writing. For some years Murray was manager of the Surf Africa shop but in 2015 moved into a position as surfing instructor to locals and holidaymakers.

Shelley's Story

Unaware that we'd be leaving Roodepoort for cousin Anthony Morris' farm within the year, Shelley registered at the teachers training college in Johannesburg in January 1987 and moved into the student hostel to begin her training. The first few weeks of classroom assignments in a very rough neighbourhood were tough as she felt out of her depth to deal with the unruly behaviour in that environment. In great distress she phoned us asking for permission to leave college and I did my best to persuade her to give herself time to adapt. In tears she explained that she needed to give notice before Easter to avoid being liable to pay back the loan so I advised her to speak to the principal. To her great relief he agreed to release her as it was still within the first quarter. She packed up and caught the train home feeling emotionally vulnerable about quitting and apprehensive about finding work without any qualifications.

The morning after she arrived I woke very early and prayed earnestly into the rather bleak situation. I had faith to trust God to make a way where there seemed to be no way and felt Him directing me to building societies in our city to enquire about job opportunities. As soon as phone lines opened, I rang them all and only one had vacancies. The Allied Building Society had place for two young trainees – specifically not 'school-leavers' but girls with some experience. Speaking on behalf of my daughter, I made an appointment for later that day and woke her with the unbelievable news that she had a job interview lined up. The interview went well and out of several young applicants Shelley and an ex-Varsity student were selected. Amazingly, God had turned the apparent negative of leaving college to a positive point in her career. Having been well grounded at the Allied, she went on to a fruitful span of years in the Natal Building Society until she was married and fell pregnant with her first baby.

Marriage and Parenthood

Richmond

On arrival at Maywood Farm in the Richmond district, Peter and I joined the Methodist Church and became fully involved in fellowship with a new circle of friends. The church was led by a retired pastor, Len Collins, who, with his wife Joy, had moved to their smallholding with the intention of resting from fulltime ministry. However, under pressure from the congregation to help out temporarily, he led the church for four years. When he stepped down due to frail health, the deacons appealed to Ray Oliver, lead elder of New Covenant Fellowship (NCF) in Pietermaritzburg to help with supply preachers and worship teams, which they provided faithfully every Sunday until a new pastor was appointed.

Maywood Farm

We had often visited cousin Anthony's parents, Ruth and Edwin Morris, when they were living in the big house at Maywood Farm so it felt very strange for us to be moving into it as our home. Years before while Anthony was away at agricultural college, his older brother Ian had worked the farm with his dad and built a house next door for his bride Barbara. When they bought their own farm in another district, Anthony and his bride Carol moved into the house and helped Uncle Edwin with the running of the farm. When Uncle Edwin remarried and moved into Pietermaritzburg, he left the farm in Anthony and Carol's hands.

Our son Justin was halfway through Standard 9 when we moved to the farm and caught the school bus to Pietermaritzburg daily. Loving the outdoors, he enjoyed farm life immensely and after school was often seen helping the farm labourers mulch the mature silage in the pit. The pungent odour that clung to Justy's feet was so overpowering that I insisted he scrub up outside before coming into the house to bath!

With Peter's efficiency and beautiful printing, he produced new dairy charts for the office wall and settled into the challenging schedule of rising at 4.00am to start the milking. He loved the animals and embraced the physical work with great enthusiasm, giving all his energies and commitment to the job. At the same time, a local farmer, Tom Gemmell, approached me to promote the sale of his 'Ivanhoe' yoghurt in supermarkets in Pietermaritzburg, so I became his PRO for a year until he decided that the production of yoghurt was not financially viable.

We cleared and planted the vegetable patch on the farm that Aunt Ruth had started years before, and with farm compost it yielded abundant supplies of fresh vegetables for the table. We were all in our element on the farm but at fifty-four years of age, the strain of the twelve-hour working day with half an hour lunch break began to tell on Peter. Having a slightly longer lunch break could have enabled him to cope with the long hours but when he asked for this small respite, it was denied.

After eighteen months I feared that the strain would take a severe toll and encouraged him to hand in his notice and look for alternative employment. His contacts with the dairy industry opened a door for him as a sales rep with 'Creamline Dairies' based in Pietermaritzburg. We left our short but happy season at Maywood and rented 'Highmoor', a large red brick house at the entrance to Richmond village, for the next nine months.

With capital from the sale of our home in Roodepoort, Peter and I made a carefully considered choice to clear all our debts and move into the future debt-free. Anticipating that we'd never be in the financial position to buy property again, we decided to go the route of rented accommodation. But we were in for a big surprise!

In July 1987 when our mother died, my siblings and I were amazed to discover she had left each of us a portion of her legacy from Saxon. At the point when all our children had left home, Peter and I decided to put my gift into a savings account to spend on travelling to new places – but God had higher plans!

Marriage and Parenthood

'Man Proposes, God Disposes!'

One glorious spring morning in September 1989 Peter and I drove around Richmond village to admire the 'Open Gardens' on display to the public annually. As we headed home and crested the hill in Victoria Street, my attention was drawn to a small 'For Sale' sign on the grass verge outside a charming house. Suddenly I felt a compelling urge to view the property and said, "Pete, please stop. I want to have a look at this house." Puzzled by my request, Peter stopped the car and followed me. The house appeared to be empty but I approached the gate cautiously and found a heavy chain and padlock looped around the latch. It wasn't locked so we walked slowly round to the front. The sight of an English garden with sundial, rose bushes and flowering shrubs at the bottom of the garden set my heart racing. I turned to face the front verandah and said, "Pete, I know this will sound crazy, but I have the strangest sense that God is telling me he intends us to have this property." In a state of awe, I walked slowly round the whole garden praying that if it was in God's will, it would become ours.

I took note of the agent's name and local phone number on the sign and we drove home in silence, deep in thought. My honouring husband had learned from past experience not to dismiss the promptings I received from God but to take heed and wait for confirmation. As soon as we arrived home I went into the kitchen to prepare lunch. Unbeknown to me, Peter sat down with pen and paper to calculate, if we were to buy, how much we could afford to pay in monthly mortgage repayments. From that figure he estimated a purchase price we could consider of no more than R80,000.

Restless to know the price of this lovely home, I dialled the number on the 'For Sale' board with thumping heart. The subagent, Derek, answered and without hesitation volunteered the information that Mrs Jean Nicholson owned the house and her son Lynton, pastor of the Howick Assembly of God church, was handling the sale. To my question about price he quoted the bitterly disappointing figure of R90,000. I thanked him politely, explained that the price was well out of our range, and put the phone down. After telling Peter the price I went back to the kitchen feeling really dejected after being so sure I had heard from God!

Laying out the bread for sandwiches, I was startled by the voice of the Lord beginning to speak very clearly into my thoughts. His directions were specific: "Ask your friends Arthur and Zoë Duncan in the Howick Assembly of God to give the owner, Mrs Nicholson a message. Through her son Lynton, tell her three things: 1) you are born-again Christians; 2) you are serious buyers; 3) you can only afford R80,000."

I hurried through to share this amazing word with Peter, who urged me to phone Zoë at once. Our friend received my request without question and promised a quick response. True to her word, Zoë phoned back after church the next day with wonderful news. She had spoken to Lynton and he was happy to accept our offer of R80,000 on behalf of his mother! *Wow!* Praise God, I had heard His voice correctly after all! No haggling, no long wait for an answer but another miraculous piece of God's puzzle falling quickly into place.

The property exuded peace so we named it 'Shalom'[49] and our artist son Steve painted a handsome black and white sign for the front gate. It was quite clear to me now that my inheritance from Mummy was meant for the deposit on this delightful house for purposes yet to be revealed. So with travel dreams put on hold, the purchase negotiations were completed in December 1989 just in time for us to welcome all our children and grandchildren for a celebration Christmas in our new home.

Our attractive four-bedroom home 'Shalom' had once been converted into two self-contained flats with bathrooms en suite, but was now beautifully restored to a single home. God's purpose for us buying this house was revealed a month after my visit to Andy and Lynne in Swaziland, when we had a significant phone call from our son that was music to our ears: "Mom and Dad, I

---

[49] Hebrew for 'peace'

Marriage and Parenthood

have resigned from my job and need to get away from this situation to start afresh. Please may we come home and stay with you?" Peter and I were overjoyed with Andy's decision and welcomed the little family with open arms. Being conveniently placed at the centre of the village, our little family could live in one wing of the house without feeling that they were disturbing our peace.

It was a joy to be able to watch our little grandsons' progress every day. Two-year-old Jonty loved being out of doors with our Zulu gardener Albert. Much to Albert's delight, he took to sharing his morning tea-breaks, sitting alongside him in the garden with his own mug of tea and slice of bread. He joined a little playgroup down the road and made friends with companions of his own age. Dominic was fast developing into a most engaging little man, winning the hearts of everyone with his sparkling hazel eyes and wide smile. One of Dom's endearing habits was to fall asleep at the drop of a hat wherever he happened to be. Sometimes his little eyes closed midway through a meal and his head dropped forward on to his dinner plate. At other times we found him lying fast asleep in unexpected corners of the lawn or curled up in an armchair.

Andy's physical and emotional restoration was a process. He was very thin but after weeks of home cooking began to put on weight and the effects of the drugs in his body gradually diminished. When he felt ready to look for a job, a local farmer, Malcolm Nicholson, employed him as a temporary hand on the farm. From there he was offered the position as Farm Manager, with the bonus of being able to move his family into the manager's house on the farm. What a blessing of God's provision for all of them! Malcolm's wife Colleen was a caring, generous friend to this little family in need of loving acceptance and nurturing at this time in their lives, and we were able to visit them often.

When Malcolm made decisions which resulted in the sudden closure of this chapter, another local farmer, Hennie van Niekerk, and his wife Ina employed Andy to manage their farm 'Welkom' on the outskirts of the Richmond village. Once again there was a free house available and this Christian couple became close friends as they all belonged to the Richmond Christian Fellowship. Hennie and Ina were exceptionally generous to the Hurd family in many ways during the years that Andy worked for them, and farm life offered the continued blessing of outdoor living in which they all flourished.

Prayer for Israel Group

A small group of Christians from different churches in the village met monthly to pray for Arabs and Jews to receive revelation that Jesus Christ, the Prince of Peace, is the awaited Messiah who has already come. Having been deeply impacted by our visits to the Holy Land, I was eager to join the group. In 1990 Janette Ross from the organization 'Churches Ministry among the Jews' (CMJ) visited and shared about her work within the large Jewish community in Johannesburg. My heart was quickened on hearing about her earlier ministry in Old Jaffa for twenty-five years before moving to South Africa, and I told her of the desire Peter and I shared to serve God in the Holy Land.

When Janette visited again the following year, I'd begun to feel God stirring my heart to prepare for Israel in answer to our prayer. I asked her how we could find work in the Christian community and she described the four CMJ centres which accepted volunteers from around the world: 'Christ Church' in Jerusalem; the 'International School' in Jerusalem; 'Beit Immanuel' centre in Old Jaffa; and 'Stella Carmel Conference Centre' on Mount Carmel. Janette explained that the volunteer programme was suspended because of the current Gulf War, but gave me the address of the director, Ray Lockhart, and encouraged me to write and start the application process. Filled with excitement I ran up the road from the vicarage where Janette was staying to share this exciting news with Peter. Oh dear, my enthusiasm was faced once again with a negative response: "No, we can't go away for months now, Honey! What about my job and what would we do about the house? Let's wait until I retire in a couple of years, then we'll be free to go."

In my heart I knew that it would be sooner and in spite of his negative mindset, Peter gave me permission to write to the director. My airmail letter brought a speedy reply from Ray and Jill Lockhart, containing full information about volunteering and the reference forms to be completed. While I waited for God to confirm His plan to Peter, I didn't talk about it but he was aware of my quiet, unwavering conviction and began to pray that God would speak to him personally. His answer came while driving on a business trip, when God said simply, "Peter, *go!*" He came home in high spirits, energised to start planning and having sent all the documentation ahead of us, we were ready for departure by the end of September 1991. Our son Murray moved in to house-sit and our daughter Shelley took responsibility for our financial affairs in the building society.

A Seven-Month Israel Adventure

On 7th September 1991 we flew by El Al Airlines, well prepared for the daunting Israeli security procedures at Ben Gurion Airport and on arrival next morning were met by Ray Lockhart in the Stella minibus. I couldn't sleep a wink overnight for the excitement and nervous tension, but despite lack of sleep my senses were on high alert as we drove along the coastal road past landmarks I remembered from our tours. Climbing out of the plain from the old port of Haifa, we wound our way up the forested mountainside eager to reach our destination after hearing glowing reports about Stella Carmel from previous volunteers.

When eventually we reached the summit and faced the driveway on to the Stella property, I had a fleeting feeling of déjà vu. Suddenly it came back to me. We had passed this spot on tour seven years before on the road to where the prophet Elijah called down the fire of God on pagan sacrifices. How amazing that God had brought us back to this place to serve Him!

Riding High with Jesus

As we drove on to the Stella property, my first impression was one of deep disappointment. The grassy slopes were parched and brown, the ground bleached and chalky. Where was the beauty that other volunteers had spoken of? The main building was impressive in architecture and size, surrounded by a wide porch on two sides, but there was no beauty to be seen in the gardens. However, once inside I could appreciate the interior – the wide stone corridors, the large dining hall and kitchen, and the wide upstairs balcony. In the main lounge there was a sense of Middle Eastern charm in its carpets, woven wall hangings, huge brass trays and brass ornaments. Leading from the main house was the director's flat and a small chapel. On the slope just below the main building there was a flat for a husband and wife team of maintenance manager and housekeeper, and a laundry with large space for hanging washing to dry in bad weather.

After the first spring rains there was an astonishing transformation as the grounds became covered almost overnight with a bright carpet of red poppies and yellow daisies. In every nook and cranny between the rocks, miniature pink cyclamen appeared and in the little grove of trees beside our annex tiny purple, yellow and white crocuses pushed their way up through the hard earth.

The group of young volunteers who had completed their term and were about to leave were Andrew Lessey, Kathy Mc Clean and Pam Taylor from England, Adéle Jack from Ireland, and Paula Johnston from South Africa. The five young volunteers who arrived with us ranged between eighteen and twenty-five years old – Simon Rideout, Debbie Montcur, Debby Jeaco and Deborah Hamilton from the UK, and Jonathan dos Santos from Brazil. Already in our fifties, Peter and I were able to give these young ones loving support and encouragement as surrogate Mum and Dad while we all worked through the challenges of community living in a foreign land. Being far from our loved ones, we were soon forged into a close-knit family and had great fun together. Other 'vollies' who came to continue the work when we left were Andrea Cockerton from Bury-St-Edmunds, Joy Marshall,

Marriage and Parenthood

Dawn Craig, Peter Frith and friends Pat and Audrey from South Africa.

On arrival we were disappointed to find that Ray and Jill Lockhart had been relocated from Stella to Christ Church in Jerusalem, and in their place two retired Church of England vicars were sent out from the UK to hold the fort for the duration of our time there. Leslie Rowe arrived first for three months, followed by Peter Cottingham from Wales for the remaining four. Both men appreciated the mature support Peter and I offered while they found their feet in the role assigned to them, and we grew to love them both dearly. Soon after we left Stella, Peter and Jan Acton took up their post as the new directors at Stella Carmel.

When it came to assigning roles to the volunteers, because of past experience in his own business Peter was given the task of manning the reception office while Richard Ritter was on leave in England. It transpired that Richard would not be returning so Peter held the post for the duration of our stay. With years of experience cooking for a family of seven, I was posted to the kitchen as assistant to the young American cook, Michael Guberman.

Within a month of our arrival Michael and his French wife Beatrice left on a month's honeymoon, and I faced the daunting responsibility of running the kitchen with the help of volunteers which entailed some unfamiliar challenges. One of these was identifying commodities with Hebrew labels in the pantry. The best way was often by the tongue test as I discovered when I mistook white powder in a packet with a baby picture on it for baby formula when it was cornflour. Another challenge was working out quantities for meals when large groups of a hundred guests came to stay.

White Christmas – in Israel?

Peter and I were assigned a cosy bedsit annex separate from the main building, which opened out on to a small grove of pine trees. We soon settled into our private lodgings with jay birds building their nests in the branches above, and the flash of their beautiful turquoise wings in flight becoming a familiar sight.

On 2nd January 1992 I woke early to a very dark morning and finding that the power had gone off, I opened our bedroom door for light. During the night it had snowed silently and I was astonished to find the whole world before me covered by a thick blanket of pristine snow with an uncanny hush hanging over the earth. In great excitement I woke Peter to share in the surprise discovery, and soon the sound of happy laughter from Druze children in the valley below echoed up to us as they enjoyed the novelty of playing in snow they had never seen before.

The two Druze villages closest to Stella on top of Mount Carmel were Isifiya and Daliyat el Carmel. The core tenets of the Druze faith are secret, comprised of a mix of worship of Allah and their prophet Jethro, with Mount Gebal as their holy place of worship. All Druze men wear Cossack-like trousers with a pouch between the legs and the weird explanation we were given was that they expect their Messiah to be born of a man and he will be caught in the pouch! Peter and I befriended Aamer Mansour, son of the Druze owners of the shop next door, and asked him about their faith but he refused to talk about it. We were honoured to be invited by Aamer to his family home for a meal to meet his father Abu Faddle and family, the men eating around a low table while I joined the women in the back room.

We learned from the local villagers that this was the first snowfall in living memory, so they were completely unprepared for the chaos it caused in the community as it continued to snow for days. The fall was so deep that it was impossible for scholars and workers to travel down to Haifa and for deliveries of goods to be brought up the mountain. Everyone on the top became isolated; backpacking visitors to Stella were marooned at our Centre and those caught down in the town couldn't make it back home for days.

The enjoyment of seeing falling snow was balanced by freezing temperatures which brought serious practical issues at Stella. The oil providing heating for the building froze in the pipes

Marriage and Parenthood

causing them to burst and the electricity cables snapped under the weight of the snow. So we had no lights and no heating for weeks! With temperatures dropping below freezing, our saving grace was the huge gas range on which we boiled drums of water in the kitchen for all purposes including cooking, hot drinks and ablutions! We cooked meals with fresh supplies until they ran out, then raided the store cupboards and improvised with what we found. We used our limited supply of candles sparingly and dressed in several layers of clothing day and night to keep out the freezing cold!

Sitting at lunch one day in the gloomy dining room, we heard a deafening crack like a gunshot at the side of the house. Rushing on to the verandah, we found that a massive bough of a tree next to the building had snapped like a twig as the sap froze and made it as brittle as a matchstick under the weight of the snow. We marvelled that it had missed hitting the corner of the main building by inches! The forest of firs on the mountainside near our property was transformed into a winter wonderland, providing me with spectacular photos while out walking with Sam the Stella dog. Even after the snow stopped falling, chaos continued when the melt began, and cars which attempted to travel slid into multiple pileups in the mush and blocked the road for others. There was total confusion, with no traffic authority present to direct operations, and tempers flared under the stress of the moment. Eventually technicians made their way up the mountain to repair the burst pipes at Stella and order was restored, much to everyone's relief.

On our first weekend off Peter and I were given a lift by Richard Ritter to the apartment of Richard and Margareta Mayhew at the International School in Jerusalem. Thousands of believers had come to Israel from around the world to celebrate the annual 'Feast of Tabernacles' and on the Sunday afternoon we were thrilled to join the 'Praise Walk' down the hillside from the Haas Promenade at Talpiot to grassed terraces below, where hearts and voices were raised in prayer and songs of praise to the Lord. From this magnificent spot overlooking the old city of

Jerusalem we watched the sun set over the city with a golden glow reflecting in the golden Dome of the Rock on the Temple Mount. An unforgettable experience!

Our seven months of ministry for the Lord in Israel were a rich experience like no other before or after. Peter was in his element, assigned to the reception office to handle the administration because of his experience of running our own business. I helped Michael Guberman in the kitchen but took part in housekeeping duties once a week. The volunteers' duties in the Centre covered polishing all the massive brass trays and ornaments in the lounge, cleaning the wide passages daily with wet cloths wrapped around rubber squeegees[50], dusting, scrubbing showers and toilets, loading washing machines with mountains of bed linen and towels after visiting groups left, hanging them very precisely on lines to dry and ironing them all with the electric press.

Soon after Peter and I arrived, a Christian Chinese couple, Cee and Vin, chose Stella as the venue for their wedding. The ceremony took place on the top balcony in sunshine and we helped to prepare for the reception on the ground floor balcony. It was a very happy occasion shared by many of their friends from Haifa.

Midway up the mountain from the old city of Haifa was the new university building. From the thirty-second floor we captured the magnificent panoramic view over the city of Haifa on the coast up to Nazareth and Mount Hermon in the north! We worked hard in the guest house so made the most of our afternoons off to relax and explore the countryside around us. From Stella to Haifa and back there was a constant flow of 'sheruts'[51] so on our days off Peter and I got up early to catch one at the bottom of our drive. On foot we explored the fascinating old parts of the city of Haifa and the surrounding area, enjoying simple lunches of fresh sesame seed bagels with spreading cheese, 'falafel'[52] in a pita pocket bread with salad, or 'shwarma'[53].

---

[50] goomis
[51] seven-seater taxis
[52] deepfried balls of minced chickpeas
[53] sliced lamb and salad in pita bread

Marriage and Parenthood

Most times we caught local buses but once took a train to spend our free weekend in the charming little seaside town of Nahariya, established by immigrant Jews from Germany. On the beach we found a beautiful sculpture of seagulls in flight above the wooden wreck of the boat 'Aliya' – one of the small boats smashed on the rocks while attempting to bring immigrants from Europe during the British blockade of 1947.

Over the months that we served the Lord in the Holy Land, we met many lovely folk living in the land who added to the blessing of being there. Some were on limited visas like ours, some on longer term working visas and others were citizens. One elderly couple who became dear to us were Ronald and Laura Adeney, because of their warmth and kindness in helping all the volunteers to settle into the unfamiliar culture far from our own loved ones. I remember Laura coming up from Haifa one afternoon to teach the ladies how to make festive candles for Christmas, and recall the joy of celebrating Advent in their home with warming mulled wine made with apple juice, cinnamon and nutmeg spices on a freezing winter's night.

Our Holiday Breaks

Every three months the volunteers were given a full week's leave, so Peter and I enjoyed two off-peak holidays at minimal cost in our seven-month stay. The first was by ferry to the island of Cyprus and the second by plane to Istanbul.

Cyprus

On the ferry to Cyprus we met a couple stationed at the RAF base who kindly offered us a lift into Limassol and dropped us at a reasonably priced furnished flat for rent on the seafront. Hiring a small car, we set off every morning at 5am with a picnic basket to spend a full day exploring the coves along the Greek coast or heading inland to explore the ornately decorated monasteries and picturesque villages in the Troodos mountain range. From a distance the autumn coloured leaves of the forests on the mountainside created a stunning patchwork collage of gold, brown, copper and red. We came across scenes of village life that had not changed in generations, such as old lacemaking women of Lefkara dressed in black, sitting at their doors working their age-old handcraft with gnarled but nimble fingers. On other occasions we found little groups of elderly men sitting chatting in the sunshine while watching the world go by.

Istanbul, Turkey

For our second break we flew from Ben Gurion to Istanbul in Turkey. Landing at Ataturk Airport in mid-winter snow, we booked into a cosy room in a small hotel at cheap out-of-season rates for the week. I had dropped my camera on the way and was dismayed to discover that the winder was damaged, so before we started to explore the city my priority was to find someone to fix it. Not far from our hotel we came across a little shop with a faded advertisement in the window which suggested a photographic business. It was clear that the old Turkish owner couldn't understand a word of English, but from inside the shop someone else answered me in broken English. He came forward and in answer to my question directed us to an address with a simple diagram, to the small premises of a camera technician who identified the fault and agreed to mend the cracked shaft if I left it for a few hours. We made our way to the quayside and watched fishermen selling the catch from their boats, one enterprising Turk having set up a stand with open fire to sell his fish freshly grilled.

A few hours later I collected the camera, thanking the young man as best I could and we started to walk through thick snow to the famous mosques. The cold was even more intense when we had to take off our boots to enter the Blue Mosque, a regular place of Muslim worship to Allah with partial remains of painted mosaic on walls from the era when it was a place of Christian worship in Emperor Constantine's day. The pink Haga Sofia Mosque is not a place of worship now but a museum, and

Marriage and Parenthood

standing inside these massive buildings with their towering spires brings a sense of awe at the history that is captured in their domed grandeur.

From there we visited Topkapi Palace with its treasures of the past, and made our way to the warmth of a restaurant overlooking the waterway for a cup of hot chocolate. Trudging through the snow, we viewed life on the street that continues unabated despite the weather. Customers browsing in front of shops simply shook the thick layer of fallen snow from garments for sale and at the centre of a traffic junction one tradesman had laid clothing items for sale on giant plastic sheets on the pavement, leaving me wondering how clean they would be!

Catching the ferry up the Bosphorus waterway was a great experience, stopping to drop workers at jetties along the way or picking up passengers who were heading for the city. From the water it was interesting to view the architecture of the buildings along the banks, and at the last stop we left the ferry to search for a fish restaurant that had been recommended to us. Later, on the ferry up the Golden Horn we were accompanied by a group of little Turkish girls in uniform who turned their faces away shyly when I smiled at them.

Back at the hotel that evening I stopped at the reception desk to ask the young Turkish receptionists if they could suggest places of interest to visit. They spoke good English and were keen to teach me their alphabet when I engaged them in conversation. One suggested we take the bus to his hometown of Bursa where there was a famous open market, so the following day we caught a bus over the bridge that spans the Bosphorus. Through the window I glimpsed the sad sight of an old performing brown bear being led along the road by a rope through its nose. Locating the stop for the Bursa bus, we had to wait on board for some time until it was full, but enjoyed the novelty of being among peasant folk in a foreign country. Before we departed, a young lad climbed on board the bus balancing on his head a large round tray full of fresh bread for sale.

Riding High with Jesus

Eventually the bus was full and a couple of hours later we arrived at our destination. Making our way through a shopping mall full of individual shops displaying jewellery and other glittering items, we found the open market. Here we explored the interesting selection of fruit and vegetables, crafts on display and more traditional clothing at low cost. In late afternoon we boarded a bus back to town but discovered to our dismay that the journey ended at a terminus some distance from our hotel. We had no idea where we were and found it quite scary to be lost in unfamiliar territory, unable to speak the local language, with very little money between us. We appealed in vain to the crowd of bemused Turkish men who shook their heads at our efforts to communicate, and I sent up a quick prayer for God's help. To our huge relief, out of the semi-darkness a kind taxi driver approached who understood a little English and agreed to take us to our destination for the few coins we had left. How grateful we were to be back in the safety of our hotel where a hot bath eased out the tiredness and stress of the day.

Volunteer Outings

Every quarter the CMJ leaders took volunteers from all four Centres on outings to interesting locations not included in tourist itineraries. One memorable winter trip was to snow-covered Mount Hermon, where our young vollies had fun sliding down the slopes on cardboard toboggans before tucking into our delicious picnic lunch.

In absolute contrast, on a blazing hot day we ventured into a dry wadi[54] in the arid Negev desert overlooking the Dead Sea. Our guides explained how desert dwellers of old had survived in this arid landscape by watering their crops with the dew that formed under stones in the fields. A distant rumble of thunder caused our guide to hurry us out of the wadi because of the danger of possible flash floods which gush through the wadis at frightening speed and

---

[54] deep gully

Marriage and Parenthood

have been known to sweep unsuspecting tourists away to their death.

The guide took our party down into the incredible underground labyrinth of tunnels in the hidden Bar Kochbar caves which the Jews had excavated to hide from the Romans during the revolt. Our group was divided when we entered the second small chamber, and we had a long wait in the confined space for our first group to move forward behind other tourists. I had never suffered with claustrophobia before but in the airless space under the low ceiling I was suddenly overwhelmed by the most terrifying panic attack. I couldn't face the thought of the long succession of airless passages ahead, so making a hasty decision, I turned around and pushed frantically past an incoming party to reach the entrance and scramble up the ladder to ground level. Peter followed me out into the fresh air and as the panic subsided, my heartrate returned to normal and we explored above ground while waiting patiently for the group to emerge, very relieved that we had made a timely decision.

Peter's Life-changing Encounter with God

Peter had always looked forward to the Saturday Shabbat[55] services in our chapel with Messianic believers from Haifa. But one Saturday shortly before we were due to leave Stella Carmel he was in a very bad mood, angry at someone on the staff who had been a thorn in his flesh for months. In our bedsit he announced that he was not coming with me to the Kehilah Service and wouldn't be persuaded to change his mind.

As I was about to leave the room, I felt God drop a word into my spirit for him: *"Peter, God says, 'Your problem is not Norma but your pride – and I need to deal with that.'"* He became furiously angry with me but I knew the message was from God, so turned quietly and returned to the kitchen to pray for him. Not long afterwards he came to me in the kitchen to apologise and tell

---

[55] Sabbath

me that the Holy Spirit had convicted him of his need for a change of heart. He asked me to pray for him so we went upstairs to his little office and I simply prayed for the peace of God to fill his heart and mind.

We entered the chapel together as the service was about to begin and took the last two empty chairs. The Japanese preacher Peter Tsukahira stood up and announced, "My sermon for today is on *pride* and *humility!*"

Peter turned to me with a wry little smile and said, "I knew I shouldn't have come!"

As the message unfolded we both knew it was straight from God's heart to his, and at the close, when the preacher invited anyone who wanted prayer to come forward, Peter tried to stand. The presence of the Holy Spirit was so heavy on him that he couldn't get up and said, "Honey, please help me!" so I linked my arm in his, pulled him to his feet and he ran to the front. As Pastor David Davis laid hands on Peter's shoulders to pray, he sank to the carpet under the power of the Holy Spirit and lay receiving God's divine ministry, while I sat with tears of deep gratitude streaming down my cheeks.

Many others had gone up for prayer and returned to their seats but I could see no sign of Peter. Suddenly he stood up from the carpet, embraced Pastor David with a bear hug and walked like a man in a trance straight down the aisle into my arms. While the congregation moved into a Communion service, we headed for the privacy of our bedsit, where we stood in a warm embrace, weeping tears of joy and thanks to God for His love, mercy and deep work of grace. I could see that Peter still needed time alone with God so suggested he lie down on his bed while I fetched him tea and a sandwich. In the months that followed, Peter never spoke about his encounter with God, but it was clear from the change in him that God had dealt deeply with the root of pride. He displayed a quietened spirit, was reconciled with the person on the team that he had resented and, at our farewell service on the Sunday before we departed, humbly testified to the Stella family of God's profound work in his heart.

Marriage and Parenthood

Our Future in God's Hands

Like countless other Christians, Peter and I felt a deep spiritual bonding with the land and the people of Israel that was hard to put into words, and both felt heart-sore at the prospect of leaving after seven months. We were intrigued when John Chorlton, principal of the International School in Jerusalem, asked to meet with us briefly on our last day. He came quickly to the point: "I have received very favourable reports about you from all the CMJ staff and I'm satisfied that you are the kind of people I want on my staff at the school. So I am inviting you to consider accepting positions on a two-year contract as Building Maintenance Man and Tuckshop Assistant. I want you to go home and pray for confirmation while I am away in England at a CMJ council meeting. Let me know by fax at the end of the month whether God has confirmed that this is right for you." Fifteen minutes later we were out of his office with the incredibly exciting prospect of returning within three months as part of the official quota of salaried CMJ workers in the land.

Before flying home, we decided to spend our last three days at Eilat on the Red Sea, an all-year-round Mecca for wealthy tourists and penniless backpackers because of the constant sunshine. We set off on the long journey by bus through the hot, dry Negev desert having booked simple cheap accommodation for a couple of nights at the rustic centre called 'The Shelter', started by John Pex. Run with the help of volunteers, The Shelter had become a place of ministry over the years to many young people drawn to the 'hippie' lifestyle, who made their way around the globe to Eilat and ended up living on the beach.

Several years before, John Pex had come as a carefree hippie himself, but his life was changed when he met a Christian gentleman on the beach who told him that Jesus Christ had died for his sins. John came under conviction of sin, repented and accepted the gift of salvation. He knew from experience that many young people look for purpose in life down blind alleys with drugs and alcohol, and having met with Jesus who is the Truth and the

Life, he wanted to introduce others to the Saviour. So he built a simple structure from palm tree trunks and branches to serve as a small Christian Rehabilitation Centre. As the word spread, hundreds of young people from many nations came, heard the Gospel message and through the power of God's Holy Spirit found freedom from addictions and God's purpose for their lives.

In this peaceful spot Peter and I spent three refreshing days after a very busy season at Stella Carmel. We swam in the clear blue waters of the Red Sea and explored the spectacular beauty of sea life among the coral reefs through viewing panels in the underwater tower. With our sights now set on home and our family, we left Eilat and prepared to face once again the stringent security checks of the Israeli Airport Customs and security officials at Ben Gurion Airport before the overnight flight home on 9th April 1992.

On the day we had left South Africa seven months before, our daughter Shelley had shared the thrilling news that she was pregnant and her Dad promised to have me home in time for the baby's arrival. Working on a tentative date of the baby's arrival, we prayed for God's Holy Spirit to guide us and booked a flight to arrive on 10th April. We spent six precious days with Shelley before Hayley Beth was born on 16th April, and rejoiced at the birth of our beautiful little granddaughter.

God Closes the Door to Israel

We shared the exciting news to our children about the offer of work in Israel, and at the end of the month faxed the principal to say we would be delighted to accept. By return fax we received a devastating reply: "While praying at the council meeting in England, I felt a block in my spirit. I'm sorry, I no longer feel you are the right people!" That was all – no explanation of why! I felt crushed with bitter disappointment and sobbed before the Lord, imploring Him to show me the reason, when we were the same people who had seemed so right only a month ago! Six months

Marriage and Parenthood

later I would receive the answer to that prayer in a dramatic way I could never have foreseen.

Within the next four months the Stella administrator Richard Ritter wrote to Peter confidentially to tell him that his position as Administrator/Receptionist plus the Handyman and Housekeeper positions would soon be vacant as he, Dennis and Norma were all returning to England. Richard urged Peter to apply because he knew we could have filled these jobs perfectly. However, it was not to be. We did apply but Jos Drummond, CMJ Board Director, explained that for daily communication with local Israeli businesses and residents, a practical decision was to appoint a Hebrew-speaking member of staff – which we understood – and the Housekeeper and Handyman positions were to be filled by volunteers for the time being.

With those doors closing, I felt God clearly impressing on me, "You will not be returning to Israel." So we settled to waiting for the Lord to open the right door into other Christian ministry of His choice. Life continued and we celebrated happy milestones with family at home.

Barry Smith Prophetic Teaching

In August 1992 Evangelist Barry Smith from the Island of Samoa paid South Africa a visit of spiritual significance to our country. Travelling the world with his wife, Barry brought a series of teachings on prophetic revelation from passages in the Bible that concern the events of the 'end times' before Jesus Christ returns. We attended his teachings at the 'Living Waters Church'[56] on three consecutive evenings, and his incredible in-depth coverage of the whole of Scripture clearly revealed the mercy of God Almighty who has done all He can to save mankind from hell. The sober warnings of the consequence of rejecting Jesus and his gift of salvation brought our younger family members Stephen, Karen,

---

[56] A church in Durban

Village Life Continues

Back in our lovely Richmond home, Shalom, after seven months away in Israel, Peter and I made the most of the time with our family and close friends, sharing about our deep experiences with the Lord in Israel. Friends Daphne and Henry Kegel came to visit from Johannesburg and took us back to the Reef with them for four days. While there we had the joy of a brief but special time with my sister Enid and Doug Crankshaw in Northcliff and several close friends: Pioneer Avenue neighbour Ethel Forgey, Roy and Daphne Lambert, Bun and Joy Heaton, and Ike and Issie Liebenberg from the Roodepoort Assembly. Renewing special friendships always brings refreshment, and we returned home by Translux Coach, very grateful for this time with them all.

Sharing Jesus

In the course of daily activities, I had spontaneous opportunities to share the Gospel with many people in our village. Permission was granted for me to visit the black nursing staff at the Richmond Chest Clinic with freedom to teach from the Bible. At the conclusion of several weeks of sharing the good news, Daphne Mbele made the joyful decision to accept Jesus as her Saviour.

The Anglican Women's Fellowship invited me to tell them about my Holy Land visit, which gave opportunity to emphasize the significance of Israel in God's divine plans for the whole world.

One day I was walking past the army compound in the heart of the village and found three off-duty black soldiers – Oscar Mtjali, Vincent Mbonambi and Cyprian Madladla – idling away the hours close to the security fence. I stopped to chat to them and asked if they knew that God loved them and Jesus had died for their sin. Other soldiers drifted up to listen and I invited them to repent and receive salvation, which left these men deeply touched by the good news of God's love for them.

Ministry with Jean Guthrie Cosmetics

Months before going to Israel I attended a workshop of Jean Guthrie Cosmetics, a cosmetic company with a real difference. Jean Guthrie had launched it under instruction from God to bring him glory in sharing the Gospel of salvation, and to help women see themselves as he sees them: unique, beautiful and worthy of His love. Having represented a leading cosmetic house for years Jean was qualified to bring this unique Christian company to birth, and the more I heard about the Christian ethos, the more impressed I became.

I had been praying for a means of reaching women of all races in our village with God's grace and love, and came away convinced that God had opened this door of ministry to me. I travelled to Durban for training by Michelle Hardy and once qualified joined the Pietermaritzburg team of consultants headed by Pearl Gilson from Hilton.

In the course of village life, I met and invited many ladies to my home for a free gift facial, with beautiful relaxing worship music playing softly while I shared very simply what Jesus has meant to me all my life. Applying soft make-up after each facial, it was my joy to watch less privileged women who had felt unattractive see their transformation in the mirror. In earning their trust, I had the privilege of inviting them to enter into relationship with God through His Son Jesus, so they too could draw on His power to help them cope with life.

My goal was to bless women and make them feel special, and my reward lay not in selling products but in seeing them leave with hope and awareness of God's unconditional love for them. They left carrying in their hearts the secret from the Bible passage found in 1 Peter 3 verse 4: *"[True beauty] should be that of your inner self, the unfading beauty of a gentle and quiet spirit, which is of great worth in God's sight."* Many were the hearts I saw touched by the sweet presence of God's Holy Spirit in our home through the years that I was with the company.

Prophecy from Pastor Amaci Unfolds

Once Peter and I knew we would not be returning to Israel, we prayed for God to reveal his plan to us. Our friends Colin and Maureen Fayers had a guest from Mauritius, Pastor Vasee Amaci, staying with them, a man anointed with the prophetic gift of hearing words from God for people. After being introduced to him at our ladies' meeting, I suggested to Peter that we should ask him to pray with us about our future.

On 25th August 1992 we walked down the road to the Fayers' home with our sons Steve and Justin, both in their twenties. When Pastor Amaci prayed for the lads, both felt a powerful touch of God's power throughout their bodies and returned home filled with praise.

The pastor then prayed for Peter and I, laying his hands on our shoulders. We felt the supernatural presence of God upon us as he began to share a prophetic vision that the Lord was giving him:

> *I see both of you holding hands, with the glory of the Lord shining round about you. You are standing in a dry place with a waterfall pouring out the glory over you. Your ministry together will be a great blessing to many people. 'Wait!' says the Lord. 'I will show you in My time.'*

Putting his hand on Peter's left shoulder he continued:

> *Peter, my brother, you are very special to God. I see you dressed in a white suit with a <u>red rose</u> in your buttonhole. You have the seal of <u>victory</u> on you. Move out in faith and victory.*

Marriage and Parenthood

Mindful that all prophecy needs to be tested, we hid these words in our hearts and waited for the fulfilment, while we enjoyed the peace of our lovely home and involved ourselves in the work that God was doing in our village.

Three weeks after receiving the prophecy from Pastor Amaci, on 14th September my sister Lorna phoned me to say that she'd seen a mutual friend Malcolm Graham at church that morning. Malcolm had enquired after us and hearing we were back from Israel he had said, "Please ask Colleen to give me a call tomorrow."

I came off the phone with a tingling sense of anticipation in my spirit and went through to Peter in the lounge. "Darling, Lorna has just given me a message from Malcolm Graham at AE[57] that he wants me to ring him tomorrow. I feel that this phone call is leading somewhere!" Sure enough, the next morning when I called Malcolm he invited us to meet with him at AE the following day.

I had known Malcolm and his wife Bertha since I was a shy teenager at the Central Methodist Church in Durban, when they were youth leaders. I hadn't seen them for years but Lorna had updated them with our news. Malcolm was now Financial Director at African Enterprise – a Christian parachurch organization founded by Michael Cassidy in Pietermaritzburg in 1961, which Peter and I had supported in its early days.

We were surprised to hear that the AE ministry had expanded from a small town office into a conference centre on a magnificent property in Town Bush Valley, Pietermaritzburg. The original farmhouse was transformed into an impressive guesthouse, with a spacious auditorium, several guest cottages, two family homes and two staff cottages. A complex of offices covered the slopes beyond a charming, picturesque little chapel floating on a pond in the middle of sprawling green lawns. Many years before, in the early days of developing the property, my brother-in-law Brian Christian had helped to landscape the

---

[57] African Enterprise

gardens with flowering shrubs and perennials while he and my sister Lorna lived in one of the first staff cottages built.

Before leaving to meet Malcolm on Tuesday 15th, Peter and I attended the Richmond Ladies' Fellowship meeting where Pastor Hilton Toohy and his wife Rhoda were ministering. At the close of the meeting they prayed for everyone present, and once again Peter and I felt the power of God move upon us. Rhoda laid her hand gently on my diaphragm and spoke this prophetic word over me:

> *Rivers of living water will flow so fully that you won't be able to contain the flow. God will use your mouth to speak out with boldness.*

My AE Interview

We left feeling grateful to God for His encouragement and headed for African Enterprise. Malcolm wasted no time in giving us the reason for his call: "We've been praying for some time for the right person to fill the role of Hostess in the AE centre, and when I heard that you and Peter were back from Israel, Colleen, I felt God say that you're the right person for the job."

After a brief chat he introduced us to centre manager Steve Bollaert who gave us a tour of the property. I felt an excitement mounting in my spirit as Steve detailed the aspects of the Hostess role, because I recalled God's words to me one day in the kitchen at Stella Carmel: *"This is not just a 'scrapbook' experience. I am preparing you for something more."*

Having noted our positive response to the fact that this position was perfect for me, Stephen turned to Peter and said bluntly, "This may be right for you, Colleen, but I'm sorry, Peter, we don't have money for two. The position is designed with salary and benefits for a single lady!" Without hesitation Peter replied that even if there was no salary attached, he would be willing to accompany me as a volunteer on the Garden Maintenance team.

After prayerful consideration of all the conditions over a matter of days, I accepted the position to commence duty from

Marriage and Parenthood

Monday 2nd November 1992. We drove home reflecting quietly on God's awesome answer to prayer, directing us into ministry where we expected to serve him together for many years to come. The Application for Employment forms arrived in the mail, followed within days by my Contract of Service which I completed and returned.

Prophetic Words Spoken in Jest

Two weeks before I was due to start work, Peter and I sat quietly on our front porch. Studying the small print details of my contract, Peter looked up at me with a mischievous twinkle in his eyes and said, "You know, Honey, you would be better off without me, because there is a clause stating that in the event of my death you would receive a substantial insurance payout!"

With a broad smile I got up, placed my hands on the arms of Peter's chair and leaned forward to look deep into his eyes – "Oh no, I would *not!*" – before planting a kiss on his forehead with the words, "I *love* you, Peter Graham." There was no way I could have known the awesome significance of Peter's words soon to be revealed!

Now that our prayers had been answered we began to prepare for the new season at AE with great enthusiasm. On 25th October, at our final service with the Richmond Fellowship, we were prayed for by the elders and enjoyed time with friends over a farewell tea. A family lunch at home with our children Nick, Shelley, Andy, Lynne, Justin and three little grandchildren Jonty, Dominic and Hayley brought an emotional day to a close.

Peter measured the rooms of our little cottage precisely and chose pieces of furniture to fit perfectly. Moving day arrived and with his cousin Anthony's truck and our sons Andy and Justin to help, he loaded furniture and set it in place in the cottage 29th October 1992. I followed in the car with personal possessions and the next morning we were up early to start unpacking. There was no stove in the cottage as our midday dinners would be supplied from the main dining room, but we had a two-plate table-top burner for preparing light meals. I unpacked our clothing and personal effects while Peter hung curtains and pictures, and by Sunday evening on 2nd November we were comfortably settled.

My first day on duty was spent meeting household staff and exploring the property. On Tuesday morning we were welcomed at the weekly devotions with eighty staff and guests, when team leaders gathered around to lay hands and commission us into God's work as part of the AE team. It was an emotional moment for us as we felt God's plan unfolding for our future together.

God's Higher Plans Unfold

The summer days were glorious and at 5am the following morning, November 4th, Peter set out on his daily constitutional walk. He had already mapped out a route along the country lanes surrounding the AE estate and as he walked more briskly than I could keep pace, he went alone. I spent a quiet hour reading my bible and praying before getting dressed in readiness to sit on the porch and enjoy the beauty of the morning with him when he returned.

At precisely six o'clock Peter called to me from the front steps in a perfectly normal tone of voice before sitting down. "That was tough going this morning, love. I really battled." As there was no suggestion of a problem, I thought he simply meant he was short of breath. However, as I stepped out on to the porch, my mind was catapulted into shock as I saw him breathe his last breath – and in an instant he was gone beyond my reach!

In unimaginable anguish I cried out to God my Father, who enfolded me with his awesome presence and spoke these words audibly: *"Be at peace, this is not a mistake. I have chosen to take him. I healed him once, but this time I've chosen to take him."*

God's declared intention to take Peter brought tender reassurance to my heart that I had not been meant to call for help. My spirit was set instantly at peace with unquestioning acceptance of his sovereign will, but my mind was spinning with shock. Suddenly I was bombarded with wonderful memories from our

Marriage and Parenthood

last year together in the amazing Israeli adventure and the joyous times with precious family on our return. Memories came rushing at supernatural speed, like little shining arrows – *ping-ping-ping-ping* – each one reflecting facets of God's character of love, mercy, compassion, tenderness and grace. From deep within me a fountain of praise and thanksgiving gushed forth, lifting me up into a place where I was lost in worship before the bright 'shekinah'[58] cloud of God's glory! When I came back into the present I found the shock had been lifted, my whole being was drenched with God's divine peace and my heart was overflowing with such a full measure of his love, peace and joy that it has continued to spill over and touch the lives of people ever since.

I phoned each of our children to break the sad news to them before calling my new boss, Stephen Bollaert, who came running down the hill at speed carrying his boots in his hand. On arrival at work a couple of hours later, all the members of staff who had been introduced to us the previous day were deeply shocked at the news of Peter's death. Our children Andy, Murray, Shelley and Justin came as quickly as they could, with Steve following a day later from a job some distance away in Pongola, Zululand. We spent the days of the next week together in my cottage, reminiscing with tears and laughter over the good times we had shared as a family with their beloved dad.

I was grateful to have the help of my boys Andrew and son-in-law Nick in identifying Peter's body at the police station. As a family we gathered in the lounge to plan a Thanksgiving Service in the AE auditorium, followed by a family service at the Pietermaritzburg Crematorium. Seated in his dad's armchair reading Peter's bible, Justin was led to Psalm 34 verse 18 with the comforting words, *"The Lord is close to the broken-hearted and saves those who are crushed in spirit,"* a passage that spoke so intimately to our grieving hearts.

By God's grace I had been placed at AE with facilities at our disposal for the Memorial Service for Peter three days later. In the

---

[58] Hebrew for 'glory'

face of deep loss, the joy and peace that radiated from me was evidence of God's supernatural anointing when I shared testimony of God's sovereign work in Peter's life, for friends who hadn't seen him for years. My cousin Aubrey McAravey wrote his impressions in a letter to my sister Enid: "I attended the Memorial Service and words fail to express my admiration of Colleen's composure and fortitude. I could never under similar circumstances have addressed the mourners and friends as she did. Her faith is an inspiration to all of us." Knowing that my radiant joy was the result of God's anointing, I gave all the glory to Him for His presence and strength.

Following the service, our extended family gathered for a private cremation at the Mountain Rise Crematorium, and three days later Andrew and Nick collected Peter's ashes. Our children weren't all serving God at the time of Peter's death, but on Sunday 8th November they attended worship with me at NCF, which blessed my heart and would have thrilled their dad. We draw comfort as Christians from our belief that death is not the end of life but simply a passing through, because we have the promise of God that our spirits will live on in eternity with Him and our Saviour Jesus.

Days later our boys gathered in my cottage to share some of their dad's personal possessions, each choosing items of clothing that had special significance for them. Steve who loved hats inherited his dad's selection from our Israel trip – the navy blue woollen Turkish fisherman's cap bought in the marketplace in Istanbul, the white pilot's hat with gold braid from Cyprus, and the furry Arab hat bought in Isifiya village. Andy chose his home-knitted cardigan, Justin his bible and Murray his leather belt. We gave away Peter's suits and other items that were not suitable for the lads.

When it came to deciding where to scatter Peter's ashes, I felt it was fitting for him to be near me at AE where he had looked forward eagerly to serving the Lord. With great comfort we believed that his spirit was already with Jesus, and in a spirit of joyful celebration of his life our little family gathered on the wooden footbridge below my cottage on December 28th. With all of us taking turns to scatter his ashes into the fast-flowing stream, Andy read words of encouragement from Psalm 34 in the Bible, and I followed with the passage from the first letter of Paul to the Corinthians chapter 15 verses 35-49, which describe for believers the promise of heavenly resurrection bodies to come.

Amaci's Prophecy Confirmed

Weeks after Peter's death I received revelation by the Holy Spirit of Pastor Amaci's prophetic vision. What he'd seen in the waterfall of God's glory surrounding us was Peter being prepared in his white robe to meet his Maker, while for me it was an outpouring of His anointing for service in the days to come. The testimony of that awesome experience has brought encouragement to many people whenever I've shared it.

On the night before he died, at 9pm, Peter finished a small handyman job in the cottage and said, "Well love, I can put my tools away now; we're all set." Looking back, I am struck by the prophetic declaration in Peter's words. Yes, he was all set to go Home, while I was all set to stay and serve God where He had placed me.

With hindsight, the Holy Spirit helped me to recognize the reason why we couldn't return to Israel, when I discerned that God had closed the door through the principal's sensitivity and obedience to Holy Spirit leading. I understood now that God had mercifully brought us home before fulfilling his plans to take Peter home, which had to be veiled from me at the time! The full implication of what God had spared me from brought silent tears of gratitude coursing down my face as I marvelled at our Heavenly Father's tender compassion toward us.

Riding High with Jesus

Marriage and Parenthood

Our Engagement and Wedding Day

Celebrating our engagement, December 1956

Colleen and Peter Hurd's wedding

Colleen Hurd on her wedding day, January 7th, 1961

Uncle Edwin, Aunt Ruth Morris and Michael

Eckersley family at the wedding

239

Riding High with Jesus

Pre-wedding photos on the farm

Various Hurd Family Homes

1st home, 10 Clydesdale Ave., Pietermaritzburg, 1961

2nd home, 36 Armstrong Drive, Pietermaritzburg, 1964

3rd home, The Glades, Hilton, 1966

Ndulinde, Zululand, 1967

The brown rock at Tongaat Beach

Eckersley family meal, 1961

Riding High with Jesus

Maywood Farm, 1987

High Moor, Richmond, 1988 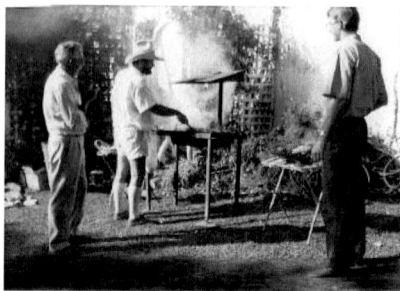   *Enjoying the garden, Shalom, 1991*

Shalom home in Richmond, 1989

Peter and Dominic on the verandah at Shalom, 1991

Marriage and Parenthood

Young Family

First baby, Andrew Graham, 1962

3rd baby, Murray, with Daddy and brothers

Baby Murray with Steve, 1966

Maid Norah with Andy, 1965

Second baby, Stephen Bradley, with Gran and Grandpa, 1964

Auntie Flo with baby Murray at Mum's cottage, 1966

Riding High with Jesus

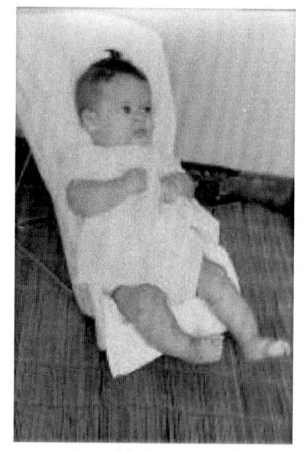

4th baby, Shelley Anne, 1969

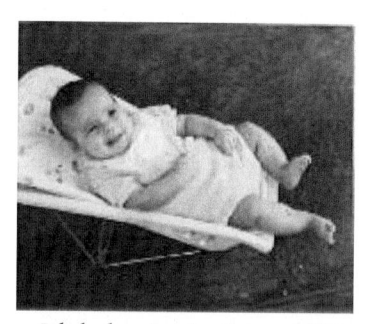

5th baby, Justin Peter, 1970

The Hurd family up a tree at Gran's, 1972

Granny's cottage at Tongaat Beach

Marriage and Parenthood

Ndulinde Store and Eshowe Life

Ndulinde Store, pension day gathering

Ndulinde home 1967-1972

Eunice's wedding at Ndulinde

Drakensburg Mountain timeshare

Riding High with Jesus

Hurd family, 1972

Servant M'sweet with Shelley and Justin, 1972

Hurd boys with cousins at Tongaat Beach, 1970s

Marriage and Parenthood

Ndulinde Store and Eshowe Life

Round Table fancy dress ball

Colleen and Peter in traditional Zulu attire for a fancy dress, 1968

Round Table fancy dress, 1973

Sun-loving Peter Hurd

Round Table Red Indian evening

Riding High with Jesus

Drakensburg Choir Boy Days

*Open Day at
Drakensburg Choir School*

Choir boy Murray, 1976

Choir boy Andy, 1972

Choir boy Stephen, 1973

Choir boy Justin, 1978

Marriage and Parenthood

Roodepoort Home and Work

Home in Pioneer Avenue, Roodepoort, 1981

Home in Roodepoort

Digging the hole for the pool

The pool lowered into the hole

Enjoying the outdoors with friends at our pool

Enjoying our pool area with friends

Riding High with Jesus

Roodeport Home and Work, 1981-1986

*Peter and Colleen's
25th Wedding Anniversary, 1986*

Lunch at the poolside

Special Roodeport neighbours

Our garden after snow

*Management at Mapp Med Aid
Brokers*

*Staff at Mapp Med Aid
Brokers, Johannesburg*

Namibia Holiday, 1987

Riding High with Jesus

Colleen and Peter Hurd's Family

Marriage and Parenthood

More Family

Colleen meeting cousin Patrick Eckersley

Mum's marriage to Saxon Groom

Mum, grandchildren and friends at her cottage Ocean View

Riding High with Jesus

Andy

Andy, Lynne, Jonty and Dom in Swaziland after Andy's accident, 1990

Andrew, Lynne, Jonty and Dom

Andrew, Lynne, Jonty and Dom

Marriage and Parenthood

Jonty and Dom, 2012

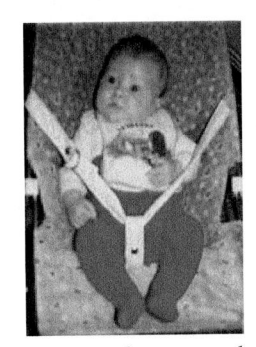

Jonty at three months

Uncle Justin with Jonts and Dom at Shalom

Jonty with his daddy

255

Justin

Justin, Mish, Jordan, Reuben, Ethen and adopted daughter Hlakanipho Hurd

Reuben and Ethen

Jordan and Roo

Marriage and Parenthood

Murray

Murray, Michelle, Jemma and Jethro, 2007

Jemma and Jethro Hurd, 2003

Murray, Michelle, Jemma and Jethro, 2012

Riding High with Jesus

Shelley

Shelley and Nick van Rensburg, Hayley and Brendon

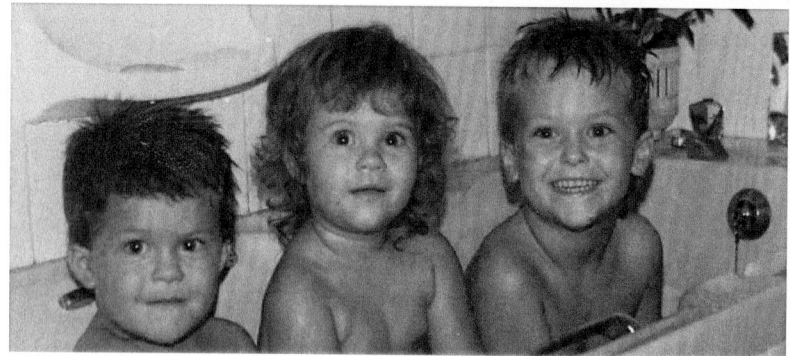

Steve

Stephen beside the pool he built for Annie

Stephen Hurd

Stephen Bradley Hurd, 2009

Steve's partner, Annie Webber, 2014

Riding High with Jesus

In Memory of Stephen Bradley, 1964-2007

Volunteers at Stella Carmel in Israel, 1991-1992

Praise walk in Jerusalem, 1991

On the Lebanese border, 1991

Benny's restaurant in old Jaffa

Peter and tour guide friend Farah

A falafel stand in Haifa

New volunteers

Riding High with Jesus

Mount Carmel snow after fifty years

Our outing to Mount Hermon

Staff and volunteers

Farewell as we leave Stella Carmel for South Africa, 1992

Marriage and Parenthood

Peter at The Shelter in Eilat with volunteers

The CMJ ministry we worked for

Riding High with Jesus

Part Two

Riding High with Jesus

4

A New Beginning

As I settled into my hostess role, the days became extremely busy and physically demanding. The shock and grief brought a deep weariness to my whole being, but I found that in quiet times spent in God's presence He was slowly restoring me.

The multiple hostess duties included taking telephone bookings and welcoming arrivals; supervising the housekeeping staff and sometimes helping to strip beds for a quick changeover; checking and preparing rooms for incoming guests with fresh flowers; arranging flowers in the main house lounge, dining room and main hall; setting up the hall for group seminars, prayer partners and team conferences as well as supervising the meals and tables for large conferences. I delighted in being available to meet guests at mealtimes in the dining room and help them in any way possible.

On a relational level it was a pleasure getting to know Zulu and Indian women working in the house and kitchen, and encouraging them. At times it was necessary to sort out staff disagreements and minister to individuals in need of personal counsel and support.

Of course in the weeks following Peter's death, it was necessary to attend to all sorts of legal matters with the police, the bank, the lawyer and the building society. However, the process was made easier by the fact that Peter had no estate to leave and there were no complications with his simple will which left his personal possessions to me.

In the four years that followed I went about my daily tasks at AE sharing freely with everyone from the fullness of God's joy, peace and love in my heart. Offsetting the weariness in body and mind in the early days, I enjoyed the task of gathering flowers from the magnificent gardens to arrange in the guest cottages, lounge and dining room. While I moved quietly among the beautiful blossoms, the balm God's love washed over me and I could give way to tears of longing, but by the time I returned to the scullery to put them in water my tears had dried and I would be smiling and humming songs of praise.

As the weeks passed I could sense that the black staff working with me in the Centre and some of the office staff were mystified by my joyful spirit in the face of my loss. I felt I needed to explain, so shared at staff devotions about my awesome encounter with God at the moment of Peter's death, to help them understand that while I was grieving deeply, God was constantly lifting me out of the place of weeping with His supernatural gift of joy that bubbled up from within.

Through the CMJ network, word spread abroad about Peter's death to those we had worked with in Israel, and I was deeply touched by phone calls from dear friends as far away as Deborah Hamilton in Scotland, Debbie Moncur in England, and Alex and Charmaine Meek in Australia.

As I cared for guests who came and went in a constant flow, long-lasting friendships were formed with prayer partners who visited AE more than once. Those who became very close friends were Dr Eizabeth Duncan from Peebles, Scotland; Rhiannon Lloyd from Rhyll in Wales; Gottfried and Audrey Osei-Mensah from Reading, England; and Catherine Hollister-Jones from Tauranga, New Zealand. The blessing of their love and tender care played a significant part in my transition into single life and ministry, and I was delighted to be able to visit them all in their own homes later. When grieving delegates came to the annual 'Grief Recovery' and 'Divorce Recovery' workshops, I was privileged to share the Lord's

A New Beginning

comforting love that I was receiving. Dallas Willard from the USA brought an impacting seminar on the theme 'Intimacy with God' which resonated with the deep work of healing that was taking place in my own heart.

There were times when the longing for Peter's human presence felt almost unbearable, as recorded in my prayer journal two weeks after his death.

> *"The past weeks have been hard emotionally as I move through the pain of intense longing for Peter's loving touch, the tender look of love in his eyes and his warm hugs. Oh God, how I miss him! My only solace is in coming into the circle of your arms and looking into your eyes. You know my pain and understand my tears. Precious Jesus, your love and comfort lift me above my sorrow, and I am encouraged that this experience of loss is preparing me for something wonderful that God has in store for me in blessings and also in service for Him.*
>
> *My victory will help others to walk this path in victory. Yes, Lord, I want to move through this pain to whatever else you have for me. There will be new lessons to deepen my understanding of your love, Father. The learning will not stop this side of heaven and you are with me in it all. Hallelujah! I dry my tears and move into a new day."*

Three weeks later, after reading Jesus' call to, "seek ye first the kingdom of God, and his righteousness; and all these things shall be added unto you,"[59] my entry reads:

> *"Father, as I meditate on these words, I thank and praise you for drawing me to this truth over the past years. I have a testimony to this truth, Lord, as you*

---

[59] Matthew 6:33 (KJV)

have opened my heart to love and obey you more dearly above all others.

I am hearing your voice more clearly and being blessed in abundance with every provision from you daily, as are the lilies of the field and the sparrows. I seem to have arrived suddenly at a place of far deeper intimacy with you, my Father. I'm sure it has been building up in past years to culminate now through Peter's passing and my entering into the close circle of your arms."

The journey of grieving takes time, to move from a place of desolation to healing, as my journal records two months after Peter's death, on Wednesday 6th January:

"My beloved Father, the past week has been the hardest yet, with an uncontrollable need to weep and the almost unbearable longing to hold Peter again and talk to him. Once or twice I have felt frantic at the reality that I am cut off from him forever, and cannot share or exchange any thought with him again! My visit to Dr Patricia Moores has brought help in a tonic for fatigue and sleeplessness, to lift me over the present phase of dealing with the finality of Peter's absence. Thank you, my Lord, for all the love and encouragement of those around me. With your Spirit's touch in the depths of my aching heart, I shall move on in victory, Gentle Shepherd."

Pastor Babaka from Kinshasa, Zambia, visited AE for a few weeks, during which time he and I talked at depth about his ministry and the overwhelming experience of my call to AE and Peter's sudden death. His Scripture blessing for me was from the book of Revelation 3:8: *"See, I have placed before you an open door that no-one can shut. I know that you have little strength, yet you have kept my word and have not denied my name."* Babaka's exhortation from the Lord on the 17th March was twofold: *"Be*

A New Beginning

the presence of God's love in this place. Become a praying person and available to God for waking you up to pray." Another visitor to AE brought this word of encouragement to me: *"Sorrow is a fruit. God does not make it grow on branches too weak to bear it."*

On 31st January 1993, two months after his dad's sudden death, our eldest son Andrew made his full commitment to Jesus Christ. Reflecting on how God had mercifully saved him from death several times, Andy repented and entered the Kingdom of God as His son. This was indeed joyful news to me as the prophetic word I had been given in Roodepoort began to unfold: *"All your children will be saved and shining lights in the Kingdom."* The following Sunday Andy and Lynne attended worship with me at NCF and my beloved boy continued to grow spiritually from that time on.

Peter and I had set out on this adventure of serving God together, committed to living simply and sacrificially for Jesus. So when Malcolm Graham called me into his office to tell me that I stood to receive a sum from the insurance company in lieu of Peter's death, I burst into tears.

Later in the privacy of my cottage, I recalled Peter's joking words – "You would be better off financially without me!" – and cried out, "Lord, I wanted to make sacrifices for you and you are giving me even more!"

His gentle reply reflected the tender heart of our Heavenly Father: *"You have made your sacrifice by surrendering Peter to me with a willing heart."*

A sweet surprise was waiting for me on a visit to my sister Coral in the form of an adorable little cross-Maltese puppy. I looked into the tiny black and brown whiskered face with an irresistibly sweet expression and adopted her on the spot. She went home with me that night and Tessie became my little companion who helped to ease the pain of loneliness. She was no trouble as she followed me around the garden or lay quietly at my feet while I worked.

Son Murray's Wedding

Sadly, Peter died just six months before we celebrated the marriage of our third son, Murray Brenton, on 29th May 1993 to his beautiful bride Michelle Lewis, in the intimate setting of the old Greys Chapel in Pietermaritzburg. The wedding reception was a very joyous occasion but – oh, how I missed Peter at my side! Sitting on my own at the main table watching everyone dancing happily with partners, I felt an overwhelming loneliness come over me, with the strangest sense of being 'in an invisible bubble' to everyone except God!

With the insurance money paid to me in 1993, I traded in the old 'Audi' car we'd had since Roodepoort days for a nippy second-hand 'VW Golf Automatic'. A constant reminder of God's provision, this car was wonderfully reliable and brought me great joy for eleven years. Recalling all my childhood years of walking everywhere, I took pleasure in stopping to offer lifts to those on foot wherever I travelled, and shared with them God's promises of help to all who put their full trust in Him.

The Call

In the early 1980's I had felt the first stirrings in my heart to take the Good News of Jesus Christ to other nations. Years later, while hosting guests from all corners of the earth at African Enterprise, the call deepened. Among those who came was a group of international prayer partners for week-long conferences in 1994 and 1995. Delegates included Derek and Ruth Prince and brothers and sisters from Lesotho, Botswana, Brazil, Mozambique, Zimbabwe, Nigeria, Portugal, Germany, Malaysia, Singapore, Samoa, the Solomon Islands, Philippines, USA, Sweden, Denmark, the United Kingdom, Finland, India, Hungary, Israel, Switzerland, Netherlands, Australia and South Africa.

A New Beginning

Testimony Trip to Israel and the UK

God had already prompted me to share my story of His amazing grace with friends in Israel and the Stella volunteers from the UK when in June 1993 Janette Ross invited me to accompany her to the annual CMJ Conference in England. So with my flight booked, I drove up to Johannesburg on my 57th birthday to spend the night with Janette before flying to Tel Aviv the following evening.

Arriving next morning at Ben Gurion Airport, we were met and taken to John and Christine Claydon's home for a restful break. It felt so good to be back in Israel as Janette and I enjoyed a walk around Old Jaffa where she'd ministered for years at the CMJ centre 'Beit Immanuel'. From Tel Aviv we took a sherut to Jerusalem and I was dropped off at the International Anglican School to a warm welcome from friends on the teaching staff, Richard and Margareta Mayhew. Being back in the Holy Land held a mixture of deep joy and pain as I listened to the familiar sounds of the city from their upstairs apartment. The school is in the large complex of buildings used as a hospital during the British occupation of Palestine, prior to Israel becoming a State in 1948. I ventured out to find my way by bus to visit Joy Marshall, an ex-volunteer we knew, now working in the CMJ office, and meeting up with these kind friends was the start to a wonderful few weeks of blessing.

Moving into Ray and Jill Lockhart's home on the Christ Church property, I was able to attend Sunday evening service in this historic place of worship, the oldest Protestant church in Jerusalem. A real delight was sharing a Passover Meal on Shabbat where I met Marcia Slaughter, a very friendly vicar's wife from Bishop's Stortford, England, who invited me to visit them. I was taken on a walk through old Jerusalem with our Arab tour guide friend Farah Salem, and on a visit to the Garden Tomb met volunteer guides Victor and Meg Jack from Bury St Edmunds in Suffolk. I found Stella volunteer Debby Jeaco working at 'Beit Jedidiah Guest House' and from there went up by sherut to Stella

273

Carmel for the next Shabbat, where every corner of the building and the gardens was filled with a host of tender memories.

On 5th July, Janette and I flew from Ben Gurion Airport to London Heathrow, where I was met and hosted for three days by two ladies – Eileen Alvis and Mary Pinkess – who had met us at Stella on their annual trip to Israel with medical supplies for the poor. These dear ladies from Cheam in Surrey were happy to see me again and treated me to an open-top bus ride around London. Hopping off to feed pigeons in Trafalgar Square and hopping on again to see all the familiar postcard sights of London Bridge, London Tower, Buckingham Palace and much more along the banks of the River Thames was a thrilling adventure.

The ladies dropped me at the National Trust mansion 'Polesden Lacey' to explore the artworks, period furniture and photographs of the original famous owner, Margaret Helen Grevill, while they went off to arrange their next trip to Israel. After wandering through the beautiful gardens filled with a profusion of roses, delphiniums and lavender, I was ready for a pot of tea in the tearoom, then settled myself on the grass against the trunk of one of the magnificent trees to wait for Eileen and Mary.

The following four days were a healing balm to my grieving heart under the tender care of Audrey and Gottfried Osei Mensah in Reading, meeting their Christian friends and relaxing quietly in the warm comfort of their home. Being driven through Berkshire and Wiltshire countryside on a trip to the circle of standing stones at Avebury was pure delight. My heart sang at the beautiful scenes of wheat fields full of blood-red poppies, harebells, cow parsley and golden rape blossoms, and the villages with their quintessential thatched cottages, climbing roses and pretty gardens, which perfectly represented the England of my childhood storybooks.

From Reading I caught a train to Cambridge for a brief 'hello' to our young friend Andrea Cockerton and her parents in Bury-St-Edmunds. From there National Express coaches took me on the long journey across country to join the coastal route

A New Beginning

through charming Cornish seaside towns to the little village of Rock, every twist of the road opening up thrilling vistas. I was reunited for six days in Rock with Peter's and my dear friend Muriel Currant, who had met us in Pietermaritzburg many years before. This became a very poignant visit as I discovered on arrival that Muriel's terminal cancer had reappeared after some years.

We spent precious hours together in her cosy cottage, sharing heart to heart the faithful promises of God in His Word. Muriel told me that she lacked certainty of her salvation which was making her feel very anxious, and I was able to put her fears to rest and encourage her in this time of emotional and spiritual need, knowing that her end was near. She was unable to leave her cottage but insisted that I take the ferry cross the lagoon to explore the seaside town of Padstow. Here I was caught up in the holiday atmosphere of a bustling crowd enjoying the music of a silver band playing on the quayside. When I received word that Muriel had died soon after my visit, I felt immensely grateful to God for making that visit possible and for the privilege of bringing reassurance and peace to her heart.

From Cornwall I took coaches up to Birmingham to spend a weekend with Deborah Hamilton, followed by a most memorable visit to my cousin Joyce Hall in Broxburn, Scotland. I expected to spend a quiet week with Joyce, catching up on family news and exploring her neighbourhood, but she broke the surprising news as soon as I arrived me that she'd booked us on a ten-day tour of the Scottish Highlands with David Urquhart Tours! Like two schoolgirls we enjoyed every minute of this excellent tour which was filled to the brim with interesting places, people and scenes of breathtaking beauty. Sharing a keen sense of humour, Joyce and I had plenty of laughs, on one occasion having to move away from a stand of 'saucy' Scottish postcards to gain control over our laughter before it was too late!

Janette Ross and I met up again on 30th July at the CMJ Conference in the gracious 'High Leigh' centre in Hertfordshire. In her 'report back' time she invited me to share my testimony, which was an emotional time in the company of lots of familiar faces from Israel, including Ray and Jill Lockhart, Jos Drummond, Michael Bulman, Pedro dos Santos and his wife Anu from Beit Immanuel, who had all loved Peter. Among the delegates, I met Allan and Sue Wootton, a couple from Bristol where my cousin Dawn Pettit, husband James and two young sons Lloyd and William were living. At the close of the conference they were kind enough to give me a lift to Bristol for a quick visit.

Back in Reading, Audrey Ossei-Mensah took me for a stroll along a stretch of the River Thames near their home. Whenever I had seen the Thames on postcards, it was always as a mighty river flowing through the city of London, so I was most surprised to see this rural picture of the narrow river meandering gently through the countryside. Watching narrow boats making their way slowly upstream and with cows grazing in pastures close to the bank was a delight I hadn't expected. Canadian geese, grebes and loons all shared the waterfront with swans nesting in the rushes along the banks. On the way home I made a detour to a nearby florist for a 'thank you' bouquet of flowers for Audrey who had been such an emotional blessing to me.

I caught a bus to Heathrow Airport for my afternoon flight back to Israel, looking forward to spending a day with my son Stephen who was working at the Kum Kum Restaurant in Tel Aviv. How wonderful it was to spend relaxed time with my boy, exchanging news from home and hearing about his adventures in the Holy Land!

Janette and I linked up at Beit Immanuel and left for the airport, where we discovered flight changes that meant a very long wait. In the overcrowded airport the only place to rest our weary bodies was on the hard floor until at last our SA flight was called at 3am. At the local South African time of 12pm (noon) the next day we arrived at Jan Smuts Airport. Utterly exhausted but with no time to lose, I filled my faithful little Golf with fuel and set off on the long drive home. Arriving very late that night I fell into bed feeling immensely thankful to God for safe travels across the world and back.

A New Beginning

The Ministry of Loving Others

While praying one morning, "Lord, make me a place of shelter and warmth for others," I had a picture of myself as a ball of wool being woven in with threads of other colours, and felt that God was saying my life would be spent in working alongside many different people in service for Him. How true that prophetic picture has proven to be over the years, as God's purposes for my life have unfolded across the world!

In the three years that I lived in my cottage at AE, I became 'Mother' to young interns from other places: Jackie Martin from Zimbabwe; Christine from the States; Polly Brandreth from the UK; and Bronwyn Moore from Australia, who had a fascinating testimony of meeting with God intimately while working as a shepherdess in the Negev Desert, Israel. Living next door to these young volunteers I shared laughter, wisdom, comforting advice and encouragement, and remained on call at all hours to remove spiders from the rooms of those not used to living with African creatures.

I had the pleasure of meeting the young American actor Bruce Marchiano, who played the part of Jesus Christ in the South African production of 'The Matthew Visual Bible'. Bruce was on a tour of South Africa, sharing the testimony of how his life had been changed by a powerful encounter with God during the making of the video. While we had lunch together at AE, he mentioned how exhausted he was from all the media attention and interviews, so I offered him the quiet of my cottage while I was away for a week.

Dennis and Mary Bambury from the UK brought a group of fine young Christian volunteers called 'The Wetfooters' from All Souls Church, Langham Place in London. They set about building a block of simple dwellings in the forest on the AE hillside, and during the weeks they were with us, the Bamburys and I formed a firm friendship which led to my visiting them in their London home on more than one occasion.

The young Stella volunteer Andrea Cockerton visited South Africa with her choir from England, and popped in to visit me. In Israel she had blessed me with her piano playing and singing of beautiful Christian Worship songs; now it was good to hear her choir performing at the prestigious Michaelhouse College in Hilton near Pietermaritzburg. In my cottage at AE we shared sweet memories of Stella days and caught up on recent news.

Industrial Factory Ministry

Over lunch at African Enterprise, I met a Dutch couple, Gert and Marta van Koten, who had started a Christian work among factory workers in our town called 'Industrial Ministry South Africa' (IMSA). They invited me to bring a message of encouragement to the Indian workers at the 'Ma Baker' pie factory, which opened the door to becoming a close friend and regular member of their IMSA team, sharing the Gospel with women of all ages during their lunchbreaks. The same opportunity was extended to a small group of African workers at the agricultural research station 'Proseed' at Ashburton, where we sat out of doors in the sunshine while I shared about the saving grace of Jesus.

Fulfilling the Wish that Peter and I Shared

In February 1994 I received a late invitation to join a two-week 'Shoresh' tour to Israel offering in-depth study of the Hebrew roots of our Christian faith. Peter and I had hoped to do this tour together, so my request for leave was granted by AE administrator David Reece on compassionate grounds. Praying in preparation for the tour, I had the following specific thoughts come to me which I recorded in my prayer journal:

- *What does the next month hold for me, Lord God? What are your purposes being worked out*

A New Beginning

in and around me? I feel from the free working of this plan that you're in it.

- *Whom will I meet? What relationships will be formed? Whose lives will you touch through me?*

- *Where will you take me, and what will you teach me, this time?*

Knowing no-one else in the tour group that I was about to meet, I reflected on these searching questions wondering what relevance they might have in the coming days. Thinking back to simple ways in which I had blessed others on our previous tours, I felt the Holy Spirit was preparing me for God's purposes in this one too.

On 12th February I flew with our charismatic tour guide Doogie St Clair Lang and a group of six South Africans strangers from Johannesburg to link up in the Negev Desert with a party of Church of England clergy from the UK. The tour proved to be all-absorbing and hugely informative as we studied places recorded in the Bible. Under the guidance of Raphael, biblical scholar of note, we visited places of biblical significance not usually seen by tourists. Looking ahead two years to the year 1996, we celebrated the anniversary of the historical fact that Jerusalem had been Israel's capital for three thousand years! By the end of the tour, I was able to discern answers to the personal questions I had raised to the Lord, as I brought encouragement to some in the group and gave prophetic envisioning to one person who had come to Israel earnestly seeking fresh purpose from the Lord.

God Intervenes to Save South Africa from Civil War

For forty years under the white Afrikaner Nationalist Government, South Africa had been in the grip of the Apartheid regime of racial discrimination and segregation. Now there was a battle for dominance between the leading black political parties, which was bringing the country to the brink of civil war. The month of April 1994 marked a significant turning point in the history of South Africa, as God intervened in response to the desperate cry of Christians for peace to fill our land. Political tensions were miraculously diffused by God's Holy Spirit when a call went out to the churches to gather for prayer at a large stadium in Durban.

Led by a Christian farmer, Angus Buchan from Greytown, thousands of Christians of all races travelled to attend the peace rally on 17th April 1994, repenting for the sin of our nation and crying out to God to save us from a catastrophic eruption.[60] In answer to our cry God changed hearts miraculously and brought key political leaders to the point of peaceful dialogue in the presence of spiritual leaders. As a direct result, the momentous event of free elections for all races took place across the country on 28th May 1994, with black citizens voting for the first time in the history of South Africa.

At Africa Enterprise in December 1994, an atmosphere of great excitement was generated among the staff when a crew from the South African Broadcasting Corporation (SABC) came to film our staff devotions for a New Year programme on television. For many this was a nerve-wracking experience as the large cameras zoomed in for close-up shots during the service, but great was the excitement when the programme was broadcast and we watched ourselves on national TV!

Sunday, 29th January 1995 was a red-letter day for my son-in-law Nicholas van Rensburg when he gave his heart to Jesus and was born again into the family of God. Over the next few years his faith deepened and the day came when he was taken on to the NCF eldership team, where he served until he and my daughter Shelley left to plant 'Bay City Church' in Port Elizabeth.

---

[60] You can read the story of Angus Buchan and the peace rally in 'Faith Like Potatoes'; Monach Books (2006); ISBN 978-1-854247-40-7

A New Beginning

Irish Visitors to AE

At AE it was my pleasure to host a couple from Northern Ireland – the Rev. Cecil Kerr and his wife Myrtle, visiting from the Christian Renewal Centre in Rostrevor, Newry. Coming from a war-torn country themselves, they had come to South Africa to learn about the impact of violent tribal unrest in the province of Natal. As our friendship developed, they invited me to visit them in Ireland. So in June 1995 I caught a flight to London Heathrow where a friend met me and we drove on to the ferry leaving Holyhead for Dun Laoghaire. Docking there in the morning we drove north to spend three days in the warm fellowship of the team at the 'Centre for Reconciliation'. Invited by the staff into their daily prayer meetings, I shared personal testimony of the situation as a South African, and explained the political factors underlying the unrest between factions in South Africa.

Captivated by the evocative strains of Irish music coming from the visitors' lounge one morning, I was drawn to find the source. Entering slowly, I discovered a video recording playing of Michael Flatley's 'Riverdance' show, which had just taken the world by storm at the Eurovision contest in Dublin. I wasted no time in purchasing copies at the nearby 'Woolworths' shop to take home to family. No matter how often I watch the video, I am always moved by the hauntingly beautiful, magical sound of the Irish fiddles, the pipes and the Bodhran drum. My short visit to the Centre at Rostrevor was indeed memorable for many reasons.

From Ireland it was back to the UK for a couple of days before setting off for Sweden at the invitation of Costin Bacruban, the young Romanian doctor I'd prayed with at Stella Carmel for his visa to come through in time. From Harwich Port my friend and I caught a ferry bound for Amsterdam and then a train through the beautiful rainbow tulip fields of Holland, across Germany and Denmark. At the coast a single coach from our train was uncoupled and ferried across to continue the rail journey from Malmo to Vasteros. Costin met us and drove to where he, his wife

Riding High with Jesus

Adele and her parents and aunt had made the traditional move into their summer house deep in the forest.

On arrival I was surprised to find that Sweden is such a forested country, and discovered that we'd come at the most significant time of the year, the Summer Solstice. What a delight it was to watch beautiful little girls dancing around the traditional maypole on the village green dressed in white with circlets of flowers in their blonde hair. Back in the forest house, celebrations continued through the night with feasting on a large selection of traditional fish dishes accompanied by free-flowing schnapps. At 1.30am my friends walked us out of the forest into a clearing to witness the amazing spectacle of the sunset. As the golden ball of the sun sank to touch the horizon it began to rise again immediately – the briefest sunset ever, to be found only in this part of the world!

A long walk through the pine forest on a sunny day was followed by a refreshing swim in the champagne-coloured water of the lake, tinted by the roots of the trees. At dusk Adele's father invited us to accompany him on his regular round to check his lobster baskets in nearby lakes. When we left the following day, I carried a host of rich memories of our fascinating time in this totally different culture and environment!

Back in South Africa, Steve and Barbara Arbo from the USA led our AE Team devotions in testimony and song, before praying for many of the team for a fresh touch from the Lord. The presence of God fell powerfully on me as Barbara brought this encouraging word:

> *God has been doing divine surgery and the healing from the operation will be instant. He says that you have been ploughing in hard ground for some time but now the spring rains have fallen and softened the earth, so the work will be much easier. Even the difficult people will be easier to handle! There is a fresh anointing to go forward with the work.*

Strategic Changes to AE

After serving as Hostess for three years, with the resignation of the centre manager Steve Bollaert, my role changed. I was asked to relinquish my hostess role to the wife of the newly appointed manager, Pieter van der Merwe, and was assigned to a new post as Communications Assistant to Ralph Jarvis. In the first year I was sent out to visit every vicar, pastor, dominee and minister in the city, to share about the ministry of African Enterprise and to invite them to partner with us. I felt led by the Holy Spirit to encourage the leaders personally and to pray for fresh anointing on them for ministry and for their families. My next visits fell within a radius of Pietermaritzburg in the small towns of Richmond, Camperdown, Cato Ridge and Ladysmith, with the intention of extending further north the following year.

While working with Ralph Jarvis I enjoyed the experience of a 'Mission to Margate' on the Natal South Coast to bring the Gospel to elderly residents in 'The Village of Happiness'. Hosted for the week by local Christians, we visited and prayed with residents individually in their cottages and held a Sunday service in the local Methodist Church. Although many had been regular churchgoers for years, it became evident that some hadn't understood that being a Christian required repentance of sin and acceptance of Jesus Christ as Saviour. As they grasped the truth shared from God's Word, we had the privilege of seeing some 'born again' and brought into relationship with God. With hindsight I see the hand of God preparing me for similar ministry to come in England ten years later.

Sudden Closure of my AE Season

During my fourth year at Africa Enterprise, donations to the ministry fell significantly and at the beginning of December 1996 all staff members were called individually to the boardroom. Having no idea that others before me were being offered redundancy packages, I went in to meet with the team leaders expecting to discuss expansion plans for the coming year. To my utter astonishment, Michael Cassidy's personal assistant Nellis du Preez announced regretfully that my post as Communications Assistant would be closing within six weeks – with no mention of a redundancy package for me in my sixtieth year!

Before I had time to register concern about my future I felt a soft mist descend upon me from above and heard the inner voice of God's Holy Spirit say, *"I am closing this door because I have another one waiting to open."* With quiet confidence in my Heavenly Father, I smiled at the group of leaders seated around the table and said, "Brothers, the Lord has just told me that He is closing this door because He has another one waiting to open, so I don't want you to worry about me." I turned and walked from the boardroom leaving the men stunned by my response, and crossed the lawn to my office with the strangest sense that my feet were not touching the ground!

With eager anticipation I prayed, "Where to now, Lord? Are you sending me to the nations?"

A month later I heard His simple to-the-point answer: *"Go and be a servant in the house where you worship me."* No, clearly it was not yet time for the nations!

A significant change that God imparted to me at this point was that I shouldn't look to a salary for my support now, but directly to Him for my provision. An exciting element had been added to the faith adventure I was embarking on, as I stood on the prophetic word I'd had – *"His supply for you will continue to be fresh, steady and at times like a flood"* – not knowing how God would honour my implicit trust in Him.

NCF Ministry Begins

Despite the abrupt closure of my four-year season at African Enterprise, I felt lightness and freedom in my spirit, knowing that my future was safe in God's hands. I made an appointment with Pastor Ray Oliver at NCF and repeated God's instruction to me. He agreed to pray about it and soon had confirmation, so I was

A New Beginning

taken on to the pastoral team with the promise that my rent would be covered by the church if I found a modest flat close by.

In January 1997 I moved to Burton Hall flats in Scottsville, deeply grateful for God's provision and His sweet presence with me. My personal needs were simple, met by a small monthly income from a surrendered insurance policy, but as the cost of living began to rise I turned to the Lord in prayer for help in finding a supplementary source of income. His instant reply was, "Ask at the Chiropractic Centre about a part-time job."

Already well-known as a long-standing patient, that morning I phoned the receptionist, Colleen Beggs, to enquire if they had need of a part-time assistant. She burst out laughing. "I don't believe it! Our 'temp' lady Jean has just told us she is going back to teaching, and we haven't even had time to think about replacing her! Why, are you interested?" The three Partners agreed to employ me as a 'temp' to relieve the two receptionists on annual leave and afternoons off, and I marvelled at the swift confirmation of God's promise to care for me.

My initial duties at NCF included supervision of Monica the maid in cleaning of the buildings, assisting the secretaries in administration tasks and shopping monthly for church supplies. Soon I was drawn on to the telephoning team, making calls to visitors at our Sunday services and to hundreds who had made salvation commitments to Jesus at the 'Alpha' course and a drama 'Heaven's Gates and Hell's Flames' which ran for six weeks. I enjoyed fellowship with the elderly 'Silver Threads' in our congregation and was invited to lead their monthly meetings, laying a foundation for similar ministry that would open up in England ten years later.

On 23rd June 1997 my brother-in-law, our beloved Harry Cockerill, went to be with the Lord after battling courageously with cancer. Harry had been a tremendous emotional support to me personally when I was involved in a car accident on my own in Durban, and on the day of Peter's heart attack when he drove him to hospital for me and saw him admitted to the ICU. Throughout our years of marriage, Peter and I had shared many wonderful times with Harry, Madeline and their children, and Harry was deeply missed.

Ministry Unfolds

At the start of my second year on the NCF team, Ray Oliver said, "Colleen, it's clear to us that your gifting lies with people, so in addition to your pastoral ministry I want you to be at the church door to welcome everyone at our three Sunday services." So every week for six years it was my privilege and joy to welcome worshippers into the house of God, my heart profoundly moved by the fullness of God's love flowing through me to every individual that I welcomed into his house.

After three years at Burton Hall I was offered the position as Caretaker with the bonus of rent-free accommodation. During the next year I had the opportunity to assist tenants in many different ways, and my heart was touched when a young lady tenant Ntokozo Gambu gave me the Christmas gift of a diary with the inscription, "People like you are hard to find. You are a blessing to me. Thank you for taking care of us physically and spiritually. Stay as sweet as you are."

Ten months later the Burton Hall block of flats was sold and my job as Caretaker came to an end. The NCF elders offered me free accommodation in a cosy flat adjoining the church's 'Home for the Aged' and until the flat became vacant, farmer friends Guy and Daphne Tedder offered me their retirement cottage in 'Azalea Gardens' where I camped out happily on a mattress with my little canary and essential items for three months.

A Visit to CMJ Friends in UK

In May 1997 I started another exciting adventure to the UK, crisscrossing the country to visit cousins and CMJ friends from Stella Carmel. The trip started in Sidcup, just outside London, with cousins Audrey and Andy Humphreys and their girls. They took me to see our elderly cousin Joyce Hall in Colchester, before a friend drove me down to Audrey's sister Dawn and her husband James Pettit in the village of Poltimore, Devon. A brief but very happy time with Audrey and Dawn's parents, Alex and Bobbie Eccles in Exeter, was followed by a brief stop in Axminster to say hello to Kath and Bob Chaffey, one of the sailors who had stayed with our family during the war years.

The first Stella Carmel friend I visited was Debi Moncur in Stratford, who loved Peter as her surrogate dad and found my sharing about Peter's death and my extraordinary encounter with God deeply moving. An experience I had while staying with Debi confirmed my strong sense of God going before me late Sunday night when I was returning by train from a church service at Three Bridges. Debi had sent me off with very clear directions for the Underground journey back, but to my dismay I found that the line was closed for repairs and I was totally lost in unfamiliar territory! Sending up a quick prayer for help, I scanned the platform and ran to catch up with a lady hurrying to the exit. I explained my predicament and to my immense relief she was catching the same bus that I needed and was able to tell me when to get off. Well past eleven o'clock, walking along the deserted street to Debi's flat, I sang songs of praise to God for providing an angel in disguise and for watching over me to the door, where a very relieved Debi was glad to see me safely back.

From Debi I caught a train from Euston to Colwyn Bay on the northern Welsh Coast, where Peter Cottingham and his wife Joy graciously hosted me for five days. They drove me along the coast from Rhos-on-Sea to Conwy, Delgarog, Llanrust and Abergele as far as Llandudno. Another wonderful gift was a visit to the magnificent National Trust estate 'Bodnant Gardens' where I meandered spellbound through acres of magnificent rhododendrons in full bloom covering hillsides and deep valleys.

Back in 1996 at Africa Enterprise I'd become closely bonded with a Welsh missionary, Rhiannon Lloyd, when she ran a seminar on 'Healing, Forgiveness and Reconciliation'. We stayed in touch and when I told her I would be in Colwyn Bay, she drove from Rhyll, where she lived, to fetch me for a night in her home. Next morning, we drove through the stunningly beautiful countryside of north-west Wales to Tremadog, where my friends Margareta and Richard Mayhew from the International School in Jerusalem were now living. After a few happy days in their world I made the delightful journey from Porthmadog to Aberystwyth by the little train that runs along the picturesque coastline, so close to the sea that I felt I could reach out and touch the waves!

At Wolverhampton I changed for London where Polly and Dean Baker met and hosted me for the night in the grand home of Polly's uncle, Giles Brandreth, where they were house-sitting. I vividly recall that brief visit because I'd put a load of washing in the machine overnight and woke to the distressing discovery that the spin element hadn't worked. Leaving the house in haste for morning service at All Souls Church in London, I had no alternative but to pack the wet clothes into my suitcase in plastic bags which resulted in an embarrassing trail of drips behind me as we climbed the stairs to the church balcony.

Mission to Holland and East Germany

From London I flew to Holland to attend the 1997 Leadership Training Time (LTT) conference of New Covenant Ministries International at De Bron Centre. Travelling on my own into unfamiliar territory, I was grateful to meet up at Heathrow with other South African delegates and follow their lead to the train from the airport to Zwolle, the closest town to De Bron.

Coming from our hilly South African terrain, it was a novelty to experience the flatness of Holland with so many locals riding bicycles as their daily means of transport. On a free afternoon a group of us explored the picturesque town of Ommen, capturing on film the picture-postcard scenes of riverboats on the water and contented cows grazing in green pastures close by. We walked the extent of the town which is a tourist Mecca full of shops selling wooden Dutch clogs and countless other typical Dutch souvenirs.

Adventures in Dresden

At the close of the conference, Pastor Ray Oliver and a small group from our Pietermaritzburg church prepared to cross into East Germany to visit a small church fellowship in Dresden. Their pastor was retiring due to ill health and the elders had invited us to pray with them for God's direction for their future. In a hired minibus we followed one of the elders, Peer-Olav Weniger, to Dresden, with a prayer of thankfulness as we entered the country that there was no longer any Communist Border Post to cross!

An Australian delegate, Diana Hewitt, had asked to join our mission to Germany and the two of us were dropped off at the flat of a young couple in the middle of the new Klipphausen Industrial Estate. Placed above a factory surrounded by industry seemed a strange location to me but the interior of their modern home was as warm as their hospitality. Diana and I shared heart to heart about our life experiences and discovered that we had much in common, so by the end of the two weeks we had established a sound friendship.

On Saturday we met the German congregation and walked together to a clearing in the beautiful Tharand Dert Wald forest to support two new Christians about to be baptized by emersion in the small river that flowed through the picturesque setting. Gathering on the bank under umbrellas when the heavens opened with a heavy downpour, we encouraged them with songs of faith while they entered the freezing water to confirm their commitment to the Lord Jesus. The moment they rose out of the water, the sun broke through the clouds and beamed down on them as a glorious seal of blessing from God. The beautiful setting was like something from a storybook, with the clip-clopping of horses' hooves echoing through the forest as horse-drawn carriages passed by on the road.

That evening we were treated by Peer-Olav and his wife Connie to a family meal on their small farm. Being a keen photographer I found the homely scenes in their country setting quite enchanting. As though begging to be photographed, the plump brown hens were walking up a little ladder to their coop, while brown cows grazed under the shade of apple trees in the field until they came into the barn for milking. Guests and family all helped to carry food and drinks up the ladder to the top barn loft, where we enjoyed a delicious meal in the warmth and shared wonderful fellowship with laughter and singing to guitar accompaniment.

On Sunday afternoon we gathered in bright sunshine for an open air outreach in the park. While the Gospel story was being preached through a translator, Moira Oliver interpreted God's love in free dance and artist Sheryl Thornton-Dibb illustrated the message of the life and death of Jesus on a flipchart. Our team had attached Bible texts to the stems of single red roses which we presented to ladies who passed by or stopped to listen and chat.

The next day we were taken on a walking tour through the old sector of Dresden, where massive posters showed pitiful scenes of an obliterated city after the devastating bombings of the Second World War. Looking at historic buildings which had survived the bombing but still bore signs of the destruction, we felt the pain of the past for the people of Dresden and were moved to pray for them to find forgiveness in their hearts toward our Allied Forces. Reflecting on the scale of restoration needed, we were amazed at how much they had accomplished in rebuilding the beautiful modern city of today; and on a relaxed stroll through a newly developed shopping mall, we stopped to enjoy doner kebabs at a pavement café in brilliant sunshine.

One of the real highlights of the week was a concert arranged by group of Messianic Jewish believers, under the stone arches of the massive Albert Bridge spanning the Elbe River. The singing was led by professional musicians from Jerusalem, David Loden and his wife Lisa, to the accompaniment of local musicians on violins, cello, trumpet, oboe and keyboard. The Jewish Kletzmer music, played on traditional instruments, was exhilarating and we joined the circle of dancers with joyful abandon.

At their church office we prayed for the elders and brought prophetic words of encouragement and direction for them and their congregation. After lunch our team divided and five of us

A New Beginning

drove to the home of group leaders Marianne and Christoff in the town of Meissen, famous worldwide for its pottery. After tea and delicious German cookies, Ray gave a teaching from the Bible and prayed for their home-group before we were taken on a very interesting walk through the town's cobbled streets up the mountain to the Meissen Cathedral. From this amazing vantage point we could appreciate the magnificent view of the whole city with the broad river winding its way through the town, the life-blood of the ceramic industry for generations.

Throughout all these fascinating experiences in Dresden, I felt as if I was in another world and though I couldn't speak German, God's love bonded my heart with the local Christians we met in a very deep way.

Diana Hewitt left us to fly back to Australia and early the following morning our group set out for Frankfurt Airport where we bade farewell to Sheryl, who returned the hired minibus to the Avis Hire Company. Ray and Moira Oliver, Martin and Shirley Berndt and I checked in our luggage for the flight home and with hours to wait, took a local train into the city to explore the flea market and town centre. Two uniformed soldiers were busking with an accordion and a very large triangular stringed instrument. Here I had my first encounter with professional street mime artists, and became completely mesmerized by 'Desdimona', a Berliner painted and dressed in chalk white from head to toe. I marvelled at her ability to hold her pose, moving like clockwork only when coins were dropped into the hat. When she stepped off her stand for a short rest break, I had to ask how she did it. She explained that she'd been trained in the discipline as an actor and had been earning her living this way for five years – in the theatre, on the street and at special events arranged through an agency.

We caught the underground back to the airport and, once through Customs, found ourselves in the rather posh Leonardo da Vinci Lounge. Bone-weary and absolutely parched we searched for a cold drink vending machine but there was nothing to be seen. Our only available choice was from the bar so emptying our pockets and pooling our remaining change, we had just enough to

Riding High with Jesus

order two pots of tea and a glass of beer for Martin. Noting that we were the only ones in the lounge, I took the liberty of collecting all the milk sachets from other tables, and with additional hot water from the staff we managed to squeeze out a second round of tea. Suddenly, overcome by the humour in our pitiful situation, like children we dissolved into uncontrollable laughter around the table until our sides ached!

Sitting in the busy departure area of Frankfurt Airport waiting for our flight to be called, I suddenly had the surreal experience of hearing what sounded like *my name* being called over the intercom! Through the foreign accent I was sure when I heard it the second time, and my heart began to race. Who on earth knew I was sitting in Frankfurt Airport and why would they be calling me here? Feeling apprehensive I made my way to the Information desk but my fears were quickly dispelled when I heard my German friend Michael Köhler's voice on the line, just wanting to say goodbye! Once on board we enjoyed plentiful free drinks and the evening meal before a welcome sleep, and next morning in Johannesburg caught a connecting flight to Durban. Waiting with a warm welcome were church elders Guy Veltman, Russ Kain and Gary Vaughan, and within the hour I was reunited with my family, all thrilled to have me home again.

In September 1997 at a Worship Workshop with Fini and Isi de Gersigny at Victory Faith in Hillcrest, I went forward to receive prayer for fresh anointing. Back at my seat, Dee Andrews handed me a note with a prophetic word she'd just received for me:

God wants you to know that you need never doubt the amount nor the strength of His supply for you. It will continue to be fresh, steady and at times come like a torrent.

This personal promise from the Lord encouraged me to keep unwavering trust in Him through uncertain circumstances that lay ahead in the future.

A New Beginning

God's Grace Brings Freedom

Three years before joining the NCF team in October 1997, I'd had an experience which God instructed me to share with our Pastor Ray. I had met someone abroad who had been brought very low in spirit through illness and a broken marriage. From the deep well of God's love in my heart I had reached out to restore self-worth and hope for the future that had been lost. In doing so I'd acted beyond God's intended purpose, and despite having repented at the time I discerned that God was asking me to share the incident with my pastor. Without hesitation I obeyed, did what was required and stepped down from ministry for a period. Through this step of obedience I found closure and freedom of spirit, and learned the valuable lesson for life that I can't do God's part in ministering to others but must be led by the Holy Spirit, not by the need.

By God's grace, at that precise time I was invited by the Wendy Fath, principal of the Kingsway Preschool, to teach a small class of five-year-olds struggling to keep up with their peers. When approached, I protested that although I was a teacher I'd been out of the classroom for forty years. She dismissed my sense of inadequacy at once with the reassurance, "What these little ones need most is God's love, and you have plenty of that to give them, so just do as much of the curriculum as you can every day." The next six months were challenging, demanding but very rewarding as I affirmed and encouraged little people with the love of Jesus until the end of 1997 when Sue Jacobsen returned to her 'Elephant Class'. In thanking me for nurturing the little ones in her absence, Sue told the children in words which touched me deeply, "I want to grow up to be like Auntie Colleen – mature and gracious."

Prophecies Begin to Flow

Towards the end of January 1998 I returned to my duties on the pastoral team in time for the annual NCF Leadership Camp down the South Coast at Illovo. Before one of the sessions began,

Riding High with Jesus

Trevor and Carla Piercy and I left the meeting to release the childminders to attend. Having been with Trevor on the Dresden mission, I told him that I was sensing a growing awareness in my heart of a call from God to go to the nations. His immediate reply set me tingling with anticipation: "Colleen, I will be leading the next session and I have something important to share which concerns you!" Wow! Midway through his message Trevor was led by the Holy Spirit to pause and call out a small group of us by name, with a prophetic word from the Lord:

> *Enlarge your vision for more that God has for you. You will go out in teams and do more than you can dream of. He will equip, anoint and use you internationally.*

My heart leapt with joy at the confirmation of what I felt God had been saying to me personally.

Moira Oliver brought me a prophetic word at Jim Lamont's induction of NCF elders in 1998, which brought comfort and restoration after the painful lesson of learning not to run ahead of God:

> *Colleen, I see you taking a giant step forward across a gulf – no longer standing with one foot on either side. It is a breaking off from the past and being catapulted into new things – wider and bigger things for God than you have expected to do for Him. The timing is unclear but it will happen fast when you step across into new fields to minister God's love to people. You have been in a season of transition. The work has been done of dealing with the issues that needed attention; now you are moving forward into the new season of ministry.*

During the Alpha course at Cedara, Ray Oliver's word to me was, *"I feel God saying that you mustn't expect the anointing to flow in a constant straight line, but expect an ebb and flow in valleys and on hilltops."* Though Ray didn't know the significance of his word, I did, and was encouraged that even in the valley I'd been in for four years, God had been pouring out His anointing through me to bless others.

During a weekly prayer meeting we broke into groups to pray and ask God for words of prophecy for one another. In that time of waiting for God to reveal His plans, I felt uplifted by the following words of great encouragement.

Rus Eales:

I see you as a tree with two sides – one with gnarled, old bark symbolizing the past, not negatively but representing the old experiences in God. On the other side fresh, smooth new bark as you relax in the Lord and stop striving to please Him. The tree is firmly rooted in God and begins to put out new shoots and blossoms as you move on in new things for Him. I feel a powerful sense of God's love and acceptance of you. He has always loved you and knows that you love Him. He sees the depth of gratitude in your heart toward Him for what He has done and is doing in you and your family, and just wants you to know that He appreciates you for who you are, not for what you do for Him, and for just 'being' – and He loves you passionately.

Martin Bouwer:

I feel the deep love of God which He expresses to you today by wrapping you in red ribbon as one would wrap a gift. I sense strongly the word 'increase' and believe that you will enter into deeper intimacy with God which will result in an increase in your ministry here in our own body[61] and beyond.

---

[61] meaning the local church

Carmelle Oosthuis:

I see a spray of beautiful blossoms, with a sweet fragrance which draws the bees to collect nectar from them. Just so, the sweet fragrance of Jesus in you draws, touches and blesses others.

Jacqui Dinkelman:

I see you dancing with a bright pink ribbon in a ribbon dance for the Lord.

During a music ministry evening, all in the music team were invited to come forward and sing a new song to the Lord. This was daunting for all of us and when no-one else made a move, I took courage and stepped forward very nervously to take the microphone and sing a simple love song to the Lord. When others had done the same, the elders prayed for us individually and Ray Olivers' prayer for me was, "Pour in more of your sweetness, Lord. More of your sweetness."

Guy Veltman:

God has given you a gift which He wants you to use increasingly. I see you singing with groups in different places. You are a worshipper and God will use your gift to lead others into worship. I see a little dust on the gift, as dust collects on something that is not used often. Dust off your gift and begin to sing anywhere you feel a prompting. I see you singing over people who are on a lower level than you are – perhaps the sick in bed? Begin to use it as you have tonight, at every opportunity.

Fourteen years later in the UK, I have indeed been using God's gift to glorify Him in song, leading worship every week with elderly residents in rest homes. I have also had the privilege and joy of singing in choirs of five hundred voices at 'Praise Prom' in the Albert Hall, London. Guy's prophetic picture was clearly accurate.

At the NCF staff meeting on 16th September, Gerda Catterall said:

> *I see you as a sturdy tree with a strong taproot holding it firmly in the soil. As the root develops smaller roots so it is held more securely and draws up nourishment into the branches which begin to spread and reach out further.*

Guy Veltman:

> *I saw you in the woods where it was dark in the shadow of the trees, but as you raised your arms in worship the darkness began to lift. You have been through a time of uncertainty but God is soon going to take you out. He brought you from the city into the woods, but you will not be returning to the city when God calls you into the new things He is calling you to.*

Steve Wimble:

> *I see you in a forest beneath tall trees, where God has placed you for the purpose of waiting and resting in Him. In His time He will take you out.*

Jéan Seevaraj:

> *I see you as a salmon swimming upstream against the tide, fighting through difficulties toward the goal. You're pressing on strongly to the destiny God has for you and will not give up.*

Russel Kain:

> *I see you as a malachite kingfisher hovering over the water watching for little fish. I feel that you are one*

who looks out for those in need who may not be noticed – overlooked by others – to love and care for them with sensitivity.

A Leadership Conference in Australia

While together in Dresden, Diana Hewitt had invited me to be her guest for the 1999 LTT in Adelaide, so in February I accompanied Ray and Moira Oliver on a ministry journey to several churches in Australia and New Zealand. We started with a visit to the North Shore International Fellowship in Fremantle, Perth on the West Coast. As we explored this friendly old city on foot, I saw clear reminders of the British Colonial days in the architecture of buildings in the town centre.

We moved on to Adelaide where Diana welcomed me warmly into her home. Regrettably she was working and unable to attend much of the conference, but offered me the use of her daughter's car to drive to the meetings daily and to explore the residential suburbs of the lovely city. As I drove around the spacious parks full of giant eucalyptus trees and watched flocks of wild, brightly-coloured parakeets swooping back and forth to take cover in their foliage, I was reminded of the avenues of gum trees on our farm that I'd loved as a child. The homes of Adelaide retain a strong colonial feel too, with many architectural features similar to that of the old Tongaat dwellings. I had great fun driving round neighbouring suburbs, and on the seafront one afternoon at low tide, watched a class of preschoolers on the clean sweep of sand at the water's edge being given a lesson in respecting the sea.

The fellowship and teachings at the New Covenant Ministries International Conference were inspirational as always. At one point after Dudley Daniel encouraged us not to hold back on what God intended to do for us, I went up to ask the leaders to pray for God's clear leading. Leon and Pat van Daele, a mature couple in the Body of Christ, prayed for me with simple words of encouragement.

A New Beginning

Leon: *"God is delighting in you, Colleen. I feel He is chuckling with delight over you."* Then, after a quiet wait, "No, He is not going to tell us any more at the moment!"

Pat: "Are you on your own, Colleen?"

"Yes Pat, I am widowed."

"God wants you to know your ministry is not over. He has much more for you to do."

Once again the message confirmed unseen things to come.

While in Adelaide I phoned Australian friends Charmaine and Alex Meek from Victoria, whom Peter and I had met at Stella Carmel. They were thrilled to hear I was in the country and told me they would be ministering in Warnambool over the weekend. The only possibility of meeting up was for me to take a coach to Mount Gambier and they would drive up to find me at the small 'Avalon Motel' close to the Stateliner Coach stop. I booked in on arrival and when they arrived we drove straight to the Blue Lake in the volcanic crater of Lake Gambier, which mysteriously changes colour from slate grey to cobalt blue every November. We walked and talked for two hours in the wildlife park while viewing koalas in the trees, emus, wild birds and roaming wallabies.

At dusk we returned to my motel room where Alex linked his video camera to the TV set and showed me their recent video of ministry in Asia. With loving concern these dear friends were eager to hear all that had happened in my life since Peter's death. Within the intimacy of my little room I shared how wonderfully God had provided for me, and confessed that in missing him so deeply I'd asked God if it was His will to bring me another husband to partner with me in ministry. While praying for God's discernment about this, Charmaine had a picture:

> *I see a wedding cake with you clearly standing as the bride, Colleen, but the figure of the bridegroom is shadowy and unclear.*

It was wonderful to spend time with these dear friends who had known Peter, and I was so grateful to them for making the journey. They prayed for me with encouraging prophetic words for my future before they drove back to Warnambool and I settled down to sleep, returning by the coastal coach route the following morning. The following year I received an email from Charmaine and Alex with prophetic counsel from God:

> *Do not make the dream of another husband an idol. Do not lose focus on Jesus and His plans. Do not accept an Ishmael instead of waiting for Isaac.*

This word of caution would hold me firmly obedient to God's call in later years as I sought to fulfil God's plan for my future.

New Zealand

From Australia Ray, Moira and I flew to Auckland, New Zealand, where Ken Jeanes met and drove us down through Napier and Hastings to Havelock North, where he and Janet had planted the 'Celebration Christian Fellowship'. They had arranged for me to stay with a friend and my time with Ro was a real blessing as she had the gift of prophecy and encouraged me to develop the same gift in my own ministry. After a weekend of ministry in Havelock North, Ray and Moira left to visit churches in Auckland while I visited Janet's parents, my very dear friends Terry and Elaine McKenzie, in the small town of Waipawa.

They lived in a one-hundred-year-old two-storey home called 'The Pines', originally owned by the local doctor who kept carrier pigeons in the large dovecote at the back of the house to keep in touch with his patients in outlying areas. It was wonderful to see my friends in their charming home and garden abounding in beautiful blooms, a tribute to Elaine's hard work and green fingers. She and I took a picnic basket to the closest beach at Porangahau where I collected a few unusual shells. Later she took me on a delightful walking tour of the town, popping in to meet some of her closest friends in their homes. Taking my leave of

A New Beginning

these special friends after four days was hard, especially as my dear Elaine was receiving ongoing treatment for cancer.

Terry drove me to Havelock North Coach Station and along the journey to the north I enjoyed beautiful country scenery of mountains, forests and waterfalls with sheep grazing peacefully in green pastures. After brief stops at Rotarua and other strange-sounding Maori towns, we arrived at Mount Maunganui where I was met by Graham and Rhona Harris, friends of Catherine Hollister-Jones my dear missionary contact from AE. They had kindly offered to host me for the weekend while Catherine was away on a prayer vigil, and treated me to a visit to the hot springs of Rotorua and the Te Puia Sacred Meeting House of the Maori. Here we were welcomed with traditional songs and dances before being shown through the museum housing interesting relics of the past. On another occasion, a walk through the streets of the fascinating little town of 'Katikati' was full of delightful surprises; there artists have turned the walls of buildings into masterpieces of art, capturing people engaged in all aspects of life during the early settlers' days.

When my friend Catherine returned, she and I spent three very rich days of bonding, sharing heart to heart about God's goodness to us. She told me about her childhood in India and of a recent emotional return to her home village where she had been reunited with Indian servants who had become like family to her as a child.

Being a prayer warrior, Catherine fulfilled her deep desire to bless me with a visit to the beautiful YWAM property 'Gideon's Fields International Prayer Forest'. In brilliant sunshine we arrived at the forest beside a fast flowing river with spectacular waterfalls, where Catherine left me to take the prayer trail on my own. I was deeply moved as I made my way prayerfully from point to point through the forest of tall trees and giant tree ferns, stopping to pray for each designated country described in the information packs protected from rain inside wooden desks. The lush growth here thrives on frequent showers and while on the walk the heavens opened suddenly with a heavy downpour and I left the forest drenched, feeling I had received a double portion of blessing from the Lord.

After an extraordinarily full and wonderful time with friends in Australia and New Zealand, my heart overflowed with gratitude to God when I met up with Ray and Moira Oliver in Auckland for the very long flight home to South Africa.

The Power of Prayer

On 29th June 1999 my youngest son Justin rang to tell me that his wife Mish had gone into labour with their first baby, and as the hours passed waiting for news I felt a growing urgency in my spirit to pray for Mish and the baby's safety. Later it became apparent that my prayer was prompted by the Holy Spirit because she and her baby were in great difficulty and needed an emergency caesarean section for the delivery of their beautiful baby boy Jordan Alexander. How gracious God is to alert mothers to partner with Him in prayer for our families in times of need.

Personal Visit to England and Scotland

In July 1999 I was thrilled to make another visit to friends in England and Scotland, flying to London Heathrow via Paris. After two nights with Dennis and Mary Bambury in London, I caught a 'Stuart of Carlisle' coach to Edinburgh where my Scottish doctor friend Lysbeth was waiting to meet me. It was good to pick up our friendship again on the drive to her home 'Ahlaine'[62] near Peebles.

Lysbeth Duncan, a woman anointed with a prophetic deliverance ministry, was brought into my life by God to open my eyes to aspects of the spiritual realm of darkness that I hadn't experienced. On a scenic drive through the beautiful Border hills and lochs she showed me signs of regular occult activity in the area. Pinpointing the visible signs of standing beacons and copses of trees, she described how Satanists meet to pray against

---

[62] meaning 'hello' in Arabic

A New Beginning

everything of God in society, especially Christian marriages which are the sound bedrock of every nation. On our return we even found fresh witchcraft symbols of bird entrails laid out on top of the wooden gate to her property, a clear indication of the need for constant prayer covering.

Lysbeth is a prayer warrior who knows that Satan is a defeated foe so does not live in fear, but for me this was a sobering and eye-opening experience into the reality of the forces of darkness. While I shared my life with her at a deep level, tracing right back to ancestral links, she discerned that although I had repented of the sins of the past, the door might not have been closed to bondage and she offered to pray for me. I renounced known sins of my ancestors and then as she prayed with the authority given her by God after each confession of my own sin, I felt release and closure deep in my spirit.

We spent relaxed times chatting together while preparing and eating meals in her cosy cottage, and in her garden I helped to pull raspberries from their canes, picked fresh peas and weeded the 'veggie' beds. At the local village market full of interesting wares, Lysbeth blessed me with the gift of a lovely warm zip-up jacket. At the end of the week I left much wiser about spiritual matters and grateful for a delightful peep into Scottish life at a friend's wedding in Peebles, celebrated in true Scottish style with kilts, bagpipes and traditional dancing at the reception.

I accepted Lysbeth's gracious offer to drive me across to the Scottish town of Dunblane, to spend a couple of weeks with a South African couple, Trevor and Linda Lovegrove, who had recently started a church there. Taking the route over the Clyde River Bridge we called on her artist friends at Strachur, passing through the picturesque village of Luss on the shores of Loch Lomond. My decision to visit Dunblane was prompted months before in South Africa when I heard the tragic news of school children being gunned down at the local junior school and knew that the Lovegroves were grieving with the local community. My heart was moved to share with them the comfort of God that I'd received in my own loss, and I was given leave to go by our eldership.

During the next two weeks I was exposed to the challenges this Christian family was facing, mourning with the whole town while being up against spiritual forces of opposition that I had encountered in Peebles. While able to offer them comfort I also helped with cooking and practical tasks in the home while Linda was busy elsewhere, and I took part in their church-launching activities.

These celebrations included a colourful flag display by a visiting team from Crawley on the streets of Dunblane and neighbouring towns of Stirling and Calendar. A personal joy for me during the rich experience of the outreach was sharing the Gospel with two young men, Peter and Billy, who both made a personal commitment to Jesus and linked up at once with the church. My desire to support Trevor and Linda's family in every way I could was rewarded by Linda's words when she said goodbye: "Thank you for coming, Colleen. I don't know how I would have coped without you this week."

From Dunblane I caught an overnight coach to Victoria Coach Station arriving at 6.45am. A couple of connecting coaches brought me to Axminster where friends Bob and Kath Chaffey lived. Bob was keen to share his life story with me he talked freely about his youth, but as soon as I began to share about my faith, he closed the conversation and adamantly refused to continue. He gave no reason for this but his strong opposition to the Gospel made we wonder if he was in bondage to the spirits of Freemasonry from the past. Putting aside any controversial topics, we chatted as we walked their little Scotty dog through the nearby forest and around the beautiful property of 'Killerton House'.

Return coach journeys brought me back to Victoria Station where I was met by Lisa Schemilt, a friend from Pietermarizburg, then working at the St Raphael's Christian Care Home in the London Borough of Bromley. We enjoyed the warmth of renewed friendship during quiet times of chatting in her flat and took a drive to visit a friend at the pebbly beach of Whitstable.

A New Beginning

Discovering my Granddad's Ancestral Home

I had long carried a burning desire to trace our Granddad Fredrick Long's birthplace in the small town of Manningtree in England, and on this trip the longing intensified. In the short time remaining before I flew home it didn't seem possible – but there was a surprise waiting round the corner! My nephew Bradley Porter, living in Battersea and working as a sales rep in Greater London, phoned to say hello. When he heard I was in Bromley he popped round to see me between business calls and I shared my dream of going to Manningtree. Brad responded enthusiastically, "Auntie Col, I would love to come with you. If you can wait until I've finished my business calls tomorrow morning, I'll drive you there." As I was to catch a flight home to South Africa that evening, it would literally have to be a flying visit. I phoned the Tendring Council Offices in Essex to ask for directions to the Long family's old residence and they referred me to the Manningtree Library for directions.

Next morning Bradley picked me up and we drove as fast as possible to the little town at the mouth of the Stour River in Essex. Stopping at the library, I showed a Polish member of staff the old photograph from the 1800's and she recognized the house immediately. So following her directions to South Street, Brad and I raced up the hill on foot searching frantically for the property.

I was overjoyed to find it looking the same as the photograph taken so long ago, except for the absence of Virginia creeper covering the walls. The name plaque 'Prospect House' was still above the door and a Victorian streetlamp stood on the same grassy patch in front. With beating heart, I knocked on the door which was opened halfway by a poker-faced lady who stood looking suspiciously at me. I explained that I was the granddaughter of Frederick Long who had lived in this house in the 1800s and wondered if there were any Long relatives living there. Maintaining a frosty stance, she said, "No there are no Longs living in this house and I'm sorry but I am just about to go out." As she was about to close the door on me, I managed to ask if there were any Longs still living in the town and she grudgingly told me that there was an old lady called Winnie Long living at the top of the hill in a cottage called 'White Wings'.

With little time to spare I took quick photographs of Granddad's home before we ran up the steep hill. Searching from right and left at the junction of roads, I suddenly spotted the name White Wings on a cottage and called, "Bradley, here it is!" The house appeared to be in darkness but I rang the doorbell and stood praying for someone to be home. To my delight the door opened a crack on the safety chain and I could see a diminutive little lady with a mop of soft grey curls, gold spectacles and a kindly face.

When I introduced myself as Fred Long's granddaughter from South Africa, she broke into a smile and opened the door immediately, drawing us inside with a warm welcome. Winnie was delighted to meet us and with great enthusiasm shared all about Granddad and his siblings as she remembered them in their young days. She recognized and named everyone in the old photos of the Long family I had taken with me from Mum's memoirs, and she showed which of William's sons she had married. It was very hard to bring our brief time to a close but I explained that I had a plane to catch back to South Africa, so after taking photos with 'Win' we exchanged contact details and with the promise of further contact soon, raced down the hill to the car.

I marvelled all the way back to London at the miracle of answered prayer, finding in that brief window of opportunity the last member of the Long family who had known our Granddad in person! Brad and I sped back and pushed through heavy London traffic to make it in time for my evening flight home from Heathrow. I wrote a letter to Winnie Long as soon as I got home and had high hopes of visiting her the following year on my next visit to England. However, I learned with great sadness from another cousin that she'd had a stroke and was deeply disappointed when her son would not allow me to have any contact with her. She passed away soon afterwards so the efforts that Bradley and I had made to find her were even more

A New Beginning

significant, and the precious photos I took of Winnie are treasures which we're all so grateful to have.

A Fascinating Mission to India

In December 2001 I set off with a team from NCF to visit a church and attend the LTT in New Delhi, India. We flew with Emirates Airline from Durban to Dubai, arriving in the early morning with a whole day to wait until the evening connection to India. The young ones in the group paid R350 for Airport Visas to see something of the city of Dubai, but Bheki Zulu and I opted to remain in the airport. Surrounded by a moving sea of passengers making their way to or from departure points, Bheki and I took advantage of the delicious refreshments laid on for transit travellers before settling in recliner chairs in one of the waiting areas. After a few hours the hard plastic recliner became very uncomfortable and every bone in my body ached by the time we boarded the plane that evening.

New Delhi

Touching down in New Delhi at 3.00am was an experience to remember! Arriving in the dusty, dilapidated airport building we made our way to the Customs desks which operated on an antiquated system dating back to colonial times. Gathering our luggage in the almost deserted hall at that hour, we moved through to where our host Russel Eales was waiting with his welcoming smile. He organized us into two taxis and we set out into the waking city with the roar of traffic already starting to build up. New Delhi is a fascinating city of rich colour and interest but with evidence everywhere of heart-breaking poverty among the poorer caste. One of the strangest sights was that of holy cows wandering unheeded through the chaotic traffic on the streets or resting on islands in the middle of roads. Instead of grazing in grassy meadows these pathetic animals scrounge from the refuse

Riding High with Jesus

bins along the street, looking completely out of place in the hustle and bustle of city life.

'Rus' and Glyn Eales graciously invited our group of six to share their second floor flat in Kalkaji, the young ones sleeping in sleeping bags on the lounge floor while I was privileged to have a bed. As soon as we'd carried our bags upstairs and had a cup of tea, the others were eager to make the long journey to the Taj Mahal, but feeling a bit queasy I chose to stay with Rus and Glyn.

Suddenly, through blaring Indian music from loudspeakers on the street I heard Rus call, "Colleen, come quickly and bring your camera!" I hurried out on to the small balcony in time to capture pictures of a Hindu procession passing below. A brass band followed the carriage of a bearded Holy Man in robes and turban throwing dry rice as a blessing to the people on the street. Plodding along at a sedate pace in the procession was an elephant decorated with embroidered drapes and jewels, followed by a span of oxen pulling an open wagon carrying a group of elderly Indian women in saris around an open fire. I took as many photographs as I could before the long procession passed, glad that I'd been there to capture the essence of India in this traditional Hindu celebration.

In the morning I accompanied Russ to shop for fresh produce from a wide selection of vegetables and fruit at the local market. At pavement stalls many different dishes were being prepared over kerosene stoves and sold on the street to queues of customers. Having grown up in the Indian village of Tongaat, I was familiar with some of their local ingredients while others were quite new to me. In the alleys large sacks of dried items stood beside trays of syrupy sweet pastries, plucked chickens lay exposed on counters next to various kinds of fish, while sad-looking turkeys stood with their legs bound on top of cages holding live poultry.

Rus and Glyn took us on an exhilarating and nail-biting journey across town in little green and yellow 'tuk-tuk' taxis to the conference venue in a hotel. These minicabs weave their way bravely through the chaotic surge of bicycles, buses, trucks, cars and taxis, all hooting to announce their presence to vehicles on

A New Beginning

either side. The cacophony of sound was deafening, and squeezed three-up in a tuk-tuk, I was careful to keep my elbows tucked in to avoid having them clipped in the mad race.

At the conference, worship was led by Indian ladies looking splendid in their beautiful traditional saris. At one session Ian McKellar gave a teaching from the Word of God that the gift of prophecy is available to *all* believers, and then sent us out in groups to pray and trust God's Holy Spirit to give us words for one another. I had never considered myself as having the gift of prophecy and felt very nervous and apprehensive. However, when I quietened my mind in prayer and focussed on hearing from God for two of the delegates in the group, I was rewarded with a clear picture for both which came together with spiritual interpretation of the pictures. In both cases the individuals confirmed that what I had shared brought meaningful insight into their situations, which was a great encouragement to me. I learned the significant lesson that the prophetic gift is not dependant on me, but on my willingness to listen for the Holy Spirit's voice to give me words for others that will bless and enrich them.

Strolling home at dusk one evening, in the distance we could hear loud music approaching and soon found ourselves caught up in a large procession of Hindu wedding guests. In the middle, seated high on a splendid white horse, sat the smiling bride and groom, beautifully attired in rich, traditional finery while their friends surged forward in dance around them! The joyful spirit was infectious and we continued on our way very happy to have been touched momentarily by the unusual and memorable event.

The ladies in our group had great fun exploring the wide variety of Indian shops, while the men's interest lay in the sight-seeing tour of historical buildings from the days of the British Raj. Shortly before our visit ended I had a last-minute opportunity to visit the Taj Mahal with a group who had a spare seat in their taxi. Standing before this iconic building felt quite surreal after seeing pictures of it in books, photographs and television documentaries. On the long journey back to Kalkaji my heart was moved by the sad sight of families living in absolute squalor in hovels beside the road, a harsh reminder of the gulf existing between the quality of life for high caste Indians and those of lower caste destined to live in abject poverty.

Mussourie Village

A thrilling part of our Indian visit was a trip to the village of Mussourie high up in the slopes of the Himalayan Mountains. Tony and Linda Johnson who had planted the church in New Delhi years before, had started a fellowship there among the local residents, which was now led by Kieran and Ramon, descendants of Anglo-Indian ancestors. We started the journey from Derradun Station in one of the original steam trains still in operation from the days of British rule in India, and as we boarded the train I felt I was stepping back in time to that era, except that the carriages had long since been stripped of any sign of opulence and were now spartan in comfort. We were interested to learn that the rail service is still run today by direct descendants of the Indian station masters, engine drivers and mechanics who had run the railways in the days of the Raj. With fierce traditional pride passed down through generations and a great deal of tenacity and ingenuity, they work constantly at maintaining the ageing engines, the rail track and the coaches to keep the train service running.

At the foot of the mountain it became clear that the gradient was far too steep for the train, so we transferred to taxis and embarked on a nerve-wracking journey sweeping round hairpin bends at breakneck speed with no regard for any oncoming traffic! Once in the village of Missourie we booked into a cheap hotel perched on the slope of the mountain. Doing our best to communicate by sign language with hotel staff who spoke no English, we were assured that there would be hot water on our return. We had a meal in a small Chinese restaurant and began to explore the local shops that lined the steep path up the mountain. By 9.00pm the cold drove us back to our hotel, only to discover that all the staff had gone off duty and there was not a drop of hot water. We had a quick wash in freezing cold water before creeping into bed fully clothed but I barely slept a wink because the thick padding in the duvet gave no warmth against the bitter cold and was so heavy that I couldn't even turn over under the weight of it to ease aching hips and legs.

Sunshine brought a lift to our spirits the following morning when we gathered with the local congregation at the church house, looking out on to spectacular views across the mountains and valleys. At this high altitude I noted that the facial features of the locals bear a strong resemblance to their close Nepalese neighbours, and their crafts, handmade blankets and clothing are very similar to those in Nepal. From a viewing platform on the top of the mountain we gazed in awe at the breathtaking view of the Himalayas clothed in mist, and felt the heady effects of the chilled air on our lungs at this altitude, in spite of bright sunshine.

Before leaving Mussourie I bought seven warm woollen rugs as gifts for my girls, with an extra-large 'Adidas' holdall. At the Customs desk I was greatly relieved to pass through without paying any excess as my overweight bag was absorbed into the group's luggage allowance. We returned to family and friends eager to share with them about our colourful Indian adventure.

A God Appointment at Church

One Sunday morning in 2002 two ladies I'd never seen at church before slipped into the pew beside me. At the close of the service when I greeted them, Lynne Hackland introduced herself and her friend Rosie before explaining that she wasn't a regular churchgoer but had come seeking comfort because her husband was dying from cancer. Lynne turned to me and said, "Colleen, you have a beautiful voice and during worship while you were singing, I felt God's presence in a way I've never felt it before." I explained that it was the presence of God she was sensing because when we praise God, He draws near and touches our hearts. In chatting we discovered to our amazement that her husband Don was a cousin of Daryl Hackland, a close friend and Best Man at our wedding! I felt an immediate bond with Lynne and before we parted, offered to drive out to their farm 'Shiya Moya' at Bishopstowe, just outside Pietermaritzburg, to pray for Don. Lynn gratefully accepted. What a God appointment this meeting would turn out to be!

Within the week I drove out to the farm and found Don's sister Sally Johnson and friend Irene Peens at his bedside. After praying for God to watch over Don and fill him with His peace, I was about to leave when Lynn arrived home, so I arranged to go back the following week to see her. Four days later I drove out and found Sally, Irene and Lynne's sister Colette there. I shared the Gospel with Don and gave him opportunity to make right with God, before Sally and I sang softly over him, ushering the sweet presence of Jesus into his room. His mum, Dulcie, came across from her cottage to join us for tea, and as I drove away I felt a deep bond with this family after just two meetings.

It wasn't long after my visits that Lynne phoned to tell me that Don had passed away peacefully. The family was planning a Thanksgiving Service on the farm on 6th February 2002 and I was deeply honoured to be asked to sing the hymn 'How Great Thou Art'. A large gathering of family members and friends including Don's friends from the Motorcycle Club came together in brilliant sunshine on the lawn of their beautiful garden. After the solo, Don's cousin Daryl Hackland shared an encouraging word on 'Jesus, the Good Shepherd' from Psalm 23 and invited friends to surrender their lives to Him.

The following week I drove out to the farm and shared more of God's promises from the Bible with Lynne, adding my own experience of God's grace and faithfulness in the loss of my husband. A week later I met her again with Mum Dulcie, to continue building their faith in Jesus, the source of comfort and help through all life's challenges. A trust had developed between us and Dulcie invited me to visit her on her own to share more about God's character and my story of his love, mercy and faithfulness. This time she introduced me to her son Richard, who chatted briefly before returning to his duties on the farm. In confidence she shared motherly concern for her family and was reassured when I

A New Beginning

told her how God had faithfully answered Peter's and my prayers for our children's salvation, and encouraged her to pray and to trust Him with hers. As I prepared to leave, Fren met me with a bouquet of gorgeous blooms from the garden, which Lynne had asked her to pick for me.

On Sunday, 24th February Lynne and Rosie came to the morning service at NCF and when both ladies responded to the invitation to dedicate their lives to God, it was my joy and privilege to pray with Lynne. I introduced them to Pastor Grant Crawford and told him about our first meeting which had led to my ministry to the whole Hackland family, at which he put his arm around my shoulders and with a smile said, "You couldn't be in better hands, ladies."

Missions to Zimbabwe and Mozambique

I was keen to be a part of the team to attend the 2002 Leadership Training Time in the Zimbabwean capital Harare, having had strong family links to the former Rhodesia. After the conference I was privileged to take part in team ministry to Pastor Sam Ndlovu's congregation from Gweru, formerly Gwelo. We met daily with the local members of the church, seated on wooden benches in their simple church structure with compacted mud floor, corrugated iron roof and window openings without frames or glass panes. With the help of an interpreter I brought three teachings on 'There is Power in the Blood of Jesus', 'The Need to be Saved from Sin' and practical suggestions on 'How to Live for Jesus Every Day'. It was truly a blessed time of fellowship with Sam and his generous family, and very humbling to witness this family's commitment to Jesus in their daily Christian walk while struggling to eke out a simple existence. Years later we were all deeply saddened by the news that Samuel had tragically been killed in a motor accident, leaving his courageous wife and children to continue serving the Lord.

On another occasion Wolf Binder led a small group from NCF on a mission to Mozambique, the country of his birth, where he often ministered to the local population. On arrival after the long journey, the men in our party put up our tents while the ladies were introduced to the rustic toilet in true African style – a deep pit surrounded by poles covered with plastic beside the maize field! We held our meetings with the local congregation of Xinavane Church in school classrooms on the Xinyaganine Compound and were inspired by the young Mozambican leader Martha Sherindza who was on fire for the Lord.

At the end of our first visit, Martha invited Toni Oosthuis and me to come back and run a weekend course for the ladies. We were delighted when our elders gave their blessing on a return visit the following year. We were grateful to have Christian brothers Gerald and Michael share the driving and put up our tents on arrival. I felt humbled and honoured to bring teaching to these rural black women through an interpreter, on the theme 'Raising Godly Families as the Foundation of our Nations'. We helped them to understand the practical outworking of the Bible, stressing the importance of fulfilling our most important role in the home: being godly wives honouring our husbands, and mothers who teach our children about Jesus. After three days Toni and I left feeling closely bonded with these sisters in Christ across language and cultural differences.

A New Beginning

African Enterprise, 1992-1996

The chapel on the pond

The main building

My cottage at AE

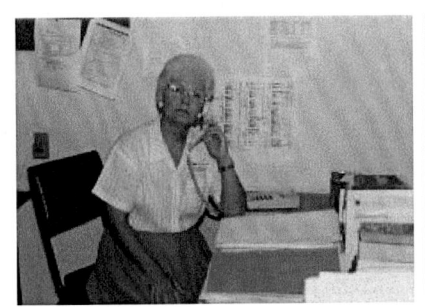

My office

Some of the AE prayer partners from around the world, 1994

315

Riding High with Jesus

My ministry to Indian workers at Mama's Pie Factory, 1993-1996

The West-footers from St Albans, 1995

AE prayer partner, 1994

AE in 2015

African Enterprise estate

A New Beginning

Visit to England, 1993

Murial Currant between me and Betty in Rock, Cornwall, 1993

Colleen and cousin Joyce with tour guide

Riding High with Jesus

Dresden, Meissen, Frankfurt

Elbe River in Meissen, Germany

Two believers baptised

De Bron International Conference Centre

In the Tharan Dert Wald forest

Desdimona mime artist in Frankfurt

Strange instruments in Frankfurt

Song and art open air ministry

A New Beginning

NCF Mission to Australia and New Zealand, 1999

Flying to Oz with Ray and Moira Oliver

Alex and Charmaine Meek in Oz

Diana Hewitt in Australia

Perth, Australia, 1999

Eucalyptus trees in Adelaide

The cross-country coach to meet the Meeks

Riding High with Jesus

Terry and Elaine beside their historic house in Waipawa

Missionary friend Catherine Hollister-Jones

Blessed moments between best friends

Penny's parents who hosted me

Terry and Elain McKenzie with original of their house

A New Beginning

Waiting for the coach to Tauranga from Waipawa

Coach to Catherine in Tauranga

Ken and Janet in Havelock North

Magnificent ferns in New Zealand forest

On the hill beside the forest and river

Riding High with Jesus

Mission to New Delhi and Mussoorie, 2001

Tuk-tuk taxis by the hundreds, New Delhi

Market stalls in Kalkaji

Street in Kalkaji

Mountain ride to the church in Mussoorie

Post boxes from the past, one present

A New Beginning

Mission to Mozambique, 2002

Colleen preaching to locals

Local people coming to greet us

Setting up camp

Women grinding maize for a meal

Stop en route

Team meeting

Rural toilet

323

NCF Send-off to the UK, 2004

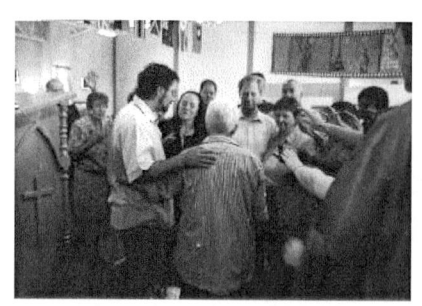

The NCF church praying for Colleen when she left for the UK

Leaving NCF for the UK

Emotional hug from son, Justin

Grant Crawford bidding me farewell

A New Beginning

Finding Granddad's Old Home in Manningtree

Granddad Fred Long's home in Manningtree

Time has stood still here at Fred Long's home

South Street down to the estuary

Winnie Long with Bradley Porter

Winnie sharing about the old days

325

Riding High with Jesus

5

New Horizons Beckon

Following several short missions to far-off places with teams over seven years, I began to sense in my spirit that change was coming in my own life. On one occasion Pastor Ray took the leadership team out of the office into the nearby Bisley Nature Reserve to pray and seek God's fresh direction for our personal lives. As I sat on a rock among the bushes listening to the chorus of chirping, trilling and piping birdcalls nearby and the honking of geese flying overhead, my whole being responded with a welling up of praise to our Creator God. I felt completely one with nature, as if I had melted into the surroundings to become a part of what I was hearing. Thoughts recorded in my prayer journal that morning reflect the sense of coming change:

Creation around me is in a time of seasonal transition. A change is taking place – it's a process of moving from one season to the next.

In my spirit I sense more and more intensely that I am 'being held' in the place of waiting to move from the past into a new season of serving God. The 'calling out' is becoming stronger as the weeks go by and God prepares my heart for whatever He has in His plan. I am reminded in His Word that His timing and plans are perfect and His promise in Jeremiah Chapter 29 verse

11 confirms this: "'I know the plans I have for you,' declares the Lord, 'plans to prosper you and not to harm you, plans to give you hope and a future.'"

There is an excitement in my spirit because through many challenges God has shown me His faithfulness and I know that wherever He calls me, whatever He asks me to do, He will equip me. There will be sacrifices to be made such as leaving family, there will be laying down of familiar securities, but I am committed without conditions to going where He needs me to be. God reinforced His promise at the leadership camp that He will do greater things than I have ever imagined, so I need to expect to leave the old behind.

Only that which God does through me is worth anything – only <u>his love, his compassion, his healing of heart and body, his encouragement, his hope</u> will bear fruit. In myself I have nothing to give, but in sharing the fullness of His love people are profoundly touched, hearts are softened and changed. Dear God, may others see Jesus in me and Him only! May He receive the glory and praise which is His alone!

God is already bringing changes in my family, a separation from one another into new things. Murray and Michelle are leaving for Cape Town. Nick and Shelley are moving house with new horizons and boundaries, physically and spiritually. Justin and Mish's future is in God's hands as a job closes. Andy and Lynne are called to be faithful to God with obedience and submission in the place of present confusion and shaking, as <u>love</u> brings down barriers and keeps hearts clear. Stephen is being brought into relationship with God his way, using his gifting to bless others and glorify Jesus. I offer up deep, unutterable thanksgiving to God *for drawing my children back to Himself in His way – by His Spirit, in His time!*

In our NCF fellowship we are rich in gifting and I delight to serve God here any way I can. But I desire to be sharing His love in places where there is a lack of such abundant expression of His love and power as we witness it – where the simple yet profound Gospel of Jesus Christ is not being lived out with vibrancy and joy. I want to go to places that need your love, Lord, expressed in quiet encouragement. Yet Lord, I need to expand my expectation of what you want to do <u>in</u> and <u>through</u> me. I need to desire and expect other gifts to be developed so I move beyond present limits and mindsets. Help me, Lord, to let go and let You have your way.

Not long after this, Gail Trollop came to share a picture with me that she'd had after the early morning NCF prayer meeting on 4th July 2000:

Colleen, you will be packing your bags soon. It will be to go to England. I see you in some kind of institution like AE in some way, an organization of some kind.

Looking back on that prophetic word, time has revealed that what she saw in the spirit perfectly describes my ministry that was to come in 2006 with the Brighton and Hove City Mission in England.

Following a time of worship when we were all called to draw deeper into Jesus, a simple word that touched my heart came from one of our elderly prayer warriors, Tiny Smith:

Colleen, I felt the Lord saying that He is rejoicing over you with singing!

I began to sense God testing my commitment in a far deeper way with the question, *"Would you be willing to leave all your family in South Africa, to serve me in another land for an extended period?"*

Having already committed myself to living at the centre of God's will, my joyful, unreserved response was, "Yes, Lord." So by 2001, I began to prepare myself to support a married couple of God's choosing who would be going to the nations to plant a church.

With the theme of 'Spiritual Rebirth' at the NCF staff meeting in February 2002 we broke into small groups to pray. Dean Barber came to me with an emphatic word:

You will birth many new spiritual babies in the Lord, with great increase in your ministry.

At a staff meeting we were given the task of creating collages with pictures from magazines, to represent our lives as we saw them in the coming year. For my prophetic picture I chose a speeding cheetah to represent the fast passage of time, a sunflower to represent joy and brightness in my heart, a boat in the shallows waiting for the incoming tide to represent waiting to go when God speaks, and leaping porpoises on the move which I expected to be when I would hear from God.

Family Times

March was a month with a couple of rare family gatherings with time for fellowship and fun. The first was a weekend with all my children and grandchildren in Guy and Daphne Tedder's large cottage at Pumula Beach on the South Coast of Natal. The second was a gathering of our whole Eckersley clan for a weekend at 'Hlalanathi Guest Lodge' in the Drakensberg Mountains. A good cross section of siblings, cousins, children and 'grand-kiddies' made for a very happy weekend of catching up with relatives we hadn't seen in a long time.

New Horizons Beckon

In June 2002 at my Drakensberg timeshare, my friend Paula Lambrecht had a prophetic picture of me:

You are dressed in a summer dress with a bag over your shoulder, looking back with a bright smile before embarking on a flight somewhere.

In September of the same year Paula gave another picture:

You are coming from a room full of furniture and warmth into a waiting room – absolutely bare of any furnishings, pictures etc. and you stand completely alone in your pain – but for Jesus, who is about to take you from that place into the next room full of joy, life and fulfilment now that you can lay down your task and move into what God has for you.

Later that year in December I went round to Paula feeling desperately low with severe physical pain in my hip and resentment in my heart over a personal issue. While she massaged my feet with oil she had a picture:

I see you digging a deep hole. The spade being used is ineffective with the big rocks that keep falling back in. It needed a grader to scoop out a big load of rocks and smaller stones. God is doing what you could not do for yourself.

This was a very encouraging word as I recognized that it referred to an emotional battle in my heart which only God could resolve for me.

At a service in September 2002 the NCMI leader Tyrone Daniel preached on the 'Abraham call' to leave country and family. I made a heart response of readiness to go and felt the power of God flood my whole being, instantly healing me of severe 'flu aches in every part of my body.

331

The New Covenant Fellowship Mantle Passed On

In 2000 Ray Oliver handed over the leadership of New Covenant Fellowship to his young successor Grant Crawford. When Grant made appointments to meet the team individually I told him about my heart for the nations.

Two years later in October 2002 I shared with him that I sensed the time was drawing near to fulfil the call. He responded instantly, "I have just the right opportunity to prepare you for this, Colleen" he said, picking up the phone on his desk. He dialled a number and had a quick chat while I sat mystified by the conversation I was overhearing. Putting the phone down Grant turned to me: "Craig and Collette Meyer are planning to go abroad for a month, and I've offered your services as 'overseer' of their flock. Well, you heard me tell Craig that you would be well able to do anything he asks you to do, and he is very happy for you to come down and help the church while he is away!" Amazed and humbled by Grant's trust in me, I planned my visit with a strong sense that God wanted me to focus on sharing with the congregation of a hundred and twenty believers the importance of developing intimate relationship with Him as Heavenly Father.

Early in 2003 Grant told me that I would be needed from 20th January to 20th February. I phoned Craig to tell him I was excited about the challenge and he sounded equally keen. My diary entry the following day read:

> *Lord, I am overwhelmed by the prospect of what is opening up right now, the door into the future and all that is waiting to happen <u>beyond</u> the <u>now</u> – the places you will send me, the people I will meet, the extension of ministry which will evolve as I trust in you, obeying your promptings and opening myself to Your Holy Spirit's presence and power.*
>
> *The years of waiting quietly as a servant, fulfilling tasks without seeking praise or attention have won your favour, Father. Now I am ready to move out with*

lessons of deep significance learned and a job faithfully done. The excitement in my spirit, Lord, is not of self-confidence as I face the challenge of standing in for Craig Meyer. It is clearly in utter dependence on you that I will grow. I recall the challenging moment on mission in Zimbabwe when my Bible and prepared notes were left with our luggage at camp and I was called on to preach without them. I sensed your anointing presence and preached the message led directly by your Holy Spirit, aware that this was a lesson in trusting you for the words to say as the disciple Stephen did before the Sanhedrin.

South City Church – Margate

Our annual NCF Family Camp was held at the coast over the weekend before I was due in Margate, and when camp broke at lunchtime on Sunday, a very dear friend Roy Lambert was waiting at the gate to take me to his and Daphne's new home at Amanzimtoti. This couple had become close friends in Roodepoort and it was so good to spend time catching up on news of the past few years.

The next morning, I drove down the coast and met Craig Meyer who took me straight to the home of his parents, Ken and Amor Meyer, who had offered to host me. They welcomed me warmly into their charming home, and over the next few days showed great interest in my testimony of life-changing encounters with God. The following day at the church office, Craig asked me to phone and introduce myself to all the home-group leaders before meeting them at their midweek meetings. Apart from that, he left no agenda, so when he and Colette left to catch their flight I was on my own with the Lord as my helper.

At the first Bible study I felt instant acceptance and appreciation from the group while sharing Scripture passages and my own experience of intimacy with God. I regard people's names as important to them and to God, so have developed the skill of memorising names as soon as I'm introduced. That night I put my memory to the test and surprised everyone in the large group by bidding them all goodnight by name.

Throughout the next four weeks I affirmed young and old at every home-group, sharing how my trust in God had deepened over the years through His faithfulness to keep His promises. Craig's Mum and Dad did not attend the meetings but enjoyed our relaxed conversations about the reality of my faith at home. Their warm hospitality was a gift to me and being only a short walk from the seashore, I revelled in being able to sit on the rocks and pray, or just marvel at the majesty of God's creation in the surging tides. My relationship with the South City family deepened very quickly and at my last Sunday morning service it was with real heartache that I bade them all farewell, fighting back tears as I drove away in my little blue Golf. Grant relayed to me a week later that Craig had phoned to say he was delighted with the favourable report about my ministry from his people, which really touched my heart.

Prophecies Unfold Abroad

On the NCF team I developed a close friendship with Jéan Seevaraj, a young man heading up the children's ministry. Jéan told me in confidence that having spent years of study and ministry as Youth Pastor in a church in the USA, he had begun to feel the call of God to plant a church in downtown Chicago. After seeking prayerful confirmation from the elders Jéan was released with their blessing and it was later agreed that I could go and support him for three months.

Having established a small fellowship in Chicago, Jéan returned to South Africa to renew his visa and we met over coffee to discuss practical details of my coming and set a date for my departure. Jéan flew back to the States expecting me to follow soon but plans came to a sudden, disappointing close when the world was rocked by news of the bombing of the Trade Centre Twin Towers. With the country in turmoil the door to his re-entry was closed and Jéan returned to Pietermaritzburg and his home church, NCF. In spite of that closed door we both believed God would call him to plant again and with hindsight it is fascinating to see that God was already laying His plans behind the veil.

During Jéan's absence I had befriended Nicola Hayes, a beautiful young musician in a group of young volunteers serving NCF church for a year. On his return, Jéan met Nicky in the youth group, they fell in love and it soon became clear that she was the girl God had chosen to fulfil His future plans. Within their first year of marriage Jean and Nicky felt called to plant a church and I knew that this was the couple I would be supporting. Delighting in the blessing of our friendship, we welcomed the New Year 2003 and prayed for God to reveal His plans for our future together. My life experience of trusting God implicitly was a great encouragement to this young couple starting out on the challenging journey of faith in marriage and in building the Kingdom of God.

Church Planters Revealed

During worship at a prayer meeting in early December 2003, Pastor Grant called Jéan and Nicky to the front. He explained that a few days before, he had invited them to pray about a ministry opportunity in England. Turning to them he asked, "Jéan and Nicky, do you have an answer concerning the church plant in Hove?"

Jéan replied, "Yes, Grant, we have prayed about it and feel God is calling us to Hove."

As I heard these words I felt a powerful surge of exuberant joy take my breath away, because I realized that I would be going to support them in the country of my ancestors!

The young couple were able to leave within the month on Nicky's British passport and I began the process of applying for an Ancestral Visa through my British granddad, Frederick Long, which would entitle me to work in the UK for four years. Locating and collecting all necessary legal documents, references and proof of arranged employment abroad for the Visa Application took nine months, during which time I packed all my possessions in cardboard boxes to await my return when the season was over.

Isabel Malan, a young friend from my African Enterprise days, came to stay with me at Burton Hall, eager to share with me a prophetic word from God she had received on her holiday:

> *Colleen, my daughter, your feet will be anointed by me wherever you put them, and you will spread the Good News.[63]*

God's Provision

In January 2004 God went before me in an unexpected way when I was asked to take on the salaried position as Receptionist in the NCF office. For the next nine months I earned enough to cover the cost of an air ticket to England before the year was out.

In May of that year while preparing for the UK visa, I attended a meeting at the Richmond Christian Fellowship where a visiting prophet of God, Kerry Southey, gave me an impacting word from the Lord. Without any knowledge of my unfolding plans, Kerry spoke a prophetic word that later proved to be of such accuracy and significance that it could only have come from God:

> *Plans, plans, plans... so many plans! Put her anywhere and she will not be bored, I promise you! You know, some people are like a Ferrari, but she is like one of those rocket ships that has just departed, and she has got more plans and more projects in her hands than she can handle. Everywhere you go you make plans, and you see strategically. God has given you an ability to see strategically; to look at things strategically; to see strategically; to work and then when you believe God, I*

---

[63] See Nahum 1:15: "Look there on the mountains, the feet of one him who brings good news, who proclaims peace!"

New Horizons Beckon

believe God has given you favour. I believe God has given you favour to cut red-tape. I believe He has given you favour for projects. I believe He has given favour for provision.

You can get anything out of anyone. You smile that sweet smile and they just fall on their backs like dummies. God has given you the ability to get plans going where people have said, "It is not possible," and you have said, "Well, let's talk about it." And when you talk about it, you tie them in fifty million knots and in the end they say, "I give up. Maybe it can be done."

And God says this will be a season of resources and birthing. This sounds very funny, but the Bible says the Egyptians, the midwives, were given their households. Midwives are the ladies who come alongside the people and help them bring things to birth. God says you are a lady who comes alongside people in projects; plans; feeding people; caring for needy people – and breaking through into land and property; and you cause them to have the ability to be there. God says, "Trust me, because the midwives are given their households," and God says, "Your household is on my agenda."

You are a 'party animal'! The older you get the more 'partier' you are! You love a good party and you are going to love good parties more. Parties are 'celebrations' as God does things – and you can really celebrate!

You are wise. God says He has given you wise council and wisdom. This sounds really funny but sometimes you are like a judge – like a 'legal judge'. You have to make judgement; you have to make right decisions; you have to discern what is true, what is fake and what is not. And God says you are going to have very good ability to see what is true – and you won't have to worry because He will guide and protect you.

What powerful confirmation in this word that I was indeed moving into God's plans and purposes! Nicky and Jéan had flown to the UK on the 28th December and with everything finally in place, I followed them nine months later to face the adventure of a lifetime!

A Victorious Send-Off

My memorable farewell to the NCF church took place on Sunday 4th October 2004, in the newly completed auditorium during worship when Pastor Grant Crawford called me to the front. He told the congregation of well over a thousand believers that I was about to leave for England to serve God there, and I shared briefly that God had been preparing me for years to take this step of obedience to His call. The elders gathered around to lay hands of commissioning on me while my son Justin prayed a deeply moving prayer of thanksgiving to God for my life and commitment.

Grant followed this with an intriguing announcement: "Will all those who have something for Colleen, please come forward?" From across the auditorium I stood amazed as a stream of two hundred friends begin to move toward me with personal love messages on notelets given out in secret by my daughter-in-law Mish. Sheryl Thornton-Dibb led the way carrying a beautiful bouquet of flowers picked from her garden, with a pair of warm gloves and woolly socks in a little gift bag. The flow of tears as I hugged each one was an emotional expression of our deep bonding over the years and the love-notes were tucked safely into Sheryl's handy gift bag.

Soon it was time to leave for the airport, and choked with emotion I began to walk down the aisle to the front door, bouquet in hand. An explosion of clapping and cheering broke out as dozens of mini streamers were tossed right across the church, forming a rainbow canopy of streamers over my head. In that moment I had the most awesome sense that I was a bride walking to meet her bridegroom, Jesus, and in my spirit I clearly heard God say, *"You will not be returning to this spiritual home."*

Justin, Mish and their little boys were outside waiting to drive me to Durban Airport where family members Stephen, Annie, sisters Lorna, Coral, Beth and Madeline had gathered to say goodbye. With my case checked in and last hugs exchanged I headed through Customs, turning for one last wave before finding a seat at the departure gate in a bubble of mixed emotions. Once aboard, when the passengers in my row were finally seated and we'd taken to the skies, I sat back in my aisle seat and relaxed, closing my eyes to reflect quietly on the overwhelming impact of my send-off. With meal trays cleared away, most passengers settled for the night, the lights were dimmed and a hush fell over our Economy class cabin. I took out the little bag of love-notes and read every message by the spotlight overhead, giving thanks to God for all the love expressed in them while tears flowed silently down my cheeks.

Riding High with Jesus

New Horizons Beckon

Adult Siblings

Eckersley siblings and spouses, 1970s

Mum and her girls on Tongaat Beach, 1980s

Enid and Doug Crankshaw, 2009

Sisters Lorna and Colleen, 2012

Sisters Beth, Madeline, Coral and Colleen, 2010

Riding High with Jesus

Sisters Coral, Madeline, Beth and Colleen (2010)

Colleen's brother Stanley Eckersley

6

A New Life in England

Touching down early the following morning at Heathrow Airport in England, there was a joyful reunion with Jéan and Nicky Seevaraj who had driven up from Hove to meet me. Feeling mentally and physically drained by the busy weeks of preparation, the emotional departure from family and church and little sleep on the flight, I recovered quietly in their flat at 55 Clarendon Villas, taking walks with Nicky to explore the local Hove area.

My Home Care Experience

Months before leaving I had registered with the South African agent of Cooksbridge Care Services in England to work as a live-in carer, and with some trepidation anticipated my interview within a week. Feeling utterly lost in the totally strange environment, I was grateful to Jéan and Nicky for driving me to the nearby town of Lewes where I met Kathy Murphy who registered me and explained the basic details of the training. Cathy Berlanger then took me through intensive cover of every legal aspect of Caring contained in a thick training manual, with questions to be answered at home within the month.

Unbeknown to me, Cooksbridge had been misinformed about the date of my arrival and as a result they had expected me a week earlier. Kath informed me that I was assigned to a client in

Ardingly Village from the very next day, which sent me into shock! I sent up an urgent cry to God: "Father, you know all things. *You* already knew this would happen, so I'll trust you to help me find my way there." Waiting at Lewes station for a train back to Hove as night was falling, I approached a young lady on the platform and discovered she was another Cooksbridge trainee. Sharing the same feeling of inadequacy enabled us to comfort and encourage one another as we chatted on the journey.

Facing the daunting prospect of finding my way to Ardingly, I asked Jéan to help me plan the train journey and was astonished at his replied: "Col, I am delivering mail for a security courier service in the very same area of East Sussex, so I can take you there." With immense gratitude I cried, "Oh God, how marvellous are your ways as you go before me to prepare the way!" Jéan offered to drop me at my client's door if I was willing to make an early start and my joy knew no bounds at this perfect answer to my prayer.

Prepared with a small case containing clothing, my Bible, mobile phone and personal possessions for the next three weeks, I was ready early the following morning. In very thick mist on the outskirts of Ardingly Village, it wasn't easy to locate my client's property because the wooden sign had fallen from the big tree at the entrance to her drive and was almost buried under fallen leaves. After searching the area for a while, by a small miracle Jéan spotted a hint of white between the leaves and when I brushed them aside, there was the signboard with the name of her property.

I was greeted at the back door of the cottage by the previous South African carer, Etta, waiting anxiously to show me the ropes so she could leave on holiday. Having just been warned by Etta that my client was very deaf, I felt quite apprehensive as I followed her upstairs to be shown the room I would use, and then to meet my client Martha in her room at the end of the passage. Back in the kitchen I was given a hasty explanation of the weekly routine and pointed in the direction of a pile of handwritten notes from

A New Life in England

previous carers. At precisely eleven o'clock a taxi arrived and Etta left, assuring me that I would soon be familiar with everything.

Feeling totally out of my depth, I stood in the middle of the kitchen and sent a quick prayer heavenward before glancing quickly through the notes. Putting the meat pie and vegetables Etta had prepared into the oven, I was ready promptly at one o'clock to take the tray up to Martha who appeared at first to be stern and intimidating. However, my heart reached out with compassion to the old lady when she confessed that her deafness made her feel vulnerable and nervous every time she was faced with a new carer. I was immediately put at my ease and tried my best to be sensitive to her every need.

Throughout the early days of isolation and silence due to Martha's severe deafness, I experienced loneliness more intense than I had ever known. Having had no time to buy airtime for my mobile phone, I felt completely cut off from everybody and found solace in sitting at my upstairs bedroom window, looking beyond the hedge to the tranquil scene of sheep grazing in lush green meadows. The vista stretching away to the distant hills of the gentle English countryside fringed by magnificent old oak trees brought a balm to my homesick heart as I repeated Psalm 23 to myself:

> *The Lord is my Shepherd,*
> *I shall not be in want.*
> *He makes me lie down in green pastures,*
> *he leads me beside quiet waters,*
> *he restores my soul.*
> *He guides me in paths of righteousness*
> *for his name's sake.*
> *Even though I walk through*
> *the valley of the shadow of death,*
> *I will fear no evil,*
> *for you are with me:*
> *your rod and your staff, they comfort me.*

You prepare a table before me
  in the presence of my enemies.
You anoint my head with oil;
  my cup overflows.
Surely goodness and love will follow me
  all the days of my life,
  and I will dwell in the house of the Lord for ever.

Music has always been an integral part of my life and the presenters of Classic FM provided welcome company in the kitchen with uplifting music on a small digital radio. In my bedroom I fed my soul with comfort and encouragement with beautiful worship CDs played on the treasured gift of a small portable CD player from my sister Coral. Daily I recorded my thoughts in the spiritual journal the elders at NCF had given me as a farewell gift, and pictured the precious faces of family and friends far away, often bringing out and re-reading the cluster of little love notes.

I found pleasure in wandering daily through Martha's small garden and apple orchard, listening to birdsong and picking delicious sweet apples from the laden trees before they were stung by fruit flies. Some I took indoors for eating and stewing but most were stored on shelves in the cool of the old garage, where they lasted for months.

Martha's only visitor in those three weeks was her daughter-in-law who came every Tuesday. I served tea and biscuits to the ladies in the study, and every week made tea for two gardeners at the back door, welcoming their company and a brief chat while they took their break. The only other face I saw at the house was the British Gas man who serviced the boiler, so I looked forward to my Thursday morning walk through the village to the farmers' market in the Village Hall. Martha's weekly order consisted of eggs, home-made marmalade and a Victoria sponge with the firm instruction, "Remember, no icing, just cranberry jam filling and a light dusting of icing sugar on top!" Grateful for friendly conversation with the ladies at their produce tables, I lingered

A New Life in England

awhile before making my last call at the homely bakery around the corner for a fresh loaf of wholewheat bread.

Although I couldn't make calls from my phone, I received loving text messages from a dear South African friend, Dot Mundy, who had emigrated to Guildford the year before. On my arrival in Hove I'd been deeply touched to find a 'Welcome' card from her waiting at Jéan and Nicky's home with a generous cash gift of twenty-five pounds. Now in my lonely bubble I was delighted to receive a call from Dot to say that she and her husband Hugo were coming down from Surrey to take me out during my two hours off on Sunday.

We drove to 'Wakehurst Place', the National Trust property nearby, enjoyed lunch in the restaurant and had a leisurely browse through the choice items in the shop before a wander around the beautiful gardens. On the dot of four o'clock they dropped me back in time to make Martha's tea, feeling uplifted and encouraged by the joy of contact and laughter with friends!

After three weeks I was excited at the prospect of a week's break with friend Pam Bebb and her family in Hangleton before my next assignment. I knew that my next client, Leah, lived in Hove, and hoped it might be possible to rearrange my afternoon hours off to attend church on Sunday morning or an evening home-group meeting. However, after agreeing to my request, my client changed her mind for no reason at the last minute and refused to let me go. Having heard from other carers that she was a very difficult person, I had determined to show her the love of Christ in all my daily tasks, but it was soon clear that she had a controlling spirit opposed to the Holy Spirit within me and nothing I did pleased her.

After three weeks of being criticized, verbally abused in the shops and on the street, the final straw that broke me came after a shopping trip to the supermarket. Leah rode her very heavy electric chair over the high curb with a severe jolt which caused the engine to cut out in the middle of the street and it would not start again. She began to shout accusingly that I hadn't charged it, which I knew I had, and her shouting continued so loudly that I was thrown into a panic and nearby residents were drawn to see what was happening. A couple of gentlemen came to my aid by lifting the immensely heavy chair on to the pavement, and searching frantically I found an emergency number on a small disc which I dialled on my phone. Sending up a desperate prayer for help, I was dismayed when the servicing mechanic who answered told me that he was miles away in Portsmouth. The only help he could offer was to tell me how to make the chair portable by releasing the motor with a small lever under the chair, which I did.

At the end of my emotional tether, I prayed for supernatural strength to push my client in the chair that was already a dead weight without two bags of shopping that included two large melons! After three blocks, at the top of her street, I was utterly exhausted and could go no farther so I sat her on a wall while I pushed the electric chair home and fetched the manual one. Once inside the flat I burst into tears of exhaustion and anger, which brought an unexpected softening in her attitude until my tears had dried. I phoned the Care Agency to tell them I'd had enough and was promised a replacement where I would be happy. True to their word, my next client, after a few days' rest, was the most gracious lady in Mayfield village, whose kindness was balm to my battered emotions.

'Mrs T', as she was affectionately called, was a lady of absolute gentility and warmth. She showed appreciation of everything I did for her and admired my courage in leaving all my family in South Africa to serve God in England. During our relaxed evenings in the lounge after supper, she would often ask my opinion or interpretation of Bible passages which puzzled her, saying that my answers helped to expand her understanding of the Scriptures. Our days were filled with mutual delight and I spent four happy weeks with Mrs T, exploring the village shops and integrating into the friendly congregation of Colkins Mill Baptist Church. At the village library I was able to use computers to send and receive emails that kept me wonderfully in touch with my family and friends abroad. When Mrs T's children and

A New Life in England

grandchildren gathered to celebrate her ninetieth birthday, I was made to feel welcome as one of the family.

I left Mrs T to spend my two-week break celebrating Christmas with Pam, James and Heather Bebb before returning to Mayfield for another two weeks. After my season of five months as a carer, one day while busy about my chores I felt God drop this clear word into my heart:

You can stop caring now. Go home and dispose of all those things you have boxed up, because you will not be returning to the old. I am taking you on to new things.

Confident that I had heard God's voice correctly, I booked a flight home in January 2005 to obey his instruction.

Release from Possessions

At the time of leaving South Africa I'd had no idea how long I would be in the UK so all my possessions were stored in cardboard boxes at Justin's home in Pietermaritzburg. Now God was confirming that a completely new season was opening up for me, a chapter of unknown challenges with the promise of His fresh supply as I moved forward in childlike trust. So I flew home, gave away furniture, opened my boxes and invited my children to take what they needed. Personal items including pictures, diaries and photo albums remained with Justin, and the balance was donated to NCF church for an auction sale to raise funds for the new auditorium.

At the end of that visit I returned to England feeling a release from all material possessions to follow God's plan abroad. Mrs T had warmly invited me to visit her on my return as her guest and I looked forward eagerly to seeing her again. However, it was not to be. On the coach journey from Gatwick Airport I received a phone call from Cooksbridge Care Agency with sad news that Mrs T had died from a heart attack a few days before and her funeral had already taken place. My sense of loss was so deep I couldn't hold back my tears as the coach journeyed on to Hove.

My Homes in England

Knowing that moving out of care work I would need to find private accommodation now, I had asked Jéan and Nicky to look out for a suitable place for me. In my absence they had found a lovely double bedroom to rent in a private home in Wilbury Villas, Hove. Being on the third floor, the view was straight into the green foliage of trees where birds flew in and out. Other lodgers I befriended in the house were Leandro Santos, a Christian working lad from Brazil, and a young Japanese student, Kyoko, studying English at one of the language schools in the city. Kyoko and I became close friends and after sharing my Christian faith with her, she accepted Jesus as her personal Saviour before returning home to Japan.

I was content in my spacious room with a 'No Visitors' rule for eight months, and then began to yearn for an affordable place of my own no matter how small, where I could entertain friends. Within days of praying, I was on my daily walk to the bus, past business premises, when suddenly my eyes were drawn to an untidy, handwritten advertisement pasted on the window for a bedsit in Hove Park Villas. With a quickening sense in my spirit of divine leading, I went straight in to enquire about the rental. The owner answered my eager queries with a strange abruptness that surprised me, but he agreed that I could view it after the weekend. My heart sang when I saw that it had everything I could have wished for, a kitchenette and private ablutions and a spacious first floor patio overlooking the gardens of terraced homes. The bonus was its proximity to Hove Station and a bus route, and within weeks I was overjoyed to move into my own personal space. For five years I enjoyed the company of a variety of wild birds – sparrows, robin redbreasts, starlings, blackbirds, magpies, crows, herring gulls – and even a visiting grey squirrel. My great joy was being able to open the kitchen door in the early hours of a spring or summer morning to listen to the dawn chorus of melodious birdcalls, and later to sit in the cool breeze on the patio and drink in the beauty of nature around me.

Finding Work

To supplement my part-time salary at the mission I scanned advertisements and began to apply for a variety of jobs including Classroom Assistant in local schools, Receptionist with a legal firm and the YMCA charity, 'Tesco' supermarket Shelf Packer, coffee house Supervisor and Home Cleaner – but nothing opened up. By word of mouth I met a very kind lady whose elderly husband needed someone to keep him company on occasion when she went out. But this situation didn't offer sufficient income so she referred me to a gentleman who was looking for a companion during his frequent visits from abroad.

On meeting me the elderly gentleman was surprised to find a lady of mature age, but later told me that it was my radiant smile that made him decide to take me on! Over the next two days our conversations covered many topics and gave me opportunity to share my Christian faith which he found intriguing as he had Jewish roots. At first he was charming but it soon became apparent that he had a controlling spirit which became intolerant and aggressive if I expressed any opinion contrary to his. After two days he flew into a sudden rage at something I said, told me to pack my things and leave immediately. In silence he drove me to my bedsit door, placed my case on the pavement and handed me the carer's fee. Then to my surprise he leaned forward to hug me and said, "I'm sorry, Colleen," before driving off, leaving me wondering... did he regret his impetuous decision? Sad as I was to be dismissed so abruptly, I felt relief at being set free from his dominating spirit and to show that I bore no offence, wrote a letter to assure him of God's love and encouraged him to seek the God of his forefathers for himself.

A Door Opens at Last

Spotting a small advert in the 'Friday Ads' paper for a Carer in a group of rest homes, I applied in the hope that I might be granted Sundays off to assist at our church services. On the last day of May 2005 I had an interview with the owner who said she couldn't make an exception for me, but offered a different job instead, as Activities Coordinator, which would enable me to have Sundays off. I began work on 6th June having given her my assurance that I would never "impose" my faith on residents. However, as I made myself known to the residents, they soon picked up on my South African accent and asked how I could leave all my family to come to the UK alone. Many were intrigued by my decision to put Jesus first in my life with wholehearted commitment to serve God wherever He called me, and their interest brought my Christian faith into focus very naturally. I do not believe that I ever imposed my faith on any residents, but there were several Christians who identified with my faith and asked me to pray for them which I did gladly.

I spent quality time engaging residents individually in stimulating conversation on many topics, played Scrabble with two individuals and engaged a few residents in group activities in three Homes, but this wasn't following the book of rules for Activity Co-ordinators. As the months passed I became aware of a definite spirit of opposition rising, when the owner called me out on three occasions to tell me that I had been reported for "talking religion" to residents (which could only have been one of the staff).

After a year the situation culminated in a most disturbing barrage of intimidating false accusations from the owner and one of the matrons, with no opportunity to defend myself. I discerned spiritually that the motive behind the intimidating attack was to frighten me into resigning and I left work feeling emotionally battered. That evening I shared the experience with my church group and simply asked them to pray for God's peace to be restored to me. One of the believers told me that while praying she

A New Life in England

was surprised to have the words *"Brighton and Hove City Mission"* drop into her mind. She was mystified, knowing nothing of such a mission but I sensed it was a word from God for me, so thanked her for telling me and looked forward to getting home to do a web search on my computer.

Opening up the Brighton and Hove City Mission website with eager anticipation, I read that missioners had been caring for the community and sharing the Gospel in the city since Victorian times. Next morning, I phoned the co-ordinator, Tony Smith, and shared my testimony of how God had called me to England. I told him I was in a job that I sensed was about to close and enquired if there might be a place for me at the City Mission. Tony was intrigued to hear my story of faith and invited me to meet him at the mission headquarters in Brighton.

One afternoon after work I explored the unfamiliar bus route along London Road to Preston Circus, located the office in Stanley Road and spent a delightful hour with Tony exchanging testimonies of God's calling and leading into His purposes. I heard about the two fruitful Christian ministries already in operation at the City Mission – a children's work through school assemblies and clubs, and ministry to people in crisis through a food bank where referred clients can receive food, bedding, basic appliances and spiritual counsel. He added that there was no outreach to elderly residents in rest homes, but for some time he and the trustees had been praying for God to send someone to develop this aspect. As we talked, Tony and I had the tingling sense that I might be part of God's unfolding plan. My testimony was circulated to all the trustees and at one of their meetings the chairman, John Prideaux, spoke words that were music to my ears: "Colleen, we are all in agreement that God has sent you to us. You are the answer to our prayers."

New Doors of Ministry Open Up to Me

With a light heart I resigned as Activities Co-ordinator and in August 2006 accepted a part-time position as Rest Home Team

Leader. Before starting work, I enjoyed a wonderful ten-day holiday in the south of Wales with friends and came back eager to begin Christian ministry with the Brighton and Hove City Mission.

Using the local phone book, I contacted all listed rest homes to ask permission from managers to hold short non-denominational services in the communal lounge for their residents. Delighted to find favour with two, I began to meet once a month with residents who wished to participate and it wasn't long before other homes opened their doors when I broadened my search for venues. It was quickly apparent that many Christians deeply miss being able to attend church. They appreciate singing well-known hymns from large-print sheets and enjoy the short encouraging messages of God's love that bring hope to their hearts. Over the months God has drawn alongside me a band of deeply committed men and women to share in this rewarding ministry of personal affirmation of the elderly with God's love.

My part-time salary just covered my monthly bedsit rental so I began to look for a supplementary means of income. At the mission food bank I had freedom to take 'out of date' donations that by law could not be given out to clients, and with childlike gratitude I saw this as God's unique provision. Chuckling one day at His bountiful supply I said, "Lord, I feel like the prophet Elijah in the Old Testament being fed by the ravens."

Within eight months the trustees extended my ministry hours to four days a week and with the increased volunteer team, the number of homes visited increased to twenty-five. Sadly, some rest homes had to close but in time were replaced by others. In addition to this ministry I have had the privilege of speaking at ladies' mid-week meetings in several local churches. On these occasions I take the opportunity to challenge and encourage believers to deepen their relationship with God the Father, through His Son Jesus in order to hear His voice more clearly.

Being bonded by a strong spirit of unity with the vibrant team at the Brighton and Hove City Mission has been a great blessing, with prayer the firm foundation on which all our ministries are based. We've all faced significant personal challenges

A New Life in England

through the years, and sharing my God-given gift of encouragement with the team has been a great joy. In return the love and prayer support of the mission family has been immeasurable, especially when my second son Stephen was tragically killed in South Africa.

Devastating Loss of a Son

I had already booked a flight home for February 2008 when on 13th December 2007 I had a deeply distressing call from my son Andy to say that his forty-three-year-old brother Stephen was missing. Steve had left his place of work in a cheerful mood the afternoon before but hadn't returned home or been seen by anyone since. His partner Annie set up a search at the police stations, hospitals and mortuaries in the area with no success.

After a week of desperate searching and repeat visits, Annie was given the tip-off at a police station that the body of an unidentified young white male had been brought in on 12th before being taken to a mortuary. Following this police lead, she returned to the mortuary where she'd been treated before with callous indifference by the reception desk staff. This time she was helped by a compassionate worker to identify our beloved Steve, who had been there since his death the week before. He had been hit and killed by a passenger bus speeding through the terminus and as his mobile phone, the only means of identification, had been taken by the police, he'd been labelled "Unidentified". I received a call from my family with the agonizing news of Steve's death and cried to God with groans of grief too deep for words. My booking agents arranged an immediate cancellation of my reserved flight, making it possible to fly home to South Africa the following day.

Being so close to Christmas, Steve's partner Annie had made speedy arrangements for a beautiful Memorial Service for Steve at the Mobeni Crematorium on 23rd December which some of our nearby family – Andy and Lynne, Justin and I – could attend with friends and nursing staff from Prince Mshiyeni Hospital where Annie worked. The service took the form of Scripture readings, poetry, touching tributes to Steve in song, and personal expressions of love from his friends of all races. As Steve's mother I gave thanks to God for my precious son's life and special qualities, concluding with the comforting fact that as Christians our family was drawing comfort in our grief from knowing that he was now at rest in the presence of God.

In respect of the tradition of their many African friends who would be paying their last respects to Steve, Annie had arranged to have Steve's coffin left open. On hearing this I wasn't sure that I'd be able to cope emotionally, but as I entered the chapel I felt the deep peace of God's presence fill my heart and I was able to look upon Steve's beautiful face already in eternal sleep, before kissing his forehead in fond farewell. Following this moving ceremony, close friends who had loved Stephen dearly since school days invited us to join in a sharing of intimate memories over a finger lunch at their home.

On 27th December 2007, when siblings Murray and Shelley with her family arrived from the Eastern Cape, we held an intimate family Thanksgiving Service with close friends at NCF church in Pietermaritzburg. In moving tributes to Stephen each of his siblings and I brought contributions in word, song and Scripture that celebrated his life, his character and his creative gifting. We were immensely grateful to the leadership of NCF for opening the venue to us; to Paula who provided beautiful arrangements of roses from her garden; and to friends who served refreshments. In the midst of our painful loss we rejoiced in the certainty that Steve was already safe in the presence of his Heavenly Father, together with his earthly dad and other members of our family who had gone before.

While in South Africa, I received the devastating news of the death of Jéan and Nicky Seevaraj's little three-year-old son Joseph six weeks after Steve, so my return to England on 30th January 2008 was to bring comfort to his broken-hearted young parents. Joe's tragic death due to negligence on the part of an after-hours doctor at the local Royal Sussex Hospital prompted an inquest in May, extending their anguish for months. Over the years that have followed our shared loss, Jéan, Nicky and I have been brought incredibly close in our journey, drawing together on the comfort of our Heavenly Father.

My Visits Home to South Africa

From the time I moved to the UK, I have managed to save for flights home to visit my family for five to six weeks every year, taking advantage of the City Mission closure between Christmas and New Year. My leave every year has taken on the nature of a travelling holiday as I cross the country to spend time with all my children and siblings, slipping quietly into their family routines and enjoying school holidays with grandchildren when possible.

In 2009 a significant part of my visit was spent with Steve's grieving partner Annie, visiting places where he had spent his boyhood years. As I described our family life to her and shared stories of Steve's joys and personal struggles through his early years, the pain of our shared loss drew our hearts very close and healing began deep inside as I bathed her with love and understanding.

On my return to England I became aware that in my own heart the raw agony of grief was being lifted by a gentle work of the Holy Spirit. I continued to comfort Annie in her devastating loss through long emails, texts and phone calls. Envisioning her with the new things God would open up for her, I was able to encourage her to listen for His whispers of direction at all times. It was deeply moving for me to experience the precious mother and daughter bond growing between us, and to see the expanding work of the Holy Spirit in Annie as she grew close to all Steve's siblings and their children.

In the months following Stephen's death I felt an emotional compulsion I couldn't express in words, to take all my family photos back to England with me. Spreading the sizeable collection inside my large suitcase I knew the load would be overweight and expected to pay some excess, but was not prepared for the shocking amount of R800 quoted at the airline cashier's window. I burst into uncontrollable sobs, explaining that my son had recently been killed and I needed to have my family photos with me. She referred to her supervisor who kindly reduced the fee to R500, so leaving my case with sister Coral who had come to look for me, I ran to the ATM and drew the amount from my savings account. With the case finally dispatched at the check-in counter I joined my sisters at the café, but feeling completely drained emotionally, I sat as if in a bubble listening to the conversation around me but unable to take part. Once on board I relaxed, knowing my treasured photos were in the luggage hold. The following day an indescribable joy welled up in me when I opened my case and unpacked the photographs in my bedsit, confirming it was well worth the cost to have all my loved ones with me.

Manchester Visit

In July 2008 I fulfilled the dream that I had held since my first visit to England, of visiting Manchester, the city of our Eckersley ancestors. Travelling up by train, I was hosted by an associate's friend Rebekah, in her Broughton flat. In the Greater Manchester County Record Office, I spent hours searching through the electronic storage tapes for records of family births, marriages and baptisms in Manchester Cathedral. Rewarded with some records, I printed extra copies for siblings and then spent hours exploring the vast city on foot.

On my walk to the fascinating Museum of Science and Industry a thrilling surprise awaited me when I rounded the corner on the High Street. A gap appeared suddenly in the high brick wall and, peering through, I discovered to my delight that just below me was the Bridgewater Canal, with a husband and wife on their prettily decorated narrowboat waiting at the lock for the water level to rise. Fascinated by the process I had often seen on telly but not in reality, I made my way down the steps to chat to them until they glided quietly on upstream.

Browsing the busy streets between tall buildings, another surprise awaited when I came face to face with the huge

Manchester Wheel and decided I must brave the rather unnerving experience on my own. From the dizzy height, with great caution so as not to rock my pod, I captured stunning pictures of the cathedral and the 360 degree views of the city before taking the Metro Rail out to the town of Bury to explore the massive, sprawling country market there. I meandered at leisure for hours through the vegetable and fruit stalls, the bakery, the fish market, and other stalls selling every conceivable item of clothing, household appliances, jewellery and trinkets.

At Shude Hill Records Office I enquired about possible Irish ancestral records for two of George Eckersley's children but had no success. The next day, over on Salford Quays, while exploring the waterways, I met a gentleman who recommended that I visit the War Museum, which was very interesting. Relaxing together in sunshine on the broad steps of the Lowry Art Centre, he mentioned that he was waiting for the theatre doors to open for the play 'Crown Matrimonial' with famous British cast. I made a snap decision and bought one of the last tickets for the thoroughly enjoyable show. The following day I caught the train back to Hove feeling overjoyed with all the experiences that has been tucked into my adventure in Manchester.

Divine Direction

Following my application to extend my Ancestral Visa by another year, in August 2008 my passport was returned to me by the Immigration Department with the stamp granting a further *five* years! This confirmed for me that the season of serving God in the UK wasn't over yet, and doors opened to many exciting and interesting opportunities in the years that lay ahead.

At this time a word from friend Candice Sterley was, *"Be encouraged in this next five-year chapter of your life. Be excited and expectant for God to unfold his plans."* Guy Veltman from NCF visited our church in November, and his prophetic word to me was, *"I see you having many, many seeds waiting to be planted – different kinds, different seasons, for a much bigger harvest."*

Riding High with Jesus

His friend Stuart's word was, *"I see you as a well-established tree with spreading branches. Many will come for shelter, wisdom and love in time of need."*

Mission to Romania

In June 2009 I accompanied our Pastor Jéan Seevaraj, Steve and Candice Sterley, and Margie Fforde from South City Church, on a mission trip to bless the congregation of 'Filadelfia Church' in Iasi[64], the old capital of Romania. Margie, who had previously been part of the Filadelfia Church, told us that three Christian families with little children were facing severe financial problems through unemployment and illness. So we pooled our resources and bought a generous selection of baby food, toiletries and other essential items to take to them.

The flight from Heathrow took under three hours, and touching down in Budapest we transferred to an historic ex-wartime De Havilland of the Hungarian Airlines with a young cabin attendant who was so tall and muscular that she would have done well in a Bond movie! At the Romanian airport, passing through the small arrival hall and simple Customs check was like stepping back in time. Pastor David Serediuk was waiting with warm hugs of welcome and drove us to the church house, our spacious base for five days. A large central room served as dining room / lounge and temporary bedroom for our men, while the ladies shared two double bedrooms. At the back of the house David had worked hard in poor soil to develop a very productive vegetable garden, and a flourishing grapevine covered a broad trellis above the front patio, creating a delightfully shady place to sit during hot sunny days.

The following morning, I was treated to a seventy-third birthday celebration with fancy chocolate cake at a street café, before David and his wife Stratica took us on a walking tour of the sprawling city of Iasi. Its spacious parks, passing trams, huge

---

[64] Yash

Orthodox churches, the ornate palace of King Stephen and lots of official-looking buildings made it a very interesting walk where the old spirit of Communist days could still be felt.

That evening we felt the frustration of a language barrier, being unable to communicate with thirty of the Filadelfia fellowship who couldn't speak any English. However, once the younger ones arrived and interpreted for their parents, the ice was broken and everyone relaxed.

After worship we shared a little about ourselves, with David as interpreter. I spoke of my intimate relationship with God and His faithfulness throughout my life since I was a girl, sustaining me through all of life's challenges and painful losses. David expressed deep respect and admiration for my energy and enthusiasm, explaining that in Romanian culture people my age would be regarded as 'old' and confined to home. After he had led them in singing 'Happy Birthday' I thanked them and paid tribute to *Jesus* who is the source of my joy and strength.

Visiting the local peasant market on foot, Candice and I bought fresh-cut lavender and replenished the supply of delicious sweet cherries which 'Mother' Stratika had placed in the church house for us. On the walk back along the dusty road to the house, we noted a stark contrast between extremely old, derelict hovels and new dwellings standing side by side, which reminded me of other communities I'd seen in Israel, Cyprus, Turkey, South Africa and East Germany.

We visited the three Christian families with babies and blessed them with the food and clothing we had brought. Two lived in large, grey, depressing concrete blocks of flats built during the Communist era, which they had transformed on the inside into lovely homes. But the stairwells were in a shocking state and the heavy, depressed spirit from the past still lingered over the downtrodden neighbourhood. The third family lived in a small, humble home in the small village of Erbiceni, several miles out of Iasi. Here we were touched by their generosity in providing a lunch of 'borscht', the tasty traditional Romanian soup, with meatballs and spaghetti followed by home-grown chicken roasted over an open fire, potato chips and cabbage salad. It was an emotionally moving moment when Jéan presented baby Stefan with the baby buggy which his own precious little son Joseph had used up to the time of his death.

We accepted David's invitation to take a long drive to the mountains of Moldova, past scenes which made us feel that time had truly stood still here – peasants weeding crops in their fields, others walking home in the heat of day with hoes over their shoulders or clip-clopping along the road in horse-drawn carts. Once we reached the foothills of the mountain range between Romania and Moldova, views of the majestic slopes and the huge lake were breathtaking. Architecture in buildings began to reflect the distinctive style of Swiss chalets, and all along the road we passed little shrines containing icons and statues of various religious saints. A strong-flowing mountain stream flowed through the deep gorge between craggy slopes where we stopped at rows of wooden stalls selling locally made clothing and souvenirs of all kinds. On the bank of the huge lake we laid a rug and enjoyed our delicious packed lunch followed by a quick boat ride, before being driven to see the impressive hydroelectric dam on the way home.

By the time we met for Sunday worship we all felt closely bonded as God's family and enjoyed worship in both languages led by Pastor David's daughter Gabita and her three brothers, Eddie on keyboard, Robert on guitar and Florin on drums. After a quick lunch of Stratica's famous borscht we picked up our luggage at the house and headed for the airport, leaving Romania feeling blessed by the spirit of resilience and faith we found in our Christian brothers and sisters living under difficult circumstances, and filled with gratitude for the experience of sharing with these warm, generous folk.

My Visit to Deal in Kent

In September 2009 I made my first train journey to Deal in Kent to spend a long weekend with Denise Hall, our British-born cousin on the Eckersley side. Although we'd not met before, she

A New Life in England

looked so like her mum, Joyce Hall, that I had no difficulty in recognizing her as the train pulled into the station. The Bank Holiday weekend was spent relaxing in her cosy apartment and exploring the enchanting town, which Denise was eager to show me, with its picturesque waterfront buildings, weathered fishing boats, nets and lobster cages pulled up high on the shingle.

For eight years Denise had done in-depth ancestry research and was eager to share the wealth of information spanning four generations that she had gleaned. Starting at Walmer Castle on the seafront she was also keen to show me historical landmarks of Deal, so we walked up the hill from the town to the 'Memorial to WW2 Airmen' in the meadow from which they had taken off in their Spitfires during the War. Taking a footpath down the hill past a stone church, we arrived at the seafront pub where we found a very young baby hedgehog. Denise had rescued other endangered hedgehog babies so took it home to feed and keep warm but sadly it had died by morning.

On Sunday I was treated to a delightful 'olde worlde' concert on the village green by the local brass band, from their Commemoration Bandstand built to honour the lives of eleven Royal Marine band members killed in an IRA bombing of their barracks twenty years before. In full sunshine people relaxed in deckchairs to listen to the band while children played on the lawn, and strollers passed by licking ice cream cones. In the Marine Rescue Boathouse, open to the public, I was impressed by the enormous size and capabilities of the new RNLI rescue boat, and the massive tractor used to winch it up the beach after every rescue mission.

An unexpected highlight of the day was standing at the end of the pier to watch the courageous young quadriplegic Hilary Lister sail past in her tiny craft on the last leg of her solo voyage around the British Isles. I found it inconceivable that she controlled her boat by blowing into straws, and standing alongside her friends from Whitstable Sailing Club, I felt a surge of emotion as she manoeuvred her little craft close in to acknowledge the cheers of all her well-wishers before heading out into deep water on the final lap to her destination at Dover.

Hidden Talent Discovered

After years of enjoying the lovely view of my neighbours' gardens from my bedsit patio, one day in 2009 I felt a strong prompting to sketch the scene before me. Impressed by the result, my friend Audrey bought me a set of paints for my birthday so I photocopied my pencil drawing on to thicker paper and completed a watercolour painting over a few weeks with a sense of real achievement.

One day my architect neighbour David Kemp looked over the low wall between us and asked what I was painting. Feeling shy about my first effort I was reluctant to show him but he insisted, and his reaction took me completely by surprise. Holding my painting up to the scene before him he exclaimed, "This is excellent, Colleen. You have captured the perspective in the terraced houses perfectly." Such praise coming from a professional architect was encouraging and the positive reaction from friends confirmed that I was discovering a latent gift that needed to be developed. The exciting urge to paint continued and as other pictures followed I was filled with a sense of wonder at the results.

Two years earlier I had met and developed a close friendship with Mary Taylor, a faithful supporter of the City Mission. When Mary saw my paintings she was so impressed that she decided to give me a gift of a small chest of drawers full of sketchbooks, Reeves paintbrushes, coloured paper and a calligraphy set she had always hoped to use. When I hesitated to accept this generous gift, she said, "Please take them, Colleen. Arthritis has crippled my finger joints and I can't use them anymore, so I would like you to have these and make good use of them." I was grateful beyond words for her gift and Mary was glad to find someone who would appreciate them.

A year after Steve's death my prayer of commitment to building God's Kingdom had been, "This year, Lord, I trust you

A New Life in England

will lift me above the heaviness of grief to start a new season with you – in my personal life, my ministry and my church." One step in that direction took place on Sunday, 4th January 2009, when I was inducted as Deacon at South City Church. Standing alone on the penthouse balcony of the Princes Marine Hotel, bathed in brilliant sunshine under a clear blue sky, I looked down at the waves breaking gently on the pebble beach and my heart surged with an overwhelming sense of God's love and grace. He had answered my prayer and set my heart free with his gift of unspeakable joy in the knowledge that Steve was safe in the presence of His Saviour.

UK Residency or Not?

Having been granted the extension on my UK visa to ten years, I qualified to apply for 'Indefinite Leave to Remain' or 'Residency'. Once I began to consider seriously the possibility of reducing my working hours and claiming Housing Benefit, the prospect of spending more time painting and preparing my memoirs for publication was most appealing. However, news of the sudden death of our beloved sister-in-law Joy Eckersley on 18th September 2009 threw me into emotional confusion. I felt an ache of homesickness for my family which triggered uncertainty about wanting to stay in Britain.

In addition, I considered my advanced years, my limited financial status and the strong possibility that I might be refused residency and would forfeit the application fee of £820. For three months I was in prayerful unrest. If I applied, would my family feel I was abandoning them forever? Had the suggestion of residency been prompted by the Lord, or was it just my own idea? The only way to peace was by committing the decision to prayer: "Lord, please give me the direction I need for the future. I know you've always done that but I just need to put my doubts into words."

Until the answer came I would have to be satisfied with the time I had to paint and write my story. With that act of submission, a settling peace came upon my heart and I soon felt prompted to make enquiries about the conditions of residency. Through the Brighton Community Centre I made an appointment and put some questions to a helpful solicitor, Martin Penrose. He explained that Immigration laws were under review and subject to change so advised me to decide without delay. Giving me the latest application forms, he offered to courier them to London if I chose to go ahead, which I saw as a clear answer to prayer.

Taking up his offer, I prayed, "Lord God, you know the plans you have for me, so please would you direct the Immigration authorities by your Holy Spirit to make the right decision in accordance with your will." Five months later I was called back to the Brighton office to receive my passport stamped with "INDEFINITE LEAVE TO REMAIN" which I saw as proof that God had more for me to do in the UK. My response was, "Lord God, how grateful I am to have your leading in my life!"

Midway through 2009 I was invited to lead monthly services at the sheltered accommodation complex 'Saxon Court' in Hove. Within the group of residents was an ex-missionary who was moving to the north; when she heard I was looking for a flat, she invited me to take whatever furniture and possessions I could use from her flat after she had gone! Incredibly gratefully for this amazing gift, I marked several pieces for collection, once again conscious of God's awesome provision in going before me to meet my every need before I had even asked.

Standing at the Brighton Station bus stop one day I met a bright, outgoing twenty-year-old Italian lad, Daniele, who had arrived in Brighton a couple of days ago to look for temporary work. He was being hosted by an Italian family very close to my bedsit, and sensing he was lonely, I invited him to come home with me for coffee which he accepted gladly. Enjoying the sunshine on my patio he told me about his family in Italy and his hope of finding work. Knowing he wasn't familiar with the area, I walked him to his hosts' home and he was surprised to discover how close they were. He asked if he might come again and during several visits I was able to share the reality of my faith in God which

A New Life in England

brought me to England. I corrected his view that 'being good' qualifies us for heaven, and explained that it is rather by faith in Jesus that we are saved. After several days Daniele told me with disappointment that he'd decided to return home because he hadn't found work. I wished him well and he left with grateful thanks and a warm hug. Reflecting on our meeting I saw it as one of God's appointments set up by Him to enable me to share the good news of His intimate love with those who don't know Him.

The morning after my return from South Africa in 2010, I set out to catch a bus to the mission office, eager to see my colleagues again. Descending the flight of steps at Hove Station, my shoulder bag slipped forward causing me to lose balance. I took a serious somersault tumble forward, bruising both shins severely on the metal edging and landed on my back with legs in the air, thankfully wearing trousers. While a stream of commuters side-stepped hurriedly past on their way to work, a young African lad stopped and helped me to my feet. In agony I limped slowly to the bus stop and spent the day quietly at the office recovering from the shock. Thankfully, apart from suffering a pounding headache for six weeks and severe bruising, MRI scans and tests revealed no bones broken and no sign of lasting damage.

Surprise Around the Corner

After living in absolute contentment in my bedsit for five years I began to long for space to host guests and decided to look for a two-bedroom flat. I put my name down on the waiting lists of two charities – Lions Housing Trust and Sussex Housing Trust – and at precisely the same time was surprised by a visit from my neighbour David Kemp and his brother Chris. They came to ask if I would consider becoming companion to their eighty-three-year-old mother who had taken a fall. The shock had affected her short-term memory so severely, they felt she couldn't cope on her own any longer. I considered their request prayerfully, mindful that as well as helping Rosemarie to retain her independence the offer of free accommodation would give me the means to start saving.

David took me to meet his Mum and when I felt she had accepted me, we agreed to a trial period. Two weeks later, in March 2010, I moved into her small guest room with a suitcase of essentials, and every afternoon after work called at my bedsit to collect what I needed for the following day. With the trial period over I moved my personal possessions into the large double bedroom and put my furniture into storage.

One day Rosemarie announced, "If you live here, one of the things you're expected to do is to help with polishing the household silver!" So on the Bank Holiday I came downstairs to find all the silverware waiting on the trolley in the kitchen with two pairs of old evening gloves, two plastic aprons and a basket of rags! Putting on our 'fancy dress', we settled to the job, and how I wished someone had been there to take a photo of us looking like housemaids from the television programme 'Upstairs and Downstairs'! I understood the challenging adjustment it was for the old lady to share her space after living on her own for some years, and my caring concern for her and joyful spirit eventually won her over into a relationship of warm appreciation and even affection.

My Testimony DVD is Made

In 2010 the Brighton and Hove City Mission received a financial gift to develop a Media Department. Our director, Tony Smith, decided to use my testimony as the subject of the first nine-minute DVD, so I prepared a brief script and feeling surprisingly nervous began filming. Having the large camera lens literally 'in my face' was unnerving, and I needed an occasional pause to compose myself when sharing the emotionally poignant parts of my story. We took the camera on to the street and into churches to collect scenes that might be of use but I drew the line at using British ambulances in what was clearly a South African story. I persuaded the team to delay the release of the DVD until the New

Year so I could take authentic video footage on my visit home to South Africa.

I bought a small video camera and returned in February 2011 with suitable material, thrilled to be given the opportunity to help Josh van Ness edit sections of the video. Original background piano music composed by Josh was added, with an African-style introduction on guitar and drums by Alan and Luana Hall. The DVD was ready for release in June and the finished product, though not perfect, proved to be a powerful tribute to God's faithfulness, combining good teamwork in photography and editing. As the DVD was distributed far and wide, many responses confirmed that it was achieving its purpose as an encouragement to believers and an invitation to unbelievers to trust God and submit to the Lordship of Jesus as Saviour.

Shoreham Free Church

In September 2011 Ed Squires, a gentleman from Shoreham Free Church, invited me to share more of my story at their Sunday evening meeting with their pastor, Tim Buckley, and a group of friendly members of the congregation.

The evening spent in warm fellowship with these believers was a delight and an encouragement to me.

Holland Road Men's Breakfast Talk

I felt honoured by Holland Road Baptist Church to be the first lady invited to address the men at their Men's Breakfast. Stephen Jackson hosted the meeting and during our time of prayer with other leaders, he and I sensed that God was going to use my message to bless men significantly, which seemed to be confirmed by a mysterious incident. While guests settled around their tables, Steve and I prayed quietly with heads bowed. Suddenly, without cause or warning, the heavy overhead screen behind us came crashing down on to our table, narrowly missing Steve's head and spilling my glass of orange juice over everything! Sensing demonic activity intended to disrupt the meeting, we thanked God for His Holy Spirit's presence and protection, mopped up the spilt liquid without fuss and continued with the programme.

The message God had given me challenged the men of all ages to develop a deeper personal relationship with Him, which would enrich all aspects of their lives, especially marriages and other relationships. In touching on sensitive issues which are not easily raised among men, I urged them to seek counsel and healing from past hurts including physical, sexual or emotional abuse, and to reach out for deliverance from any addictions so they could move into the future free and unhindered. It was a great joy and honour to witness how the Holy Spirit encouraged these brothers in the Lord, many of whom came to thank me personally afterwards.

Brighton Passion Plays

In 2010 a large group of Christians from several churches met to plan the first Easter Passion Play to be held in Brighton. Professional actor James Burke-Dunsmore who plays the part of Christ in the annual 'Wintershall' productions in Surrey, wrote the Scripture-based script, directed rehearsals and played the part of Christ. I joined the cast as one of the women who followed Jesus and was at the garden tomb after His resurrection. Rehearsals became a fascinating journey of watching total amateurs, some of whom could barely speak English, being schooled by James into taking their roles to a level of acting they could never have imagined.

A large stage was built on the seafront, and on Easter Sunday the play was performed in brilliant sunshine to an audience of thousands, some of whom had come prepared to watch and others walking by were drawn to stop. This powerful, free performance portraying the life and death of Jesus Christ was the first of its kind in Brighton, opening the way for the Passion to become an annual event in a city where many people do not follow the Saviour or even know that He died for their sins.

A New Life in England

The following Easter, in 2012, the Soul by the Sea organizers had to accept a less accessible seafront site much further from the crowds. The sky was low and heavy with rain so we had a run-through rehearsal with director James in our warm clothing, then dressed in costume to wait in faith for people to arrive who had difficulty locating the remote site. The sky lightened and in spite of the cold the play began with an audience of several hundred. Once again it was a deeply impacting emotional experience, the Crucifixion scene taking place on a separate stage overlooking the sea. Grateful for the offer of a lift home after the performance, I spent the evening reflecting again on the significance of Easter and the blessing of playing the servant in The Last Supper scene.

In November a group of thirty people from the previous Passion cast along with newcomers met with director James Burke-Dunsmore and Emily Swain to begin preparations for a 2013 Passion. This time it took place over three days on the open lawns beside St Peter's Cathedral in central Brighton. The part of Jesus was played by Matthew Howell, a young professional actor from London. Once again the weather was against us throughout the weekend, but undeterred the cast went on stage in sleet and bitter cold to proclaim the message of the Cross to brave guests who stood under umbrellas and passers-by on foot who stopped to watch.

The following year the Passion presentation was again held on the lawn next to St Peter's Cathedral. The skies looked threatening and as we prepared to go on stage for the first performance, the heavens opened, so fully dressed we went ahead in pouring rain to a small audience under umbrellas who had braved the weather. At the end of the play we received positive feedback from several who felt that our contemporary dress lent special impact to the Gospel story. To our delight, as Jesus rose from the grave in the last scene, the sun broke through the clouds, so for our second performance we hurriedly pulled biblical costumes over sopping clothes and did it all again in brilliant sunshine to a far larger audience who had gathered.

In 2015 James Burke-Dunsmore prepared a shorter script based on the Resurrection, which opened with the body of Jesus being carried on a bier from street level down to the tomb on the pebble beach. Under grey skies in a very emotionally impacting scene, I was one of three women who washed his wounds and would have applied spices for his burial but were stopped by the soldiers as the Sabbath hour approached. His body was laid in the tomb and in the final scene Jesus appeared to his followers in glorious resurrection triumph. Situated on the seafront, many took advantage of deckchairs provided, while many more stood to watch the action.

In a city where residents follow many faiths I am passionate about sharing the truth of the Gospel with those who need to hear that Jesus is the Saviour of mankind and that God is a Father who loves them. So taking part in the annual Passion presentation has for me been a joy and a privilege.

In the extreme heat at the height of summer in Natal my energy level has always been sapped, but the intensity has increased markedly of late. Coming from the cold winter conditions in England in December 2011 I was severely affected by Durban's heat on arrival and felt spaced out for a couple of days. Daughter-in-law Annie met me and drove to Justin and Mish's home to drop off the boys' Christmas presents, as the family was in the midst of moving from Bulwer Road to a new home. We headed for the welcome peace and quiet of Andy and Lynne's home in Cato Ridge where I spent the day resting before the Christmas family get-together the following day.

A Trip Down Memory Lane

On New Year's Eve my sisters Coral and Beth, along with some of Beth's Reardon family, took me back in time to our childhood farm. This was my first visit since I had left as a schoolgirl sixty years before, and on the route I felt very disorientated because little remained of any old landmarks. When we arrived at what had been the entrance to the farm, I was

A New Life in England

shocked to find absolutely no recognizable trace of the avenue of gum trees or the orchard of five hundred litchi trees. The whole property was completely overgrown with no evidence of a homestead or the windmill.

Parking on the road below the property we climbed the bank to where a huge concrete water reservoir had been built. Standing at height on the concrete cover, I looked out and tried to get my bearings, but the whole character of the farm had been completely obliterated. Walking down the lower road, we stood on the crest of the hill overlooking the village of Maidstone and the Tongaat Sugar Mill in the valley, and caught sight of farm workers in a field where once there had been sugarcane fields.

Still hoping to find some identifying landmark on our farm, I clambered up the bank to peer through thick growth of eucalyptus saplings, shrubs and grass. I hoped to find a recognizable tree to mark a spot – but there was absolutely nothing. As we walked back to the car I felt a deep sense of loss and sadness from the total eradication of everything that had been our childhood home, but thankfully we still have the wonderful memories captured in our hearts, memories and photographs.

On New Year's Day 2012 we took a picnic lunch to Justin and Mish's new home in at Winterskloof near Hilton. I felt I was stepping into the Garden of Eden on this magnificent property, set on the hillside overlooking a forested valley where eagles nest in the tall trees and soar on the thermals overhead. The old homestead reflected the country charm of all the old homes Peter and I had owned, with great potential for Justin to make structural improvements and for Mish to exercise her wonderful gifts of interior decorating and garden landscaping.

Early in January my son Andy drove me to Durban's King Shaka Airport on the north coast for a flight to Port Elizabeth where Michelle met me with grandchildren Jethro and Jemma. An hour's drive away, our first stop in Jeffreys Bay was to say hello to Murray at his workplace 'Surf Africa' before heading up the hill to their attractive new home built like a miniature fort in the suburb of Wavecrest. I spent a wonderfully restful week with this precious family, the cool coastal breeze minimising the summer heat as Michelle and the children took me for delightful walks along the sandy stretch of Kabeljous Beach. At their Sunday service in the school hall I was delighted to connect again with the folk in 'Face to Face Church' which Murray and Michelle had established years previously.

All too soon the week passed and Shelley arrived to take me back to Port Elizabeth for a time of quiet companionship and fun with my precious daughter, who had set all commitments aside to be with me. We discussed details of her forthcoming visit to the UK and made arrangements to meet up in Johannesburg's Oliver Thambo Airport to fly together. Our annual swim in the cold Atlantic current at Humewood beach was most refreshing and I spent peaceful hours doing my embroidery during this happy week. Shelley was devastated when her computer crashed and she lost all their family photographs, but fortunately I had brought my external hard-drive with copies from previous visits of most of her pictures so I was able to upload them along with current ones of the holiday.

On the day I was to fly from Port Elizabeth to Johannesburg to visit my sisters Lorna and Enid I had my case packed and ready, thinking that the flight was in the evening. Fortunately, Shelley thought to check and discovered it was at lunchtime so we had barely enough time to make it to the airport. There are occasions when the Holy Spirit comes to our rescue and his prompting to Shelley saved me from missing two connecting flights! Lorna's daughter Heather Farr and her husband Barry met me and drove home to a warm welcome from my sister who is as frail as a bird now, moving slowly with a walker. Enid and Douglas drove across town for a good chat over tea and a viewing on computer of my photos of life in England.

I flew back to Justin and Mish's beautiful property, where the days were busy as the boys had returned to school after the holidays. Every morning, once the family had left I sat with my embroidery on the open porch enjoying the tranquillity of nature

A New Life in England

in the company of their Zulu housemaid Joyce and Zimbabwean gardeners Kuda and his brother Makalele.

With time to reflect on the past four weeks and the potential changes awaiting me on my return to the UK in five days, I felt a strange sense of disconnection from ministry at the City Mission and the increased demands on my time as companion to Rosemarie. It was disturbing but I prayed that God would lead me to the right decision about reducing my working hours for more 'me' time.

Mish took me on a lovely scenic tour of the Devonshire Lane neighbourhood to Garlington's Estate, Hilton where she'd completed garden landscaping and interior decorating for clients. After checking on her gardeners at work she drove me to Andy's home to repack my large case with items I was taking back to the UK, including Granny Frances' oil painting of horses, the portrait of Mum as a three-year-old and my remaining diaries which I needed for reference in writing my story.

After a leisurely drive to Ballito Beach on the north coast with daughter-in-law Annie Webber, I spent the night in her home. We sat up until late sharing heart-to-heart and talking through some of the spiritual lessons that Peter and I had learned in our marriage through the challenging times and the deepening of our relationship to a wonderful conclusion before his death. It was all immensely meaningful and interesting for Annie and eventually we had soup at 11pm and fell into bed. The next day we drove to sister Madeline's home where Coral and Beth joined us, eager for me to show them a wide selection of pictures covering my life in the UK.

The girls drove me to visit our brother Stan who took us to his favourite restaurant for lunch, with lots of happy family banter around the table. The next day Coral dropped me at King Shaka Airport for the flight back to England, with time to admire the life-sized sculptures of Zulu cattle and women in traditional beadwork beside their huts, before Annie arrived to bid me farewell.

Shelley's Visit to England

As always it was hard to leave Annie waving till the very last moment at the departure gate, but what eased the parting for me this time was the joy of knowing that my daughter Shelley would be coming to England with me on a ten-day holiday. She flew from Port Elizabeth to Johannesburg where we met up and made our way to the queue for British Airways.

Arriving at Heathrow early on 1st February 2012 we were soon aboard a National Express Coach to Brighton, where Jéan Seevaraj met us and drove us 'home'. After a surprise snowfall during the night Shelley was delighted to wake to a white wonderland. Before catching the open-top No 77 Bus to 'Devil's Dyke' we searched the charity shops on George Street for a warm winter coat, woolly hat and gloves for her. Suitably clad we faced the cold to admire the view into the valley from the top of the Downs, and warmed up again in a cosy corner of the restaurant while enjoying a welcome hot meal.

Next day my friend Pam Bebb picked us up for a scenic drive to Fulking, stopping at the 'Shepherd and Dog' for a warming pub lunch before continuing through snowclad hills to Ditchling and beyond. On Sunday we were both feeling weary with cold symptoms so enjoyed a leisurely start to the day with coffee in bed, followed by cereal breakfast and a quiet restful morning at home.

On Monday morning Tony Smith, our City Mission director, picked us up for the staff prayer meeting at the office where a very warm welcome awaited us. The team were all happy to meet my daughter in person and Shelley was grateful to have the opportunity to thank them for filling the place of family for her mum in the UK. After prayer 'Shells' and I ambled down London Road, stopping for a pie en route to the Brighton Pier, Royal Pavilion Art Gallery and the North Lanes before heading home to Rosemarie.

The following day we explored the Marina and yacht basin before taking up my appointment with specialist Peter Larsen-Disney at the Sussex Gynaecology Outpatients Unit. I have been

A New Life in England

blessed with good health all my life but it had become apparent that I needed an operation to remove a large fibroid. A full hysterectomy was recommended to avoid excessive bleeding, so Shelley and I went directly across to the Gynaecological Block to complete all the pre-op tests.

At the top of Shelley's 'wish list' was a tour of London in an open top bus, so we used the Internet to plan a trip, taking details for the Golden Bus Tour Company and booking into the 'Highbury Centre' for one night. On the day of our London adventure we arrived at Hove Station to discover there were problems on the line, so had to change our route and wait for a different train to connect at Barnham. Arriving at Victoria Station much later than planned, we made our way cheerfully to the Golden Tour office and bought tickets for the two-day special.

That open top bus tour around the city of London in the freezing cold of winter was undoubtedly a memorable highlight of our time together. With evidence of snow in the very chilly air, we made the most of the view from the top deck until we reached St Paul's Cathedral where we alighted to catch a local No 4 bus to 'Highbury Centre' in the gathering dusk. After a hot shower in the snug little room we reviewed the day and my heart was touched by Shelley's words of admiration: "Mumsy, I'm so proud of you. I can't believe how much energy you have, coping with the cold and everything that we've done today!" A simple supper of cup-o-soup and rolls in our room prepared us for a good night's sleep in cosy beds.

Rising early, we enjoyed a hearty cooked breakfast before setting out on the No 4 bus back to St Paul's for the interesting hour-long audio tour before heading to the Golden Coach stop. Chatting to two tour company agents, we discovered we were an hour too early for our coach, so crossed the road for a warming cup of coffee at Starbucks to escape the bitter cold. Continuing the tour as far as Tower Bridge, we hopped off and explored the area around the Tower before catching the ferry for the free ride up the Thames to the London Eye. In chilly sunshine we ate our sandwich lunch on the square and boarded the coach on its next round, completing the tour downstairs out of the bitter cold. Back at Victoria Station we found a train about to depart for Hove and treated ourselves to a short taxi ride home from the station, carrying special memories of our wonderful mother and daughter adventure.

All too soon Shelley packed her case and on Monday morning Tony picked us up to join the staff prayer meeting at the office, after which she and I strolled quietly down London Road to Poole Valley Coach Terminus. Bravely holding back our tears I saw Shelley on to the National Express Coach and waved her out of sight before steadying my emotions and making my way to take the monthly service at 'Saxon Court'.

The Operation

On 16th February, two weeks after Shelley had left, I was admitted to the Royal Sussex Hospital for a hysterectomy. Tony Smith called at 7am to drive me to the hospital and half an hour later I was the first patient taken through to meet with the anaesthetist, who told me I would be given an epidural anaesthetic. A quick word with the surgeon followed before being prepped for theatre.

I have a very high pain threshold but when I came round in the recovery room, I was conscious of the most excruciating raw pain, as if I was still under the knife. The staff at the foot of my bed were thrown into confusion when I told them the epidural hadn't worked. They put a call through to the surgeon who instructed them to administer morphine, and I was speedily put on a self-administering drip for pain relief and taken into the four-bed ward where friendly nurses checked on me frequently.

A Quick Recovery

Being in good health helped my whole system to recover quickly, so on the second day I was ready for the catheter to be removed and enjoyed a welcome shower. Surgeon Andrew Fish called on the third morning and was very impressed with my progress, assuring me that I would be able to go home the next day. My friend Jéan Seevaraj fetched me from hospital after a delicious Sunday roast dinner and I took to my bed. Having stocked a small pantry upstairs with basic food items and a kettle, it wasn't necessary for Rosemarie to have to care for me.

The effects of my busy holiday abroad before the impact of the anaesthetic and operation brought a deep weariness so I relaxed quietly in bed for the first few weeks. By the second month I felt able to cope with daily journeys up and down the stairs to the lounge, and four months later was ready to return to fulltime ministry.

While enjoying these quiet days of recuperation at home, I made the decision to reduce my working hours and have more free time to paint and continue with my memoirs. Sharing this at the mission brought a firm response from Clive Manning: "Colleen, you really should publish your powerful story as a book to share with others." Although I'd never thought to go public, I felt an immediate leap of excited confirmation in my heart which gave me fresh impetus to complete and share it to bring glory to God!

Fully aware that reduced hours of work would diminish my income, I trusted God to make up the financial loss in His own divine way and wondered what surprises He might have around the corner to answer my prayer.

Moving On

As I anticipated, Rosemarie's memory deteriorated from Christmas and I slipped into the demanding role of fulltime carer while I was home recuperating. Keeping her on track and safe every minute of the day became exhausting in my weakened state and I looked forward to returning to work. Everyone on team expected me to take six months to recover fully, but after four months I felt strong enough to ease back into holding services in rest homes and experienced again the joy of preaching Jesus.

After meeting with her children to discuss her decline Rosemarie had an assessment done at the Memory Clinic, followed by a meeting with a Dementia Unit Official who recommended overnight agency care. For six weeks I'd prayed for God to provide someone to care for Rosemarie and when my prayer was answered, I was able to leave with peace in my heart to start a new chapter in my own flat.

With God's perfect timing I received a call from the Sussex Housing Trust offering me a flat at an affordable rent in Church Court, Hove. On viewing it for the first time, I was overwhelmed by the wonderful sense of peace and charm it exuded and the light that flooded the rooms through the large lounge and main bedroom windows. The view of an enormous Sweet Chestnut tree in the grounds of Bishop Hannington Church next door was framed by the picture windows. I discovered to my delight it was the home of a little grey squirrel.

An added bonus was the flat's close proximity to the bus route I would use to the City Mission, and the joy in my heart knew no bounds as I surveyed this amazing gift from God! Reducing my salary entitled me to apply for the amazing privilege of Housing Benefit which became available at once. This income every alternate week covers my rent and enables me to live comfortably, with efficient heating throughout the winters.

Meeting Cousins for the First Time

My cousin Denise Hall invited me to visit her again to meet Coulter relatives she had recently traced, so on the Jubilee long weekend in June I caught the train to Deal. Cousins Keith and Rita Coulter had invited their niece Sue and her husband Rob to fly over from Brussels to meet relatives Sue didn't know she had. We spent a very happy day exchanging family news with our newfound cousins while taking a leisurely walk along the beautiful coastal path, before sharing a picnic lunch.

Adjusting to the mental and emotional post-op effects on my body was strangely unsettling. Feeling concerned about prickly pain in the wound area, I asked the advice of my GP's partner, who reassured me it was normal in the healing process. However, three months after my hysterectomy I needed reassurance that I hadn't caused any damage by overdoing physical activity, so made an appointment with surgeon Andrew Fish. A quick examination confirmed that all was well and with huge relief I caught the bus home, thanking God for His healing power.

Holy Trinity Brompton Meeting

During Passion Play rehearsals in 2013, Alex Stewart-Clark invited me to his pastorate group at Holy Trinity Brompton, London to share my testimony. A warm welcome from the group soon settled my butterflies and put me at ease. My reference to the spiritual opposition I had faced in a group of rest homes was particularly relevant to Lord John Taylor from the House of Lords, who thanked me for encouraging him in his Christian stand in the political arena. Alex and the group gathered round to pray for my ministry and my heart was filled with thanksgiving when several in the gathering told me that they had experienced the presence of Jesus while I was sharing my message of encouragement to deepen their relationship with Him.

Appreciation of British Nature

In May 2013 I was up bright and early to leave for a weekend with my niece Daniela Ferguson, husband Marc and their family living at Aldeburgh, excited at the prospect of exploring their part of the Suffolk countryside. With four-year-old Travis, Marc and Daniela met the coach at Ipswich Station before driving to Yoxford to fetch their children from school – teenagers Cullum and Cayla and ten-year-old Ethan. I enjoyed exploring country lanes around their home, and a seaside trip to Southwold was great fun with a fish and chips takeaway and a meander along the pier with its fascinating water-driven Tin Clock. Other delights were visits to the 'Landmark Trust Guest House'; exploring an impenetrable brick fort on the seafront; browsing through a huge warehouse of antiques for sale with a beautiful public garden; and finally calling at their allotment to water the vegetable plants. I left Suffolk with wonderfully colourful memories, feeling I'd been there much longer than a weekend.

Having grown up with the bold colours of the African landscape, I am appreciating the subtle blends and softer shades of colour in nature, the wide variety of trees and the exquisitely lovely blossoms throughout the British countryside. Visits to some of the magnificent National Trust properties are pure delight to my heart and soul, two of which I visited recently – 'Scotney Castle' in Kent and 'Standen House' in West Sussex. The pictures captured on my camera will be a lasting joy for years to come, should I leave the country one day.

Chapter Change

At the start of 2015 I reflected on how quickly the eleven years had passed since I came to the UK, the last nine years being involved in ministry with the Brighton and Hove City Mission. Since joining the mission in 2006 and initiating the work among elderly residents in rest homes, the team has expanded and so has the number of homes visited but there is great scope for extending the work even more. Now in my seventy-ninth year I feel the Lord directing me to stand down and make way for a younger person to take over leadership, so it is with real joy and a sense of fulfilment that I have done so. The person of God's choice, Beverley McArdle, stepped into the role from February 2016 and as a volunteer I've offered my help to clients in the food bank for three months until my planned holiday from May to July. Being in the mission centre on Mondays has eased the inevitable sadness of moving out of the close fellowship enjoyed with the team daily for nine years.

Coming out of a salaried position, I stand in awe of Father God's provision for my needs once again, this time through the Pension Credit and Housing Benefits available to me as a resident of the UK. Always on the alert for changes led by God, I haven't felt His direction to leave the UK yet. So I'll continue in this new season to seek his direction in anything new he may have for me around the corner. I am already revelling in having more time to bring my book to the point of publication, and joining a small art group recently has awakened the creative juices to paint again which is exciting and energising.

During an extended visit to my family, I look forward to some additional blessings, spending a week with sister Coral at her timeshare in the Drakensberg Mountains; celebrating my eightieth birthday with all my children and grandchildren at a family gathering on the South African coast, and meeting with close friends I haven't seen for years at a special celebration tea that my daughter-in-law Mish is arranging in their beautiful country garden.

The Future

We have entered 2016 and a future in which we will all face tremendous challenges, the greatest of which will be spiritual. As Christians we are called to stand on our faith in the Saviour Jesus Christ against the raging tide of worldly humanism and rampant evil forces opposing his sovereignty – not in our own strength but by the enabling of his Holy Spirit. Having joined City Coast Church in Portslade at the beginning of 2015, Jéan, Nicky and I are deeply blessed by the preaching from God's Word and the fellowship we share as the family of God.

God is faithful to the promises in his Word, the Bible, and my family and I give him the honour, praise and worship he deserves as the Lord of Lords who will one day return to reign in the New Jerusalem as the King of Kings.

Riding High with Jesus

A New Life in England

South City Church, Hove, 2004-2014

Jéan and Nicky Seevaraj

Church service, 2003

Children's church

Seevaraj family with Granny Col

Ben's dedication day

Colleen bringing the message

385

Riding High with Jesus

Nicky and family at SCC Café church venue

Prayer for the city from the Brighton bandstand

Early days – Ziggy, Jana & Stanley

Some of the early SA members

Little Joseph (right) died in 2008

Spanish and Colombian friends

A New Life in England

Brighton and Hove City Mission, 2006-2016

Brighton and Hove City Mission team and trustees, 2013

Team leaders, 2015

Colleen's DVD of story highlights, 2010

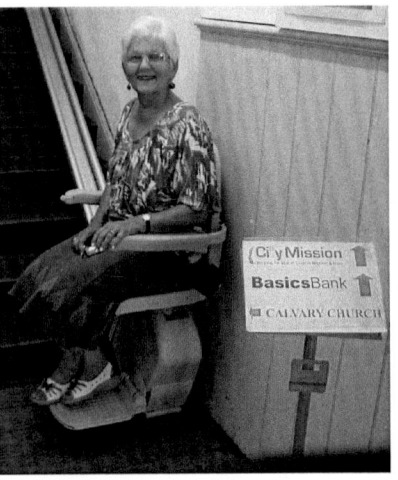

New stairlift at the City Mission

Riding High with Jesus

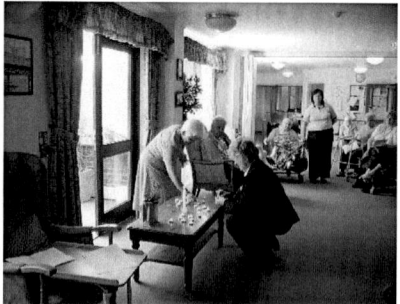

Holding a memorial service for residents

Ministry in rest homes

Celebrating my 73rd birthday, 2010

388

Artistic Talent Explored, 2010

View from my bedsit, 2010

A cottage in Shere village

Riding High with Jesus

Birthday painting for Cousin Denise

View from Devil's Dyke

A New Life in England

Rooster

Riding High with Jesus

Brighton Passion Plays, 2010-2015

2010

2014 *Crucifixion enacted*

A New Life in England

Manchester, 2008

Eccles metro-tram

Canal once used for transport

Bury Market

Inside Bury Market

Manchester library

Manchester town hall

Signs of the old days

Bury Black Pudding

Riding High with Jesus

Manchester Cathedral

The Wheel

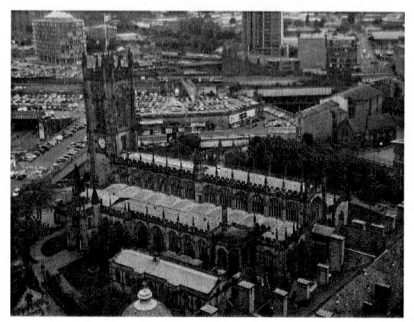

View of the cathedral from
The Wheel

View of The Wheel from
the cathedral

Baptist chapel, Shude Hill

Piccadilly Gardens

A New Life in England

The street of the Registry Offices

Public toilet on the street

Piccadilly Gardens
metro stop

Shude Hill metro stop

Old alongside the new

Upgrading the area

Riding High with Jesus

Deal, 2009

Colleen and Denise

Cousin Denise Hall and Teasel

Quadriplegic Hilary Lister

From the pier in Deal

Seafront at Deal

Remembrance Day

A New Life in England

Dover / Sandwich, 2009

Dover harbour from the clifftop

Dover

Newfound Coulter cousins

Lunch with cousins

Sandwich

Sandwich windmill

397

Riding High with Jesus

Inside the old mill

Flour collected

Old scales and weights

Samphire Ho walking path

A New Life in England

Romania, 2009

Left to right: Jéan Seevaraj, Colleen, Steve and Candice Sterley wait for flight to Romania

Changing to a Hungarian De Havilland plane in Budapest

Airport building, Romania

Fresh cherries from the market

Local market in Iasi (old capital, pronounced 'Yash')

Dilapidated bookstall on the street

Riding High with Jesus

An antique shop sign

Pastor David and Stratika Serediuk

A domed Orthodox church in Iasi

Farmer's horse-drawn wagon

River running through the mountain gorge

Tourist stalls within the shadow of the gorge

A New Life in England

The Moldovan mountains

Peaceful tourist spot on the lake

Our picnic at the lake

A wagon buried under the enormous load of hay

A family wagon

Riding High with Jesus

Another horse-drawn mode of transport

Romanian peasants returning from the field, hoes over their shoulders

Enormous fuel pipes, a legacy from the communist era

Venue for Filadelfia Church services

A New Life in England

Cobh, Ireland

A cruise liner steams into the harbour at Cobh

Friends Garth and Janet Holden, my hosts

On the coastal cliff walk at Ballycotton

A row of brightly coloured homes running down to the sea

View from the Holdens' balcony to the cruise ship mooring

The Cork Pilot boat about to guide the ship out of the bay

Riding High with Jesus

Janet and I enjoyed tea at the grand Barryscourt Castle

The Titanic Museum at Cobh

Three names for the same town. Cove until Queen Victoria's visit, changed to Queensland, then back to Irish Cobh in 1920.

Fine sculpture of mother and sons about to emigrate on the Titanic

Pupils on an outdoor education lesson

404

A New Life in England

Scenes of the bay from the
Cathedral high on the hill

The Cathedral on the hill

Janet on the path overlooking the
beautiful shoreline

Janet and Colleen enjoying a picnic
tea on the sea wall at Kinsale

405

Appendix

ANCESTORS OF COLLEEN MARGARET HURD		
	married	
JOHN WILSON b.1682	Kent England	MARY or ELIZABETH b.1686
daughter		
MARY WILSON b.1708	1725 Kent	JOHN HOWELL b.1708
		daughter
JOHN QUESTED b.1727	1763 Kent	ELIZABETH HOWELL b.1734
son		
ROBERT QUESTED b.1771 d.1831	1794 Kent	ELEANOR HUDSON d.1834
son		
THOMAS QUESTED b.1797	1821 Iwade, Kent	HARRIET SUSANNAH COULTER b.1799 d.1886
daughter		
ELIZA ANN QUESTED b.1833 d.1868	1857 Durban	JAMES CATTERALL b.1823 d.1897
		daughter
WILLIAM HENRY ECKERSLEY b.1853 d.1934	1880 Sea Cow Lake	ALICE ELIZA CATTERALL b.1860 d.1913
son		
WILLIAM COLIN ECKERSLEY b.1886 d.1966	1923	MARJORIE ENID LONG b. d.1987
daughter		
COLLEEN MARGARET ECKERSLEY b. 1936		PETER HURD b. 1933

A New Life in England

Fred Long's Family Tree

JOHN WILLIAM LONG age 19 married in 1855- RACHEL CANT age 20
children:- b.1835 Lawford - d.1900
    Rachel Elizabeth b.1861-Kelvedon
    Elizabeth R. b.1862-Manningtree
    John William b.1863 "
    Rosa A. b.1866 "
  FREDERICK EDMUND b.1867 "
    Frank b. 1874 "
    May b. 1877 "

[1861 Census- JOHN WILLIAM LONG age 25 is a Pork Butcher in Kelvedon wife RACHEL age 26]

[1871 Census- JOHN WILLIAM LONG age 35 is a Butcher living in Regent Street, Manningtree with wife RACHEL age 36 and 5 children - FREDERICK EDMUND is age 3]

[1881 census- JOHN WILLIAM LONG age 46 is now a Master Butcher employing 2 men & 2 boys with daughter Rachel Elizabeth age 20 and son John William age 18 as Assistants in South Street, Manningtree
wife RACHEL age 47, FREDERICK EDMUND age 13, Frank age 7 and May age 4 are all scholars]

[1881 Census- (Rachel's sister) Susannah Cant b.1830 Lawford is a Needlewoman living Stour Street, Manningtree with Rosa Long age 15 as a Pupil Teacher]
(Rosa is Rachel and John William Long's daughter)

JOHN WILLIAM LONG died towards the end of 1881 age 46 - leaving a young family.   His widow RACHEL LONG died in 1900 age 65.

John William Long's brother- Charles H. Long married Ellen b.1851 - Mistley
son Charlie R. b.1879 - Mistley

[1881 Census-Pork Butcher age 29 -South Street, Manningtree
-wife Ellen age 30, son Charlie R. Long age 2]

Long-Echardt Family Tree

```
FAMILY TREE
-----------
        FRANCES ELIZABETH ECHARDT  -  BORN IN CAPE TOWN IN 1869.
     OIL PAINTING DONE IN APPROX. 1896. IN HER 27TH YEAR. (3 HORSES DRINKING
AT A TROUGH) IT WAS SELECTED BY SOUTH AFRICAN ARTISTS SOCIETY TO BE
        HUNG AT THE ROYAL ACADEMY IN LONDON. THE BOAT DID NOT REACH
        LONDON ON TIME FOR THE EXHIBITION. SHE WAS A LIFE MEMBER
        OF S.A. ART SOCIETY.

MATERNAL GREAT-GREAT GRANDPARENTS- LONG
---------------------------------------
JOHN LONG (butcher)     m    RACHEL      (Gran's grandfather on
                                          her father's side)

JOHAN HERMAN ECHARDT   (German)   m    JOSEPHINE LE GRANGE
(French)
                                       ( Gran's Great-
                                   grandparents on her mother's
                                                          side)
Their son:
        JOHAN ECHARDT   m    SARAH ELIZA HOLSTEAD (Yorkshire)(2nd
                                                              wife)
1. JOSEPH (Cabinet maker)
2. CLARA  (Nurse during the boer war) m  GEORGE CHAMBERS (Mine
                                                          captain)
3. FRANCES ELIZABETH ( Teacher at 19 years. Headmistress of
Grahamstown school for girls. A pianist, violinist, artist.)
     m   FREDRICK LONG
        (Heather's great_grandparents)

4. WILLIAM ( Farmer in Paarl, Cape)
5. BERTHA GERTUDE    (Nun?)
6. ALICE JOSEPHINE *  -  ( Her daughter is Aunt Nora - aged 94
                                  living in Johannesburg)
7. MARGARET MATLIDA * (ran away from home - married British men
                        in Johannesburg)
```